The
Laywoman
Project

The Laywoman Project

Remaking Catholic Womanhood in the Vatican II Era

Mary J. Henold

THE UNIVERSITY OF NORTH CAROLINA PRESS

Chapel Hill

This book was published with the assistance of the Greensboro
Women's Fund of the University of North Carolina Press.

Designed by Jamison Cockerham
Set in Arno, Scala Sans, Serif Gothic, and Nestor
by codeMantra, Inc.

Manufactured in the United States of America

The University of North Carolina Press has been a member
of the Green Press Initiative since 2003.

Cover illustration: Margaret Mealey participates in WUCWO Study Days,
Paris, 1963. Courtesy of the National Council of Catholic Women.

LIBRARY OF CONGRESS CATALOGING-IN-PUBLICATION DATA
Names: Henold, Mary J., 1974– author.
Title: The laywoman project : remaking Catholic womanhood
in the Vatican II era / Mary J. Henold.
Description: Chapel Hill : The University of North Carolina Press, 2020. |
Includes bibliographical references and index.
Identifiers: LCCN 2019032064 | ISBN 9781469654485 (cloth) |
ISBN 9781469654492 (paperback) | ISBN 9781469654508 (ebook)
Subjects: LCSH: Women in the Catholic Church—United States. |
Catholic women—United States. | Lay ministry—Catholic Church.
Classification: LCC BX1407.W65 H46 2020 | DDC 282/.7308209045—dc23
LC record available at https://lccn.loc.gov/2019032064

Parts of chapter 2 originally appeared as "'This Is Our Challenge! We Will Pursue
It': The National Council of Catholic Women, the Feminist Movement, and the
Second Vatican Council, 1960–1975," in *Empowering the People of God: Catholic
Action before and after Vatican II*, ed. Jeremy Bonner, Christopher Denny, and
Mary Beth Fraser Connolly (New York: Fordham University Press, 2013).

For my parents

And just because some of us turn out to be the family-hearth-type woman, that doesn't mean some of us can't join the Kate Millett types and light bonfires for female freedom. (And it doesn't mean some of us can't enjoy the warmth of the flame without striking the match.)

Kathy Cribari, The Theresian *(1971)*

Contents

Figures

Acknowledgments

A book ten years in the making inspires a lot of gratitude. First, I am indebted to the many archivists who assisted with this project. Special thanks to Maria Mazzenga and William Shepherd at the American Catholic History Research Center at Catholic University. I am further indebted to the American Catholic History Research Center and the Cushwa Center for the Study of American Catholicism at the University of Notre Dame for travel grants that assisted me in getting to the archives. Roanoke College has also supported my research in the form of grants and release time.

I am grateful to the many colleagues who have provided encouragement, feedback, and support through this long process. Special thanks to Mary Beth Fraser Connolly, Kathy Cummings, Paula Kane, Jim McCartin, Catherine Osborne, Jeanne Petit, Tom Rzeznik, and Charles Strauss. I am always thankful for my friends and colleagues in the Lilly Fellows program who sustain me and remind me periodically how to be my best academic self. John Staudenmaier and Mel Piehl continue to serve as my mentors even though I should have let them off the hook years ago. I couldn't ask for better advice or greater champions. Thank you to Elaine Maisner for her work in shaping the manuscript and her endless store of patience. My colleagues in the History Department at Roanoke College have given me a warm and collegial place to teach and write, and I am profoundly thankful. I am also blessed in my parish, Our Lady of Nazareth, whose community welcomes me each week and keeps me grounded in the living church.

My family of Henolds and Carlins have been incredibly supportive as I have meandered my way through this project. My children, Ella and Hank, are a joy just because they are themselves, but also because they make life so interesting. I also appreciate how well they tolerate history lessons at the dinner table. My deepest gratitude to my husband, Tim, for his unflagging, steadfast support and his faith that I could get this done (and the knowledge that it wouldn't matter a jot if I didn't). Finally, thank you to my parents, Ken and Nikki Henold, who gave me the twin and ever intertwining gifts of an academic life and a vibrant faith.

The
Laywoman
Project

Introduction

On Their Own Behalf

When our Cardinal comes home and starts to put into practice
the decrees of the Council, he will need a strong group of laymen
just like yourselves and the Council of Catholic Women. The
Cardinal feels you are prepared, you are knowledgeable, you are
educated, you are well grounded in your faith and you are able
to do the work.... Old ways of doing things have to be changed
and that is not always easy to do and we do want to present to the
Cardinal a group of women who are zealous but not overzealous;
a group of women who are faithful and trustful and obedient.

Father James Murtaugh, address to the Chicago
Archdiocesan Council of Catholic Women (1964)

. . . .

I write as a woman whose consciousness has been raised
enough to notice that *Marriage* has fallen into the pit of sex-
role stereotyping—where "men are men and women are
women." This philosophy ignores the fact that we are, first of
all, persons.... I see no humor in this myth perpetuation.

Mrs. Lucille W. Martin, letter to the editor (1972)

Perhaps Father James Murtaugh was thinking that Cardinal Albert Meyer
had all the luck. While his boss was in Rome at the Second Vatican Council
(1962–65), a worldwide meeting of the bishops of the Catholic Church then
in its third year, Murtaugh was charged with delivering an address to the
1964 annual fall assembly of the Chicago Archdiocesan Council of Catholic Women (CACCW) in the cardinal's stead. On that occasion, Murtaugh
gave what was a very typical Vatican II–era speech from a clergyman to a
group of active Catholic laywomen. He first made clear the hierarchy under

which he and they both lived. "Our Cardinal" would be coming home, he said, and he is the one who would put the Council's decrees into practice. Following the familiar model of Catholic Action, however, where laypeople were encouraged to give their service in a program outlined by their bishop, the priest told the women they would be needed to implement Meyer's plan. Or, more precisely, that "a group of strong lay*men* just like yourselves" would be needed.

Now for the buttering up: You are smart, educated, and able! Priest speakers rarely failed to compliment the ladies, particularly when they were about to take something quite valuable away, and this speech was no different. Do not be too zealous, laywomen of Chicago; the Cardinal can't have you too excited. Trust that what we teach you is correct, be faithful, and— *please*—do what you are told. Murtaugh managed to convey that change was the dominant theme of Vatican II, yet the lingering tone was one of warning. This group in particular, these ladies in hats eating dry chicken and laughing politely at the priest's jokes: these women, he feared, could be trouble. And he was right.

This book studies communities of highly active, largely nonfeminist laywomen at a particularly unsettled moment in the history of the American Catholic Church, the roughly ten years following the start of Vatican II. Laywomen like those of the CACCW were meant to anchor the church in these volatile years, and if we think of them at all, this might be how we remember such women: ever-present, deferential, quick to serve and slow to question. But if this is all they were, why would a man like Father Murtaugh go out of his way to warn them to behave? He did so because Catholic laywomen were already signaling they were unsatisfied with how they as women fit into the discourse surrounding the Council. In the decade or so following Vatican II, these laywomen often went further than the hierarchy was prepared to go, fostering far-reaching and significant conversations that questioned basic cultural and theological precepts of Catholic gender identity. In this moment they claimed the authority to define for themselves what it meant to be a Catholic woman.

Active laywomen, especially those who channeled their energies through Catholic women's organizations like the National Council of Catholic Women (NCCW) or the Catholic Daughters of America (CDA), faced a challenging and at times frustrating set of circumstances in the 1960s and 1970s, circumstances that men like James Murtaugh merely exacerbated. Murtaugh and his confreres presented themselves as gatekeepers, authorized to interpret and implement the changes brought by Vatican II. The women of the CACCW did not challenge his right to authority; they had invited him to speak, after all. But the priest's thoughts on hierarchy and gender only highlighted what was, for laywomen, a conundrum at the center of the Council.

One of the most electrifying changes emerging from the Council was a newly emphasized, expansive interpretation of vocation for laypeople. *Lumen Gentium*, the Dogmatic Constitution on the Church, outlined their role clearly: "Upon all the laity, therefore, rests the noble duty of working to extend the divine plan of salvation to all men of each epoch and in every land. Consequently, may every opportunity be given them so that, according to their abilities and the needs of the times, they may zealously participate in the saving work of the Church."[1] Father Murtaugh casually revealed where laypeople ranked in his estimation when he attempted to convey this idea to the CACCW at the same event the previous year: "The laity can no longer be a negative element, nor can he be passive or neutral." But Murtaugh's confusing pronouns do beg the question, Were laywomen to be included in this reinterpretation? Clergy did seem to believe that the conciliar *Decree on the Apostolate of the Laity* applied to women, but they also consistently maintained, in both overt and subtle ways, that laywomen were different by nature than their husbands, brothers, and sons, and therefore retained a distinct role within the lay sphere. Because the Council made significant changes in the church's understanding of the role of the laity without questioning its core beliefs about gender, its leaders were sending Catholic women contradictory messages. How could laywomen's role as laypeople be expanded if the church still taught that woman's nature was basically fixed and subordinate?[2]

This book addresses how a particular set of Catholic laywomen puzzled out this contradiction for themselves in the years during and following the Second Vatican Council, which also happened to be, not coincidentally, the years of feminism's resurgence in the United States. In the wake of so much change, within the church and without, laywomen asked over and over again: What does it mean to be a Catholic woman? In asking and answering this question with such frequency they came to challenge the very notion that the Catholic Church's interpretations of gender, and that gender itself, were immutable. *The Laywoman Project* investigates this significant, creative work of laywomen undertaken at their own urging, and on their own behalf.[3]

It may take a readjustment to consider moderate, nonfeminist Catholic laywomen as vibrant and significant originators of discussions about gender, let alone as change agents in this area. Catholic feminists typically dominate any narratives about challenges to women's gender identity in the church during this period. They tended to distrust organizational laywomen, particularly the leaders of the National Council of Catholic Women, because they refused to support cherished feminist goals such as the Equal Rights Amendment (ERA). Feminists also believed such laywomen colluded with the hierarchy to keep Catholic women in the roles the church expected.

But such narratives cannot adequately explain the contents of the NCCW archives, for example, which are bursting with examples of their members reconsidering Catholic gender identity as early as the mid-1960s. Far from policing the boundaries of Catholic womanhood at the hierarchy's behest, NCCW leaders were questioning what they had been taught and trying to find a balance for themselves that would fit their identities to the changing times. They were among the first to openly question female essentialism, complementarity, and women's traditional roles in church service in their publications. Moreover, the NCCW leadership viewed the organization not only as a place to foster new ideas about gender but also as a means of teaching Catholic laywomen around the country to test and possibly reject the limits Catholic notions of womanhood placed on them. A narrative that attributes all discourse on gender to the Catholic feminist movement is far too simple to explain transitions in Catholic gender identity in these critical midcentury decades.

The NCCW was not alone in its project to remake American Catholic womanhood. For roughly fifteen years, from the early 1960s to the mid-1970s, Catholic laywomen wrote countless articles, memos, papers, conference addresses, and letters to the editor, guiding themselves and other women to new understandings of who they were. It was a vast preoccupation, a project in which large numbers of Catholic laywomen participated. I have come to call this phenomenon "the laywoman project." In studying it I am foregrounding laywomen as historical actors, keeping in mind historian Thomas Sugrue's lament that too frequently the study of Catholics in this era "emphasizes Catholics as the objects of change, not the agents of change." Nowhere has this been truer than in the study of laywomen, whose process of self-discovery and self-determination has been largely ignored.[4]

Before I elaborate on what the laywoman project produced, and what conclusions we might draw from the conversations in which these writers engaged, I need to situate the laywomen historically. I have elected to study in depth the leadership of four different organizations (the National Council of Catholic Women, the Theresians, the Catholic Daughters of America, and the Daughters of Isabella), one organization in brief (the World Union of Catholic Women's Organizations [WUCWO]), and the contributors to one Catholic periodical (*Marriage*). While these women represent a variety of paths, they were certainly not the only individuals involved in the work of puzzling out Catholic gender identity in the Vatican II era. Catholic feminists were also clearly part of this larger project, as were some women religious, priests, and laymen. In selecting these particular communities for in-depth analysis, I am not arguing that they are the only people worthy of study. The number of Catholic laywomen's organizations is large and includes many devotional societies and sodalities, among other groups that could help us understand gender identity. I have chosen to dive deeply into a few organizations rather than provide an overview of the many.

Furthermore, while the organizations the women in this book represented had enormous reach, they were not particularly internally diverse. While some leaned more "progressive" and some more "conservative," they can best be described as occupying moderate positions both within American politics and within the Catholic Church. Further, the majority of the laywomen in this study were white, middle-class, and middle-aged. While Catholic laywomen enjoy little tangible power in the Catholic Church, these women were able to capitalize on the privileges of their race, class status, and education level to assume leadership in prominent national organizations and achieve an audience for their ideas during a period of intense discussions about the laity's role in the Catholic Church and in the wider world. Most of the communities in this study had women of color in their memberships, so we know that diverse Catholic women participated in these conversations. However, those with the power to direct the laywoman project on the national level were predominantly white, and when they did address questions of race and racism—which was infrequently—they did so from a white perspective. The exception to this in the study is WUCWO, whose Latina leadership in the 1970s reflected the group's determination to forward marginalized voices, particularly from the global South.[5]

We must first place these women within larger conversations about the history of Vatican II. For many years historians of the Catholic Church in the twentieth century were preoccupied with asking whether Vatican II is best classified as a rupture in the church's history that radically changed Catholic culture and practice or as an event that manifested on a large scale trends already in evidence among the faithful. In the last fifteen years, scholars have largely dismissed the narrative of "rupture" in favor of that of "continuity," finding that many strands of thought and practice that came to the world's attention with the Council can be traced back decades. For the purposes of this book, I want to focus specifically on changing perceptions of lay authority and autonomy.[6]

We have abundant evidence that American laypeople, in concert with many laity globally, had begun to question the accepted perception of laypeople as passive and obedient. Under this dominant model, laypeople learned the correct paths to follow from clergy and women religious, absorbing and accepting in the process that as laity they had inferior spiritual status. To keep laypeople on the straight and narrow, religious professionals heavily emphasized sin and encouraged frequent confession. Laypeople were directed to keep their marriages open to all the children God might send their way, regardless of their ability to support them, under the threat of dire spiritual consequences. Laypeople who suffered under such teachings—or simply under the weight of the world in which they lived—were trained to seek solace and relief not only in the Eucharist but in a variety of prayerful devotions, particularly to the Blessed Mother.

But significant changes in the American church in the middle decades of the twentieth century destabilized this model. For example, this mode of structuring the lay-clerical relationship worked best with a large educational gap between clerical leadership and the people in the pew. It was also reinforced by the Catholic community's insularity; a culture that strongly discouraged "mixed marriage" (that is, unions between Catholics and non-Catholics) and sought to maintain homogenous Catholic educational and social networks was thought by many to have a greater ability to perpetuate its beliefs in changing times. But after World War II, the influx of large numbers of GIs into both Catholic and secular colleges began to narrow the education gap; clergy who in the past had typically been the most highly educated Catholics in the building could no longer rely on their credentials to sway the faithful. Moreover, the transition of large numbers of white Catholics from concentrated, homogenous urban neighborhoods to the religiously and ethnically (though not racially) diverse suburbs (and the prosperity that attended these developments) enlarged laypeople's experience and opened them to new ways of being in the world.[7] Furthermore, external developments such as the civil rights movement encouraged African American Catholics and their allies to work for justice in and outside the church, with or without clerical leadership.

Consequently, we see laypeople exploring new forms of Catholic practice and lay leadership that challenged, both implicitly and explicitly, lay passivity and the beliefs that reinforced it. Some of these developments involved direct verbal challenges to clerical authority, while others demonstrated through behavior that laypeople had come to see themselves and their faith differently. Explicit challenges usually came from a highly engaged, highly educated class of laypeople who were exploring leadership as Catholic intellectuals and/or in various forms of Catholic Action in the 1940s and 1950s. (Catholic Action is shorthand for lay involvement in many different types of projects that engaged with "the world," and originated with or were sanctioned by the hierarchy.) The laypeople who from the mid-1950s through the mid-1960s began to reject, with increasing openness, the church's prohibition of artificial contraception are an example of such a challenge.[8] A second example is the work of the interracial justice movement, centered in the Catholic Interracial Council (CIC), among other groups. According to historian Karen J. Johnson, images of marching priests and sisters often dominate our knowledge of this movement, but its leadership is best characterized as self-consciously lay. "They made racial justice a central component of Catholicism," she writes, and "challenged the hierarchy that placed priests above the laity."[9]

Several other examples of emerging lay authority can be found in the most prominent and innovative Catholic Action movements at midcentury. The Christian Family Movement (CFM) focused on progressive Catholic couples who hoped to strengthen their families in the faith as they applied that faith to solving problems of the modern world. Jeremy Bonner notes that these couples "experimented with forms of religious life in which the clergy's leadership role was either muted or absent." Similarly, the Cana movement, with its dual focus on preparing couples for marriage and strengthening existing marriages, had the unintended consequence of "decenter[ing] the moral authority of the Church. In teaching couples about the nature of marriage, Cana helped to create a generation of experts, experts who would increasingly come to value their own decision-making abilities."[10]

Historians have also provided abundant evidence in recent years for how American Catholic laity, particularly laywomen, began to transform their faith practice well before Vatican II. At times their choices indicate changed spiritual preferences or outlooks, but at other times their decisions represent true rebellion against clerical authority. We know, for example, that the way laypeople prayed changed markedly in these years as participation in traditional devotions began to decline starting in the 1950s. The laity seemed to find them less and less necessary to enacting Catholicism.[11] Likewise, declines in the number of Catholics going to confession over this period suggest that laypeople's conception of sin was changing to reflect less of an emphasis on guilt and punishment, a mindset that had tended to keep Catholics in awe of their clergy's ability to judge and forgive sin. James M. O'Toole argues that women especially seemed to be growing uncomfortable with confession, citing priests' dismissiveness and intrusiveness, along with unhappiness at always having to bare their souls to a man. Overall, the ways laypeople were approaching prayer at midcentury reflected "a good deal more than the mere repetition of words prescribed by others." They were actively making decisions about their own faith practice.[12]

Finally, we know from statistics that well before Vatican II or the turmoil of "the sixties," lay Catholics were making decisions that contradicted church teachings (or at least accepted tradition). The most important of these statistics concerns the use of birth control; Catholic women increasingly used artificial contraception over the course of the 1950s and 1960s, defying the church's authority. Already as of 1955, 30 percent of American Catholic women between eighteen and thirty-nine were using artificial contraception; by 1965, that number reached 51 percent, from which it would only increase. Rates of "mixed marriage" to non-Catholic partners were also on the rise.[13]

So what are we to conclude about mid-twentieth-century laywomen from this information? Is it safe to argue that in the case of laywomen's identity, as with so many other trends in the American church, the real transition occurred before Vatican II? Several historians ask us to consider this idea. For example, in his study of women and devotions, Timothy Kelly argues that "the changes in participation levels in the Our Lady of Perpetual Help devotion indicate that American women's ideology of gender may have changed before the feminist movement of the 1960s and 70s." He further argues that "Catholic women who once embraced a ritual that affirmed their roles as passive nurturers increasingly rejected that feminine ideal. That they did so in the years before the rebirth of the feminist movement suggests that they had begun to redefine their lives earlier than we previously believed." Similarly, Paula Kane asserts that Marian devotion declined in part due to women entering the workforce and becoming more independent. This shift, she argues, is evidence for a "Catholic women's consciousness" that originated in the 1950s, not the postconciliar period, as many have assumed.[14]

This argument fits well into the narrative of continuity. If every other change seemingly had its roots in the postwar period, why not the shift in laywomen's gender identity? I have no wish to deny that Catholic laywomen were changing in the 1950s; the evidence that laywomen had already initiated some of the shifts that would help them rethink their identities as Catholic women is incontrovertible, as Kane and Kelly have proved. But I would argue against the idea that Catholic women had a collective consciousness this early, since this implies both a desire and an ability to articulate the transition they were undergoing. That articulation would take place—it is, in fact, "the laywoman project" itself—but not until the conciliar and immediate post-conciliar period, as the evidence in this book will demonstrate.

On this point it is helpful to remember the climate in which Catholic laywomen lived in the 1950s, and the dominant messages laywomen in leadership were both receiving and perpetuating. Colleen McDannell and Kathryn Johnson remind us of the preoccupation with a particular kind of Catholic domesticity that flooded Catholic culture in this era. Fears of secularization and materialism in a time of prosperity prompted Catholic commentators to place added emphasis on patriarchal authority, not only within the hierarchy but within the family. Complementarity, the teaching that each sex was assigned distinct traits and roles by God and nature, was proclaimed far and wide as a bulwark against selfishness, secularization, and communism. A woman could not pick up a Catholic magazine at midcentury without reading about her proper role and how she put her and her family's salvation—nay, the salvation of the entire world!—at risk if she abandoned it.[15]

We know, too, that the movements in this era which encouraged lay authority and autonomy explicitly (and enthusiastically) also preached complementarity, discouraging women's leadership or sublimating it into domestic concerns. As we will see, both CFM and Cana taught laywomen to embrace and pass on Catholic teachings on gender. Furthermore, women leaders in the "progressive" liturgical movement instructed women to incorporate liturgical changes into their lives by making their homes centers for sacramental activity. Historian Katharine Harmon views this as fundamentally empowering for women, as it allowed them to "unite their role as wife and mother with that of the liturgical apostolate." Yet it did not challenge complementarity, the heart of accepted understandings of gender identity and vocation for laywomen.[16]

It is the women to whom these complementarian discourses were directed—and those who, to a great extent, had found them meaningful and influential in their life arrangements—who became the protagonists of the "laywoman project" of the 1960s and 1970s. How do these women fit into a larger history of feminism and, in a more focused way, into the history of Catholic feminism? First, should all of the women who engaged in the laywoman project be considered feminists because of the nature of this endeavor, and if so, are they Catholic feminists? It is also fair to ask, if the answers to these questions are affirmative, why write a book about what is basically watered-down feminism? If these women were doing the work of Catholic feminists—just more politely and on a larger scale—what is the point?

In fact, the majority of the women in this study were not self-identified feminists, and for the most part their project did not have the explicitly stated purpose of advancing feminist goals. Although they were working through similar questions about gender identity at the same time as early Catholic feminists, their approaches were distinct. The rhetoric of laywomen in this study was often much more circumspect, for example, and they were more careful not to offend. This can be partially explained by the fact that, unlike the majority of Catholic feminists who pursued their activism mainly through organizations and support networks outside Catholic patriarchal systems, the laywomen in this study were active in organizations and communities that were run by women but ultimately controlled by men; run by women but supervised by men; or directly run by men.

A second difference is that the laywomen in this book often discussed issues of identity centering in the home and family that contemporary Catholic feminists either found of little interest or had already moved beyond. Since Catholic feminism was dominated by women religious, the problems arising from the gendered nature of Catholic married life did not receive much attention in the movement.

Finally, since these conversations about Catholic womanhood did not typically have feminist goals and were not always informed by feminist theory or theology, the women who fostered them could end their projects with ideas that would have truly alarmed feminists. The women of the Catholic Daughters of America and the Daughters of Isabella (D of I) demonstrate that exploring questions of gender identity is not the exclusive province of feminists, nor do processes of empowerment always conform to feminist ideals. It must be pointed out, too, that the women in this study are much more representative of American laywomen as a whole than were the Catholic feminists, then as now a tiny minority of Catholic women in the United States. Almost certainly the activity of the women in this book reached far more women in the pew than Catholic feminists did in the same time period.

Recent work in the history of feminism is helpful for situating these Catholic women, who flirted with feminist concepts and may have been influenced by them, but did not choose the feminist label for themselves. This new work has encouraged us to rethink the very definitions of feminist activity. In the past, historians who were often activists themselves privileged more radical forms of feminism, particularly those centered in overwhelmingly white organizations on the East Coast. Historians, no less than the activists they chronicled, policed the term *feminist* to ensure that activists met certain benchmarks of orthodoxy before they could be recognized as such. As a result, more moderate manifestations of feminism outside the accepted centers of activity have been missed. In fact, the boundaries privileging the "second wave" caused historians to obscure much meaningful activity taking place at midcentury. This scholarship asks us to broaden our understanding of feminism so we can know the full scope of women's activism.[17]

Another set of emerging scholarship, particularly pertinent to the laywoman project, turns its focus to nonfeminist women's organizations that engaged feminist questions in thoughtful, serious ways. Feminist history has typically focused almost exclusively on those who called themselves feminist, but recently scholars have turned instead to explore how feminist ideas may have been adapted by women in diverse contexts. Melissa Estes Blair explores this narrative through such groups as the Young Women's Christian Association (YWCA), the League of Women Voters, and the National Council of Negro Women. Faith Rogow argues that the women of the National Council of Jewish Women also pursued some liberal feminist goals without claiming the label of feminist. Dorothy Sue Cobble writes of the "social justice feminism" of women in the midcentury labor movement. Likewise, historian Janet Weaver alerts us to the empowered Catholic Mexicana "barrio women" who led groups for women's economic justice in the Midwest in the 1950s and 1960s without self-identifying. Finally, what Lanethea Mathews-Gardner argues about Methodist organizational women in this era could just as easily be said about the Catholic laywomen in this study: "More important than debating the extent to which the WDCS [Women's Division of Christian Service] was or is 'feminist,' is recognizing their part in multiple struggles over the appropriate roles, responsibilities and opportunities available to women and their organizations in the mid-20th century."[18]

The larger purpose of this book, then, is not to claim there were even more Catholic feminists than we once believed. Instead, I join these other historians in arguing that one did not need to be a feminist to rethink and even challenge the limitations placed on women through restrictive notions of gender hierarchy and essentialism. Thousands of Catholic laywomen were doing just that, quite vocally, and under the very noses of the self-identified Catholic feminists who at times disdained them, not to mention the clerical and laymen who had long benefited from these restrictive notions. The 1960s provided the perfect opportunity for this rethinking to occur, not primarily because the Catholic community had become more liberal, or because the women's movement created an atmosphere more conducive to raising such questions, but because the church was squeezing laywomen into an impossible situation they themselves took action to resolve.

By the mid-1960s an active laity was showing its strength and coming to think of itself as able to exercise autonomy and contribute in meaningful ways, not only to the church's mission, but to its theology and even its governance. Some clergy were supportive of the laity's assumption of new forms of leadership, but as James Murtaugh's speech reminds us, most in the church's hierarchy were almost completely unprepared for laywomen—as women—to do any of those things. The church's teachings that had formed clergy and laywomen alike demanded sanctity of laywomen while simultaneously assuming they were inherently selfish and immature. Laywomen's primary role was in the home, nurturing Christian families, and their leadership was encouraged only if they fostered and tacitly agreed to those restrictions.

Laywomen received this message directly from the Council fathers. On the feast of the Immaculate Conception in 1965, the Council released a statement directed to the women of the world. "The hour is coming," they promised, "in fact, has now come—when the vocation of woman is being achieved in its fullness, the hour in which woman acquires in the world an influence, an effect and a power never hitherto achieved." The average woman in the pew might have been pleased to have her power celebrated (the buttering up . . .), but the singular "woman" hinted at what was coming next. "Wives, mothers of families, the best educators of the human race, in the intimacy of the family circle, pass on to your sons and daughters the traditions of your fathers. . . . always remember that by her children a mother belongs to that future which perhaps she will not seek. . . . Women, you who know how to make truth sweet, tender, and accessible, make it your task to bring the spirit of this Council into institutions, schools, homes, and daily life."[19] If the fathers were offering laywomen the world, it was a limited one indeed. It is hard to escape the sense that the Council, like Father Murtaugh, was trying to cut these women off before they even got started. If Catholic laywomen became too enthusiastic about what they heard from the Council about the laity's role, they might exceed their boundaries as women and therefore destabilize the church's teaching on gender. The remarkable thing was that for the majority of the faithful, committed Catholic laywomen in these pages, this did not stop them.

My focus in the following chapters is not just on laywomen and their ideas, but specifically on how those ideas changed over time. Each chapter focuses on a different community of women so as to trace in detail, year by year, the transitions each group made as it processed new information over the course of the 1960s and 1970s. These four chapters show the range of positions American Catholic laywomen could adopt and how drastically they could change in a short period of time. Despite the internal divergence, some conclusions immediately present themselves.

First and foremost, across the board we see Catholic laywomen claiming the authority to define for themselves what a Catholic woman was. Vatican II made it seem to some that just about everything was open for discussion, including by laity, and laywomen leaders took advantage of these unusual circumstances to effectively hijack the conversation about gender from the hierarchy. The very fact that the laywoman project took place is proof that one of the church's modern claims about men and women is false: gender is not immutable. Women revisiting what they had been told and changing their self-conception and behavior proved that gender roles were not fixed as innumerable Catholic commentators claimed in the 1950s and early 1960s. Moreover, laywomen had more power to spread this idea than we might have believed.

Laywomen's organizations chose to educate their memberships about the Council, exposing potentially millions of Catholic women to the laywoman project through their publications and programming. They did not serve merely as a clearinghouse for the bishops' information; on the contrary, leaders in these groups came up with their own programs and crafted their own interpretations for dissemination. In significant ways, these early reflections on women and Vatican II served to refocus laywomen's vocation away from expected roles and responsibilities. The laywoman project is truly an example of the "lived history" of Vatican II in which laypeople interpreted and implemented the Council's teachings as an active process in concert with the hierarchy.[20]

Overall, the laywoman project helped Catholic women transition to a new understanding of their own vocations that depended far less on essentialism, that is, the belief that each sex can be defined by a certain set of traits and accompanying expectations for their behavior. Each of the communities came to challenge the idea that good Catholic laywomen only live for others, to the point of effacing their own calls. Moreover, they largely rejected the idea that it was shameful for Catholic wives to choose employment outside the home. These communities encouraged laywomen to think more expansively about their role as persons in the world, instead of as women first.

The second epigraph for this chapter is a revealing illustration of the laywoman project's capacity to challenge gender essentialism. Mrs. Lucille Martin wrote in to *Marriage* magazine in 1972 to complain about a lighthearted article that would have caused little fuss just a few years earlier. Titled "Power Struggle in the Supermarket," the piece joked about the different nature of men and women as revealed through their shopping habits. The author—not incidentally another laywoman—revealed that this piece was not quite so fluffy as it might appear on the surface. "The sexes *are* different," the author insisted. "Androgyny (with its claim that the sexes soon will merge and everybody will be as mixed-up as milkshakes) just won't work. The sexes are not going to merge as long as there is shopping to do."[21]

Martin considered this work an example of "the pit of sex-role stereotyping—where 'men are men and women are women.'" She would no longer tolerate such an outlook in the magazine, where once it would have been second nature, and she was not fooled by the failed attempt to mask it with humor. But Lucille Martin does not appear to be an ardent feminist. Note how she opens her critique: "I write as a woman whose consciousness has been raised enough to notice . . ." Raised just enough to use her first name and not her husband's, but no more perhaps, as she takes pains to make clear. Still, she took a stand in the pages of a respected Catholic periodical for the right of laywomen to cast off ideas that no longer fit (or perhaps had never fit) their idea of themselves.[22]

The wide-ranging discussion of essentialism, and its rejection by many participants in the laywoman project, also led them to question complementarity. This is the teaching that God created men and women to complement each other with distinct natures, functions, and roles; it is the church's core modern teaching on gender roles. Writers in *Marriage* challenged the teaching on many fronts, including deeply ingrained perceptions of women's sexuality and other aspects of laywomen's roles in married life. The women of the NCCW also undermined complementarity by teaching that laywomen must rethink the roles they had been assigned as women in the gendered world of parish life; they heard over and over that they now had more to contribute to the Catholic community than spiritual bouquets and checks for the missions. These were worthy pursuits to be sure but ones rooted in an essentialist vision of what a woman was and, perhaps more important, what she should not be. The laywoman project did not reach universal conclusions on this subject, however, as we shall see.

In the prologue, I return to the discourse of essentialism and complementarity that permeated the Catholic community shortly before the laywoman project began. Through a set of popular articles responding to a "vocation crisis" starting in 1958, I examine how Catholics perceived laywomen at the end of the 1950s. Together, these articles illustrate laywomen's place in the Catholic hierarchy of vocation, and therefore their status in the Catholic community, on the eve of Vatican II. Essentialism dominated, as laywomen were blamed for suppressing vocations to the sisterhoods.

Chapter 1, on the Theresians, emerges directly from the themes of the prologue. The Theresians, a group for laywomen, was founded in the early 1960s for the sole purpose of fostering vocations to the sisterhoods. By design, the group encouraged laywomen to view their own lives and work as secondary to the superior calls of women religious. Over time, however, the Theresians show how laywomen and their allies took concrete steps to develop a vocation for laywomen that placed them on an equal spiritual footing with others in the Catholic community. Eventually, the Theresians became an explicitly feminist organization, but not before they spent over a decade wrestling with foundational questions of gender identity in the context of Catholic teaching.

Chapter 2 shifts focus from the tiny Theresians to the massive National Council of Catholic Women, which claimed to serve every Catholic lay-woman in the United States. I specifically focus on the NCCW's relation-ship to feminism as it attempted to rethink Catholic womanhood (and challenge the hierarchy) without the radical step of self-identifying. This chapter also examines the World Union of Catholic Women's Organizations (WUCWO), an organization closely associated with the NCCW that took a more self-consciously feminist path, to explain the curious nature of the NCCW's nonfeminist feminism.

In chapter 3 I move away from women's organizations to explore a com-munity of Catholic women in print. *Marriage* magazine, a periodical for Catholic couples, took changing gender roles as its particular focus during the postconciliar era, and encouraged laymen as well as women to debate controversial ideas in its pages. Unlike the organizational women in this book, the laywomen writers in *Marriage* were most preoccupied by ques-tions that centered on gender, sexuality, and other intimate matters, espe-cially the evolving power dynamics between Catholic husbands and wives. Here we see laywomen's challenges to essentialism and complementarity most strongly articulated (and most strongly opposed) in articles on working wives, sex, and male headship in the family.

Chapter 4 considers two more self-consciously conservative groups of Catholic laywomen who nevertheless participated in the laywoman project in fascinating ways. Leaders of the Catholic Daughters of America and the Daughters of Isabella took a defensive posture, proudly posi-tioning themselves as shoring up a faith under threat in the 1960s and

1970s. However, they too considered new ideas about their own identities as women in the church as they tried in good faith to adapt to the realities of a changing world. After a decade of careful thought as well as input from the hierarchy, they determined their best course was to hold on to what they knew. They found more power in an older version of Catholic womanhood than newer interpretations of gender could offer them, even as they saw the strength of their organizations diminish as a result.

. . . .

I offer *The Laywoman Project* first and foremost as a work of scholarship to add to our understanding of this time in the history of the American Catholic Church. But I also offer it as a reminder of the collective power of Catholic laywomen, who too often—even among themselves—are perceived to be powerless in the Catholic Church. At a time when the scandals caused by systematic sexual abuse by clergy and the cover-up of that abuse by the hierarchy demand an emboldened laity, the work of these women reminds us that Catholic laywomen can train themselves for self-advocacy. Laywomen do indeed have a history of challenging clerical authority, if primarily in this case by questioning and perhaps rejecting teachings central to the construction of their own identities.

The laywoman project proves that faithful, committed, nonradical Catholic leaders at the very heart of American Catholicism fostered vitally necessary conversations in the postconciliar era that the clerical leadership of the church was extremely reluctant to have. They undertook their larger project because the church wanted change in one area ("the laity"), while leaving the church's understanding of gender, and therefore the underpinnings of its power structure in institution and family, sacrosanct. Laywomen determined they had the authority to address the situation through word and action. In doing so they threw off their passivity as, in fact, they had been instructed to do as "laymen." Theirs is a legacy of laywomen thinking, speaking out, and acting on their own behalf. If their actions could not change the hierarchy, the hierarchy nevertheless could not stop them from transforming themselves and their communities—that is, the church—through new understandings of who they were and what they were called to do.

Prologue

Killing Vocations over Wheaties and Milk

I would spend a lifetime being grateful to God
for the decision He helped me make, and being
sorry for those who were unable to make it.

Sister Mary Yolanda, bvm, "Vocation:
From Doubt to Decision" (1959)

Three friends, Lucy, Ellen, and Fran, sat in the corner drugstore drinking coffee for the last time together. It was a poignant moment for Sister Mary Yolanda, née Lucy, a recent college graduate about to enter the convent of the Sisters of Charity of the Blessed Virgin Mary. This moment, her last as a typical American girl in sneakers and curls, became the centerpiece of a rumination on women's vocation published in *Today* magazine in 1959. The story neatly reveals popular conceptions of Catholic laywomen and their standing in the church at the brink of the 1960s.

The bulk of the story focuses on Lucy's spiritual journey to the moment of decision, filled as it was with doubt and uncertainty. Wasn't she too social to be a nun? Too indecisive? Too focused on the material things in life? She felt the pull of religious life yet was conflicted enough that she wore a new fur to her meeting with a priest vocation director in a bid to get herself rejected. But once he taught her how to pray properly about her incipient vocation, it led to her final commitment. "I did not dream of the hundredfold harvest of joy I would reap," she concluded, "with chalk on my veil in a yellow classroom—172 teaching days a year."

Lucy made her choice against the backdrop of her two best friends, Ellen (engaged to be married) and Fran (eager for a distinguished career in journalism and the single life). It is Fran that Lucy identifies with most closely; before her decision to enter religious life, the two spun dreams together of success and glamour in the big city. It is Fran, too, who finds it hardest to let her friend go, treating her to a new hairdo so that the "holies . . . will realize that [she] knew how to dress." Lucy speaks of her fondly but ultimately rejects Fran's path, which represents the way of materialism. "No gain, no greed, no applause, no recognition pulled me toward religious life," she said. "Here, then, was the heart of the true vocation: it is followed solely for love."

If Fran represents the single career woman, with an appropriate hard edge, Ellen is equally materialistic, but with a softer, flightier, domestic glow. Her obsession with bridesmaids, florists, and "the price of petit fours" was "the joke of our crowd." Like Lucy, Ellen faced indecision over her vocation. An earlier scene finds them ensconced in Ellen's bedroom, Ellen wrapped in a blanket, weeping over her fear of marriage. "Oh Lucy, how can you be so sure of what you're doing? Maybe I'm supposed to be a nun instead of Bill's wife." We are told that Ellen stalks about "melodramatically," and Lucy observes that "she looks smaller than ever—almost pathetic." Ellen's dilemma is not resolved until her fiancé takes charge. Lucy reports with a smile that "God had used the tools at hand, namely Bill, to steer her by the circumstances of life around her to this vocation." We are left with the vision of a deliriously happy, but decidedly passive, married laywoman.

There is another significant laywoman in this story, although we hear of her only in passing. Lucy remarks sadly that her "parents' objections to my leaving loomed large on the horizon of obstacles." Ever since her announcement, "there had been little that was pleasant at home—little that did not carry soreness with it." Thus appears one of the most common tropes in what we might call "vocation crisis literature": the obstructionist Catholic mother. We will see much more of her in the pages to come.

Sister Mary Yolanda's story is heartfelt and sincere, and it reveals much about the challenges of accepting the call to religious life. But she shows us quite a bit more about where laywomen stood in this church of 1959. Catholic laywomen may have received a variety of calls, but they were certainly not all perceived to be on the same plane. At the top of our hierarchy is the priest vocation director, the only person capable of offering sufficient spiritual guidance to Lucy. Lucy herself comes next. Her self-understanding is the most developed, as is her spirituality, and she uses both to guide and comfort her friends (with firm assistance from the layman Bill). Fran and Ellen are safe on their own paths, but they have not overcome their materialism, which will keep them from achieving a higher spirituality. The lowest rung on the ladder is reserved for the Catholic mother, who created an unpleasant home that brought only "soreness" to her daughter on the brink of dedicating her life to God. While Lucy is clearly full of love for her friends and family, she herself tells us how she views other women's vocations in relation to her own: "I would spend a lifetime being grateful to God for the decision He helped me make, and being sorry for those who were unable to make it."[1]

I doubt Sister Mary Yolanda wanted to trivialize the life choices of her friends, or suggest her own superiority. Her intent was to verbalize her dedication to this intensely challenging and rewarding vocation, in terms meant to appeal to an American Catholic girl. Those average Catholic teens of the baby boom generation would be heavily scrutinized in these years, and charged with stemming a looming crisis in the American church, a crisis born of Catholics' prosperity. As was widely reported in the Catholic press at the time, the growth in the Catholic population was rapidly outstripping the increase in vocations. For example, the Paulist magazine *Information* reported that as of 1948, 80,000 teaching sisters taught 4.5 million students in the United States. By 1958, 96,000 sisters were expected to teach 8.5 million students. That's an 89 percent increase in students, but only a 20 percent increase in sisters. And the numbers continued to rise: in 1958 alone the Catholic population grew by 1.5 million.[2]

Little wonder, then, that worried Catholic leaders took to the press to get the word out; between 1958 and 1964 the Catholic media featured all manner of hand-wringing articles on the dearth of new priests, brothers, and nuns. These articles give us the opportunity to examine not only how laywomen were viewed in the period just prior to the Council, but also the limits placed on their vocations. The national conversation about the vocation crisis was heavily gendered and saved its highest criticism for married women. A variety of experts in the field of vocation looked on the Catholic *girl* with approval, each a potential religious vocation; the married laywoman, however, bore the brunt of Catholic frustration. Most commonly, she was viewed as an obstacle to her child's vocation, either because of her lack of faith, her failure to promote Catholic values (and devotions) in the home, or her selfish refusal to relinquish her hold on her child. Anxious to prove their commitment, many laywomen, especially those in the national women's organizations, vowed to do their part to forward, not hinder, the growth of vocations. It is in this atmosphere that the Theresians came into being, as will be discussed in chapter 1. But all of the laywomen in these pages were forced to contend with the persistent stereotypes revealed here that shaped laywomen's identity and responsibilities.

The first thing to note is that these articles about the vocation crisis were usually written by priests and religious. Of forty-one articles consulted for this study, written between 1958 and 1964, twenty-three were written by priests, eight by women religious, and three each by laymen and laywomen. Perhaps this is not surprising, since priests and religious had a vested interest in increasing vocations, particularly to their own orders and dioceses. The end result, however, is that blame was placed squarely on the one area of life about which these authors knew the least: the modern Catholic home. "Since God is not wanting in the graces He gives," one editorial concluded, "we must look for the answer in American Catholic family life."[3]

Nearly half of the articles advanced the claim that Catholic parents actively obstructed vocations. Remember, though, that we rarely hear about parents' objections firsthand, only through the hearsay of priests and religious. In the same month that Sister Mary Yolanda was writing of her vocation, Father Henry Strassner outlined four potential sermons on vocations for *Emmanuel*. He described the eager young boy or girl, nervously confessing a vocation to a parent. "And thus the battle to kill a vocation is begun." These parents take a number of different tacks. You're much too young, they claim. Or they bribe the youngster with new clothes or car privileges. The mother "sobs hysterically"; the father "manfully" describes his aspirations for his boy. "Stupid parents," Strassner writes. "Selfish parents." He describes two figures in the night, looking in the windows: "The devil sneers a smile of triumph. Christ's face is wrinkled in pain." A widely reported survey seemed to justify these accusations. In the late 1950s Serra International, a group for laymen committed to increasing vocations, asked 1,561 young priests and 2,453 young nuns how their parents responded to their vocation: 59 percent of the men, and a whopping 72 percent of the women reported "parental objections ranging from simple ridicule to physical violence." As one author noted, "We can bring God's dream to glorious fruition—or we can kill it over Wheaties and milk."[4]

The discrepancy between the statistics on parental objections for nuns and priests can be explained by the fact that priests enjoyed a higher prestige than women religious, and also greater independence relative to sisters. Documents also reveal that many, even in the Catholic community, worried that convents were stifling and unpleasant places to live. A revealing comment in *Homiletic and Pastoral Review*, a journal for priests, shows how priests themselves found it difficult to speak positively about convent life. The author took his fellow priests to task: "From our point of view, Father, the convent life of today may not seem in the least attractive, but we must remember that neither of us is going to live that life. . . . If 160,000 girls in

America alone are able to do so well at it this very day, it certainly cannot be something unusually repulsive." He reminded his brethren, "Don't try to understand women! Any one of the fairer sex who is at all honest will tell you that women do not understand each other or even themselves." With all Catholic laywomen thus summarily dismissed, it was not that far of a leap to blame them for failing to bring their daughters to a proper understanding of their calls to serve the faith.

Articles often outlined the objections most raised by parents, then systematically dismissed them. Isn't thirteen too young for a boy to decide his fate? Not for Christ in the Temple! Shouldn't my child see more of the world first, so she can make an informed decision? Sure, if you want to expose her to temptation and the possibility of a mixed marriage . . . or worse! As these objections were dismissed, judgments were passed. Parents of the day were accused of being overly concerned with upward mobility and material possessions. These accusations reveal deep unease over American Catholics' prosperity at midcentury, and seem to be a manifestation of the "materialist crisis" of the 1950s. Vocation experts believed Catholic parents had chosen prosperity over spirituality, individualism over the community, selfishness over sacrifice, and were transmitting these values to their children en masse. "The real truth is that either parents lack faith," one priest concluded sadly, "or they lack a real love for their children."[5]

At first glance, these authors seem to heap equal blame on both laymen and laywomen, since the articles were usually directed at both parents, but the gendered nature of the texts indicates that mothers were being subtly (and sometimes not so subtly) blamed for the crisis. First, one of the greatest charges leveled at lay readers was that their homes were insufficiently Catholic. As the religious tone of the home was the mother's province, it was implied that failure to promote a Catholic atmosphere was her fault. What did the authors mean by a sufficiently "Catholic atmosphere"? Parents were told that a truly Catholic home featured daily family rosary, mealtime blessings, statues and holy cards representing a variety of saints, holy water and blessed candles, crucifixes, and a ready selection of Catholic magazines. Parents should set the example by engaging in daily prayer and frequent reception of the sacraments. "A home without such things is usually a worldly home," Fr. Donald Miller argued, "that is, one in which worldly ambitions will be fostered in the minds and hearts of children to the exclusion of any thought of spiritual ideals."[6]

Catholic laywomen's gradual shift away from personal, home-based devotions to a more institutionalized communal prayer focused on the liturgy began in the 1950s, and certainly predated Vatican II. As has been noted, this is one area in which the Catholic laity anticipated, and to some degree drove, the changes that would appear to be a startling break with tradition after the Council. But we cannot forget that even though the tide had shifted, change was still contested. These articles show that the backlash against laywomen for abandoning devotions was not limited to discussion of devotions themselves; here laywomen are blamed for undermining the church's most essential infrastructure: the priesthood and religious life.[7]

A second indication that women were to blame for the lack of vocations is the frequent discussion of maternal selfishness. "They are greedy. They love themselves," a priest explained. "They are looking for security with no view to confidence in God." Authors often included anecdotes to illustrate their arguments, and these usually featured a mother reluctant to relinquish her child. Such love and devotion were rarely praised; rather, a mother's reluctance indicated the failure to place God's will above her own.[8] A pair of Maryknoll vocation directors argued that this selfishness represented weakness, not intentional obstruction: "a child, whose whole juvenile life has been spent trying to please his parents, cannot be expected to be heroic in the face of his mother's quivering lips and a few tears. I'd certainly say that most parents do not encourage their children to be heroic. They would prefer that they be tranquil and prosperous, but not heroic." (It is telling that while the priests called out both parents for this, the article's headline read, "*Mothers Today Do Not Want Their Children to Be Heroic*.")[9]

The priests went on to demonstrate proper sacrifice from a proper Catholic mother: "Now I can't imagine the Blessed Mother trying to talk Christ out of the Crucifixion. I can't hear her saying: 'This is all very nice, but this crucifixion is just too much.'" The men and women of Maryknoll offered more models for Catholic mothers in *Bernie Becomes a Nun*, a 1956 book designed to appeal to teenaged girls. *Bernie* includes a series of images showing a mother succumbing to tears when Bernie gives her the news of her vocation. "Mom cried a bit," we are told. "I don't know if it was joy or sorrow." But in the end "she said at last, 'Dad and I are proud that God has chosen one of ours.'"[10]

It's ironic, then, that these authors often attempted to appeal to women's inherent selfishness as a means of encouraging them to foster vocations. They claimed that one of the most common objections mothers made to a girl's vocation was that their daughter would be lost to them forever once she entered religious life. But numerous articles assured mothers that they

I told them all about it, then. "It's the only life for me," I ended.

"You've been such a wonderful Mom and Dad, I had to tell you first."

Mom cried a bit; I don't know if it was joy or sorrow. "Go ahead, dear," she said at last. "Dad and I are proud that God has chosen one of ours."

I went back to the cake. My heart was light and gay.

From *Bernie Becomes a Nun* (1956), a book by Maryknoll sister Maria del Rey written to recruit sisters. This illustration demonstrates how a good Catholic mother should respond to the news that her daughter had a vocation. She was to put aside her grief quickly for the good of her child and the church.

actually gained more than they lost, since "a married son or daughter must leave their family for another and their interests and responsibilities will change—but a religious—they keep their family close to their heart, daily recommending them to God." A nun was often the only child available to come at a moment of tragedy, another insisted. And married daughters were distracted and wanted only to "dump their problems" on their mothers, whereas a religious would be a source of serene comfort for all of her days. So even as mothers were accused of selfishness, authors shamelessly appealed to their self-interest, reinforcing the trait they claimed to abhor.[11]

We can also conclude that many of these columns were ultimately directed at women because the solutions offered were female ones. Numerous experts praised the heroic lengths to which prayerful mothers would go to obtain vocations for their children. A priest speaker at a 1964 vocation conference told such a story of a young mother and her three children. A woman expecting her first child asked her mother, a fallen-away Catholic, to accompany her to church and wait for her while she went to confession. While in church, the woman offered up her child to God if her mother would enter the confessional. The mother went to confession, and later that year the child was stillborn. Even though the woman was informed that she could have no more children, she prayed with all her might that she would have a second child, even if it was "slightly deformed." She "modified the prayer somewhat upon reflection, asking God if the child were born deformed that it might be cured." Sure enough, a son was born alive, but with a clubbed foot. After more extensive prayer, the only doctor in the country who could perform the required surgery was located in her hometown. A few years later, the woman prayed again, this time for a child free of defect, whom she could dedicate to God for a vocation to the priesthood. Once again, the woman's prayer was answered.[12]

Such tales of heroic prayer and sacrifice were held up as the highest examples of Catholic motherhood. One priest spoke of a family with twelve children that boasted two nuns and two priests; he attributed their success to the practice of saying the rosary together as a family every day for fifty years. Another story, mentioned more than once, tells of Mrs. John Vaughan, a mother of thirteen who prayed for an hour before the Blessed Sacrament each day of her adult life, 7,300 hours of prayer in total, "begging God" that her children might be called to religious life. Although one wonders where she could have found the time, all five of her daughters and six of her eight sons answered the call, "one later to be a cardinal." Here was the ideal laywoman, the mother dedicated to sacrificing all for the sake of the church.

Yet she was also a figure of great strength, generating miracles through her extreme piety.[13]

Some laywomen definitely understood that their prayer lives afforded them a measure of power, limited though it was by the prevalent belief that laywomen's power originated chiefly in self-sacrifice and the domestic context. In a 1962 issue of the *Isabellan*, the Daughters of Isabella exhorted laywomen to tap their special powers for vocation promotion. The article begins with a question: "Christian mothers! The harvest is great . . . are you willing to help Me save the world?" The author then reminded laywomen of their authority: "The family is a parish whose Pastor is the Mother." She then named different aspects of laywomen's role—"Praying mother," "Generous mother," and "Suffering mother." In these guises, laywomen "do everything toward the end of seeing their children consecrated to God." Generous mothers "are ready to sacrifice *all* that their children might realize their true calling." An accompanying illustration shows just how generous a dedicated mother could be: a kneeling woman hands her infant child to a standing, radiant Blessed Mother. What wouldn't the perfect Catholic mother give up to help Christ save the world?[14]

But what these authors give in praise of laywomen, they could also take away. Examples of powerful Catholic mothers are undermined by the persistent sense that laywomen were inferior, sinful, and generally unworthy. A 1959 article claimed that "physical motherhood" was inherently inferior to "spiritual motherhood": "It is our task to make clear to our Catholic girls the happiness of spiritual motherhood. Physical motherhood, in itself, is no complete accomplishment, as witness those who are mothers physically, but unwillingly. Without spiritual motherhood a woman is incomplete, and opportunities for spiritual motherhood are greater in a life dedicated to religion than to family life." Physical motherhood could happen to anyone, but the more highly valued spiritual motherhood required true dedication, more likely to occur in the life of a woman religious.[15]

Others stressed the laity's general unworthiness. In the "Parents' Prayer for Vocations" (1959), parents were directed to pray as follows: "How happy would we be if You would make us the parents of a priest or religious. We know that we often offend You and are not worthy of so high a privilege. But, dear God, do not think of our many sins. Think, rather, of the many needs of Your Church." In the last stanza, parents were to ask "the Queen of Vocations" to "put in a good word for us that we too may become the parents of a priest, a Brother, or a Sister." Here mothers become supplicants on their knees before a queen, further emphasizing their lowliness. Mothers reluctant to allow a daughter into the convent were reminded that religious life was the "higher calling," and she only proved her own spirituality to be "incomplete or underdeveloped" if she stood in her daughter's way. Pay attention to your child's call, laywomen were cautioned, "Perhaps it is His way of inviting you to be worthy of such a child."[16]

Finally, these authors were not shy in naming the most practical reason for increasing vocations, the relative cost of teaching sisters versus laywomen teachers. One article quoted the archbishop of Cincinnati on the dire need for sisters. He lamented that the archdiocese saw an increase of only four religious in the elementary schools, necessitating an increase of eighty new lay teachers. "How long can we continue to operate a Catholic school system under such conditions?" he wondered.

This question echoed through every diocese in the nation in the early 1960s. Demographic changes in the 1950s put incredible pressure on bishops and pastors to expand the capacity of the Catholic schools to meet the needs of the growing Catholic population. As the number of vocations failed to keep pace with the baby boom, classrooms overflowed, forcing superintendents to hire laity to make up the difference. Since sisters took vows of poverty and lived in community, they were willing to accept incredibly low wages. Laywomen could not survive on such salaries, so hiring them strained the finances of parishes and limited growth. The situation deteriorated further through the 1960s and 1970s, as falling birth rates and white flight caused the opposite problem—empty classrooms—leaving pastors even less able to pay laywomen a living wage. The author of the article mentioned above went out of his way to acknowledge that lay teachers were "dedicated persons, worth every penny of their salaries; but there is a big difference between the salary of a nun and a lay teacher."[17]

It can be quite jarring, in fact, to see how openly officials discussed the monetary side of the vocation crisis. Girls must follow the call to the sisterhoods for the sake of spiritual motherhood, yes, but the closure of the local parish school was a much more pressing problem. A remarkably candid letter from Stephen Woznicki, the bishop of Saginaw, to the regional director of the National Council of Catholic Women, Detroit Province, reveals how one member of the hierarchy viewed women's role in the looming disaster. Woznicki confessed to losing sleep over the lack of female vocations in his diocese, which had led to the closing of schools and the hiring of lay teachers. Twice in the letter he says that bishops and priests are not at fault; they are "doing all they can . . . but nothing can be done—there are no Sisters." The fault lay in a familiar quarter: "The bottleneck to vocations to the Sisterhood must be found in the parents and also in the lack of the spirit of sacrifice, or in plain words, selfishness among the girls. It's the parents who must change their outlook on vocations, or Sisterhoods will become only token organizations in the Church in this country." We then get to the point of the letter, which is to persuade the women of the NCCW to put their energies toward advancing vocations, "since without doubt, the lack of Sisters is the greatest danger to the Church in America at present." "Why not soft pedal all kinds of far-fetched activities for the time being," he advised, "and concentrate on this problem?"[18] In one short letter, Woznicki manages to imply that it was untenable to run a school system staffed by laywomen teachers, accuse girls of pervasive selfishness, blame parents for obstruction, and dismiss the chosen work of the NCCW as "far-fetched," all while exonerating the hierarchy of any blame.

Let's state the obvious at this point. To use our opening story as illustration, Sister Mary Yolanda found her calling and fulfillment as a teaching sister. "Lucy" might also have served as a lay teacher in the same diocesan school system, giving equally of her time and talents, and finding equal fulfillment in her work. Yet Lucy would have been declared selfish because she was unwilling to enter an order and give her labor to the church at the wages paid to women religious. When Catholic pundits decried the lack of teaching sisters to staff the schools they were frankly stating that the hiring of laywomen was undesirable. In this, laywomen were blamed twice, once for refusing to enter the sisterhoods, and a second time for forcing expenditure to hire their services. Bishop Woznicki, like many of these authors, puts laywomen neatly in their place: they are of little value if they do not put themselves utterly at the service of the church.

One more trend in the articles points to the future rather than the past. A handful of the articles starting in the early 1960s take care to stress a changing definition of vocation, defining it as every Catholic's call from God to a particular form of work, and not just the call to religious life. Such a reading of lay vocation in particular would shortly be reinforced by the Second Vatican Council. The most notable of these articles were written by women religious involved in catechesis, indicating a shift in pedagogical approaches to vocation. One such article, "I Decide My Destiny," included a "vocation drama" designed for eighth graders. Students representing numerous vocations from single professional woman to married professional man, to priest and nun each have a conversation with Destiny where they state how they will answer God's call to their particular state in life, and learn of the joys and challenges of each call. The play suggests no inherent superiority in any one vocation. Similarly, in a 1962 advice column for Catholic teens, Sister M. Dominic echoed the theme that vocations are for everyone and have equal value: "A vocation is the individual life activity which determines the way wherein each one of us shares his personal wealth with other human beings in a love-service to which all of humanity is called by the Grace of God. . . . the vocation is the channel whereby that love is given from heart to heart, from mind to mind, and from soul to soul."[19]

Despite these glimpses of a new way of thinking, in the minds of many Catholics at the turn of the 1960s, laywomen did not have vocations so much as they prevented them in others. Since the ideal laywoman was a heroic sacrificing mother, anything short of total dedication smacked of selfishness. Laywomen's genuine concerns that their children were too young, or the life too difficult, were dismissed as folly, materialism, or a lack of spiritual dedication. These were some of the most powerful stereotypes by which Catholic laywomen were judged, and by which they judged themselves as the era began. It is against this backdrop that we must set the laywoman project.

1

Womanhood Is Sisterhood

Now the Theresians are an edifice built on
womanhood—not just sisterhood. (Except
"womanhood" is "sisterhood," how 'bout that?)

Kathy Cribari, 1971

Something drastic happened to the Theresians of America in 1969. After only eight years in existence, the Theresian Executive Board sat down at its annual meeting and voted unanimously to reject the organization's purpose. The Theresians to this point had a unique mission in the world of the American church. It was an organization for laywomen, founded and run by a priest, whose primary purpose was to promote vocations to the sisterhoods. Such a purpose is not obvious, perhaps. Why would laywomen by the thousands sacrifice so much time and energy to promote a call they themselves did not receive?

The answer lies in demographics. By the early 1960s, American Catholics were increasingly alarmed by a "vocation crisis." Studies in the early 1960s showed that the number of vocations to the priesthood and religious life increased by only 18 percent. Any Catholic now surviving the priest shortage of the early twenty-first century might be allowed a guffaw, but only a brief one. For while vocations were up 18 percent, the Catholic population increased in the same period by 39 percent. The reality was that 50,000 priests and 162,000 women religious were burdened with serving a population of 42 million Catholics.[1] In the early 1960s the need for vocations was clear, and thousands of prayerful laywomen were willing to lend their organizational skills and spiritual zeal to meeting it.

But if the work was so essential, why, then, would the Theresians abandon their purpose in 1969? The vocation crisis was far from being resolved; in fact, the situation had grown increasingly dire as alarming numbers of professed sisters began leaving their communities in the mid-to-late 1960s. Why, too, did the organization resolve to continue if they no longer saw their mission as either viable or desirable? In a moment when laywomen's participation in traditional Catholic women's organizations was beginning to wane, why carry on at all? But carry on they did, choosing to forge a new purpose, this time with *laywomen's* vocations at its heart.

At middecade, laywomen's voices across the American Catholic community asked over and over again the same two questions: What is a Catholic woman? What is her purpose? These questions were at the heart of the emerging laywoman project. When the board voted to change the Theresian purpose, they rejected a concept of Catholic womanhood that had started weakening in the 1950s, and was by the end of the 1960s in a state of collapse. When the leadership began to sense that the bottom had dropped out of the vision of laywomen that they were selling—that of the prayerful, respectful laywoman in service to the "higher calling" of the woman religious—they set about trying to replace it with a concept that placed both on equal footing, each prayerfully seeking to understand and fulfill her individual call from God. A lay Theresian came to understand that *her own* vocation was at the center of the group's mission and was of inherent value. The Theresians now declared themselves "an organization of Catholic lay women who are dedicated to a deeper appreciation of the vocation of the Christian woman . . . as it is lived in the religious and lay states in the world today."[2]

The Theresians offer an ideal first look at the laywoman project. Like the other communities of Catholic laywomen in this book they dealt with the Second Vatican Council and the women's movement in tandem, attempting to puzzle out their place in a changing world. Unlike the others, however, the Theresians existed from the beginning to understand and promote women's vocation. As the organization evolved through the 1960s, the definitions of women's place, ministry, and identity were always at the forefront of its conversations, offering us a rare opportunity to analyze how and why perceptions of laywomen's vocation changed over time.

This chapter will trace the Theresians of America from its starting point in 1961 to the emergence of a muted feminist, but not activist, consciousness among the Theresian leadership in the latter years of the 1970s. The goal is not to draw a straight line to feminism, which actually emerged quite late in comparison to, say, the National Council of Catholic Women (NCCW) or the World Union of Catholic Women's Organizations (WUCWO) and was never central to the group's identity and agenda. Rather, the richness of this story lies in the intervening years, as this well-meaning group of

Womanhood Is Sisterhood

laywomen, priests, and women religious picked through the jumbled confusion of ideas on offer in the culture to remake the Catholic laywoman from the ground up.

The project saw them radically reject one traditional view of the laywoman, that of inferior support to the woman religious. But in the vacuum created by that decision they returned for several years to an essentialist position. When most other national groups of Catholic women, both lay and religious, were beginning to question traditional Catholic teaching on women's roles, the Theresians opened the 1970s with a fervent defense of complementarity (albeit with the goal of saving a world in crisis, not the promotion of domesticity) and open hostility to the women's movement. In time, however, the Theresians discarded their essentialism to head in a completely different direction, adopting a view of Catholic women that was deeply rooted in "the spirit of Vatican II" (as they viewed it), cultural feminism, and the spiritual ethos of the 1970s. The end result is a strikingly modern view of Catholic women's vocation and an equally modern support system to sustain it. They affirmed laywomen's individuality and calls to work in the world, as well as what they considered to be women's basic need for a deep prayer commitment within small Christian communities. The "fathers" of Vatican II unknowingly sparked a transition that led these Catholic laywomen from self-effacement to self-possession, demonstrating Catholic laywomen's struggle to come of age in the postconciliar era.

IN SUPPORT OF SISTERHOOD VOCATIONS

It is a mark of how far the Theresians have traveled from their origins that their official history effectively ignores the first seven years of the group's existence. The Theresian Story's first chapter, "Beginnings," includes one sentence about the Theresians' original purpose. That purpose is then repudiated in passing later in the book: "The fact that early in the 1960s Theresians was considered a lay organization whose primary 'apostolate' was that of 'fostering vocations to the sisterhood' showed how separated women had allowed themselves to become in the name of religion." Note how the history limits this purpose to "early in the 1960s," even though it was in place until October 1969. This is fitting for an organizational history written to promote and celebrate the group's present-day values, which include equality for and among women. But since my interest in this group is less the end product than the transition itself, we must slog through the historical record to piece together what has been forgotten.[3]

To that end we should start with a blanket statement: the Theresians was founded to be an organization of laywomen dedicated to increasing sisterhood vocations. In the earliest days it was described as the female counterpart to Serra International, started in the 1930s as an exclusive group for middle-class, professional, Catholic laymen attempting to increase vocations to the priesthood. The Theresians was founded by Elwood Voss (1925–92), a priest and administrator in the Catholic school system in the diocese of Pueblo, Colorado. He named the group "Theresians" to suggest their devotion to Saint Thérèse of Lisieux, one of the most significant modern saints, and one who inspired a tremendous following in the United States in the first half of the twentieth century. Thérèse, a French cloistered Carmelite nun, was canonized in 1925, only twenty-eight years after her early death in 1897. Celebrated for her piety, she was a "legendary model of interiority"; Catholics were encouraged to follow her "little way," finding God in the simple tasks of everyday life. She was also associated with patient suffering due to her long struggle with tuberculosis. Both made her a highly suitable model for American laywomen, despite the fact that she was a cloistered nun.[4]

In 1985, Voss remembered the founding as a reaction against laywomen's organizations whose purpose "was generally the support of others." "There were few organizations, if any, that existed FOR the women themselves," he recalled. His solution was "an organization named Theresians that would provide an opportunity for women to enrich their own lives through spiritual development, ongoing education, affirmation and encouragement in their vocations, and a deep community experience." This description of the Theresians is a better reflection of how it perceived itself in the 1980s than Voss's original intention in 1961.[5]

To illustrate the difference, compare the above statement to one of the early documents Voss composed for the group, "The Theresian's Prayer": "Blessed Saint Thérèse, great lover of souls, guide all our efforts to foster vocations to the Sisterhood and inspire within us true zeal for this cause. Help us to foster within our homes and communities, an atmosphere in which religious vocations can grow; where young women will learn to be generous to their Blessed Lord." So far, the prayer reflects prevailing attitudes about laywomen and religious life as seen in the vocation crisis articles outlined in the prologue. A Theresian laywoman prayed for zeal in the cause of promoting other women's vocations, for a home atmosphere conducive to their growth, and for girls to be generous (implying their tendency to selfishness).

Yet the second paragraph takes the idea of service for the sake of others even further. Voss writes, "Help us to be the door-step over which many will pass on their way to God's service. And if, in being loyal Theresians, we become tired through our endeavors, remind us that we have become a stone on the highway to the Sisterhood by helping the Church in her hour of need." Laywomen's status could not be more evident: Voss (figuratively) asked these women to pray to be stepped on and passed over.[6]

The Theresians' original purpose proved popular enough that the organization grew throughout the 1960s. From a first meeting of twenty-five women in Pueblo in early 1962, the Theresians grew to 4,000 members by 1965, and to 6,000 by 1968. In that year the group had "units" in thirty-five states plus Canada, China, and West Africa. Voss further claimed the group added some thirty-five members per week to its units, which were divided into adult, college, and high school affiliates, although membership seemed to peak in the late 1960s and never gained much traction internationally. Although the organization's appeal was widespread, Theresian growth and support was always strongest in the American West and Southwest, with its most vibrant chapters found in Denver and Houston. It appears to have been predominantly white in membership and exclusively white in its leadership.[7]

Early documents from the Theresians provide a baseline for understanding these average laywomen's self-conception. How did they view themselves in relation to women religious? How did they define their own vocation, if at all? What can their chosen role reveal to us about laywomen in the Council years? In the end, it is their perceived relationship with women religious that is most revealing.

Before beginning that analysis, a methodological note is warranted. The Theresians have left behind an extensive collection of records dating back to the group's inception. These papers are comprehensive, including correspondence, newsletters and magazines, financial records, and most especially conference proceedings. These provide ample detail about the group's origins and transitions. However, they must be treated with care to achieve the end goal, that of capturing the voices of American laywomen, which could so easily be lost to us if we are not deliberate about forwarding them. The Theresian leadership on the national level was dominated by clergy and women religious in its first several decades. Elwood Voss is a towering—and beloved—presence, and his voice could easily dominate since many of the papers in the first two decades of the collection originate with, or were sent to him. As just one example of his reach, the 1972 handbook for unit presidents included four pages of quotations from Voss, printed one after the other, 53 quotes in total.[8]

Moreover, priests and women religious were the majority of speakers at most conference programs throughout the 1960s. Although laywomen did speak at conferences, their addresses had a different tone than those of the religious. I suspect that priests and sisters were viewed as experts, so their talks were often theological in nature or were designed as commentaries on other groups. A sister might speak on "the modern girl," or a priest on "the vocation atmosphere in the home." In contrast, laywomen's topics were nearly always limited to their own purview, including the practical details of running a Theresian unit, the nature of the Theresian purpose, or laywomen's role in general. Although laywomen's talks were afforded less prestige, rarely achieving keynote status, for example, they are extremely valuable for the purpose of this study.

We best begin the analysis with an understanding of where Catholic laywomen stood vis-à-vis women religious. Technically, as nonclergy all Catholic women share the same state: they are all members of the laity, regardless of religious vows. In the 1970s, Catholic feminists—both laywomen and women religious—reveled in this rediscovered fact. It proved that all Catholic women were indeed "sisters" despite their different paths, and feminists used this as a rallying cry for solidarity and justice.

But the Theresians would have found this an alien concept at the group's founding. It started its life in the middle of the vocation crisis of the early 1960s; in fact, it was a direct product of that crisis, described in the prologue of this book. Vocation crisis literature outlined the chasm between women religious and laywomen. Women religious embraced a vocation that originated with a call from God. As we have seen, laywomen were not viewed as having answered a specific call to vocation. At best, they were heroic sufferers, sacrificing for other women's vocations. At worst, they were mired in materialist values, obstructing their daughters' spiritual calls.

The perception that laywomen blocked girls' vocations to the sisterhood was only a symptom of the tension between the two groups, not its source. Religious life was afforded more status in most facets of American Catholic culture, particularly the dominant Irish Catholic strain.[9] For a woman, to be a nun was seen as the ultimate sacrifice to God, and thus the highest form of spirituality. The convent was "the higher call," a common phrase implying that married life was somehow lesser in the eyes of the church. Moreover, these women had no doubt internalized "the spiritual hierarchy," in historian James McCartin's phrase, a holdover from the immigrant church that "placed ordinary laity—the overwhelming majority of the Catholic population—at the bottom of the pyramid of power. . . . Because priests and religious sisters embodied the Church's institutional presence within local settings, they represented the most significant layer of spiritual authority in the Church."[10]

　　　　　　　　　　　　　　　　　　　　　　Womanhood Is Sisterhood

Women religious also had limited contact with laywomen after entering religious life. Even if they were not cloistered, nuns' ability to move freely in the world was circumscribed, and "particular friendships" were discouraged both in and outside communities. One feels the strain of this in the vocation crisis literature. The fear of being cut off from a child or sibling was often cited as a reason for family objection. Moreover, when sisters did have contact with the laity outside their own families, it was often when they were in positions of authority over laypeople, in schools, hospitals, parishes, and charitable institutions. While the relationships developed between sisters and laity under these circumstances were often positive and loving, as a whole they served to place laywomen in an inferior position. Religious life seemed both holier and more mysterious to laywomen held at arms' length. And laywomen certainly absorbed the message that nuns gained authority from their vocation, an authority to which a Catholic woman in the pews had little access beyond the home (and even there it was limited by the headship of her husband).

The distance between laywomen and women religious meant it was difficult for each group to see the other accurately, or view the other as an equal. When lay Theresians spoke of women religious in the early years, we can hear a certain reverence in their voices. Given a different group of laywomen you might just as easily have heard resentment, over harsh treatment in the classroom, say, or expectations of deference. But the Theresians' purpose was increasing vocations. They hoped to dispel negative views of the sisterhoods among laywomen, so they accentuated the positive. In the end, however, the vision they offered of religious life in the early years was no less stereotypical than a portrait of dour nuns smacking students' knuckles with rulers.

According to Theresian speakers in the early 1960s, sisters literally glowed. A nun had a "serene face lighted from within with a joyous fulfilled look," Mrs. John Downs claimed. A priest described nuns as having a "spiritual radiance," while Virginia Siegle (the most prominent laywomen in the Theresians' first decade) went so far as to say that this glow was the crucial characteristic of a sister: "Her life must radiate this charity. She is a living incarnation of the Person of Christ. If she . . . does not radiate—she is a failure." Finally, this idea was visually depicted in a photograph of a praying nun that appeared in a Theresian recruitment booklet in the early 1960s. The theme of the glowing nun suggests the significance of sisters' mystery for laywomen. They seemed to have an immense spiritual power within them that set them apart.[11]

Theresians promotional material showing a "glowing nun" (ca. 1964).
(Courtesy of the Women and Leadership Archives, Loyola University Chicago)

Sisters were also praised for being selfless. One speaker claimed that the current crop of women religious proved that modern women were just as self-sacrificing as women of the past. The sisters of today "can match those of yesterday in forgetting self for God and humanity." To be selfless was

Womanhood Is Sisterhood

always among the highest praises to be offered to Catholic women, and this speaker—an archbishop—wanted modern laywomen to know it was still possible, if you were a nun. Others suggested that extreme self-sacrifice was ultimately linked to happiness. A typical, if hyperbolic, take on the lives of sisters from Cynthia Bordelon was meant to be carried by Theresians to young women: "Let them know that a complete dedication and utter love of their Crucified Lord will inevitably lead to the crucifixion of their own desires and wills, so that they may be united to their Lord. Oh! But also let them know that there is never an absence of happiness. Tell them that there is always peace in the heart and a song on the lips of one who meets the challenge of a Divine Lover." Little sign of the struggles inherent to religious life here. A woman who takes vows will "inevitably" lose her own will and replace it with a song in her heart.[12]

Theresians often stressed the theme of sisters' essential femininity in their speeches. In the larger Catholic culture women religious were viewed as fundamentally asexual, their habits a means of concealing any physical attribute that made nuns womanly. In a time when domesticity and femininity were hyperemphasized in the larger culture, Theresians may have emphasized sisters' feminine side in an attempt to make the convent less off-putting to potential vocations, and to stress similarity to laywomen. A popular activity in college units was to throw "showers" for young women leaving for the convent. (At one such event the gifts included soap and black shoe polish.) Citing another aspect of the feminine role, Virginia Siegle claimed that sisters were "a witness to the Motherly character of the Church," while Marge Herrig, commenting on the changing habits, said she did not care one way or the other, as long as the garb was "fresh and feminine."[13]

You can hear the lay Theresians puzzling out their relationship to the sisters, at times emphasizing the nuns' fundamental difference (they glow), at other times viewing them as models for laywomen's own behavior (self-sacrifice), and finally stressing what they have in common (femininity). They were eager to serve these women well, but as of the early 1960s, Theresians did not yet seem able to view women religious through anything but a soft-focus lens. Mrs. Raber Taylor, writing of the "Theresian influence" in 1965, concluded that the Theresians simply want to help others "learn that nuns are real people, doing a real job with a smile." She did not seem to realize that assuming the perpetual presence of that smile limited sisters' full humanity.[14]

Of course, the Theresians' main focus was initially sisterhood, not lay vocations, so early documents speak more of sisters than of the Theresians themselves. Comments about laywomen in general are few and demonstrate an outlook heavily influenced, if no longer dominated, by an essentialist world-view. In a 1965 conference talk, Mrs. Carl Miller described her typical Ther-esian unit in Hartford, Connecticut. Charged with explaining how to start a new unit, Miller shows us first the initiative and leadership of laywomen. To begin, she invited forty laywomen to lunch, mostly NCCW members and the wives of members of Serra International. Interest was high, and regular meetings were quickly established. Miller spoke confidently about their lead-ership's relationship with the diocese, noting that the unit's first president was an ideal leader, "a gentle persuader and a diplomat" who had "deep convic-tions on the role of the lay-woman in the Church."

Their unit insisted on finding its own direction, especially on spiritual matters. Although they had a spiritual moderator who was a priest, the unit decided that "responsibility for action must be fulfilled by us and could not be left up to the spiritual moderator." But her description of these laywomen as confident leaders was undercut somewhat when she noted one of the group's activities. The local Serra Club called on the Theresians to be "host-esses" at the Serra Vocation Institute. This task was limited to "visiting and chatting with the sisters, and serving cookies and coffee."[15] They viewed themselves as highly capable but still situated within a particular role.

Mrs. Raber Taylor also spoke of laywomen's nature at the 1965 confer-ence. Much more than Mrs. Miller, Taylor veers toward essentialism. "A Ther-esian's influence is in giving," she believed. "There is inborn in woman, a loving care of living things, for nurturing, for educating, and even cultivating one's garden." She added that "the Theresian wife will make Dad the *Boss* in their home, and together they will bring the children to maturity with an objective view of life." This comment is perhaps more revealing than the speaker intended. Who is the "boss" in this scenario, the man himself, or the person with the power to designate him so?[16] But Theresians did not indulge much in essentialist rhetoric, even though it was an influence. When they discussed themselves and their purpose they were much more likely to do so in the context of their spirituality than in their role as wives and mothers, and this is where their significance lies.

Theresians saw their spirituality as their greatest strength and defining characteristic, and thus the transition that occurred in their conception of their own prayer lives deserves particular attention. Here we can trace, in miniature, the larger shift from the focus on others to the validation of lay-women's own particular vocations. This shift would not fully emerge until the late 1960s, but the transition begins in the group's earliest days, and it can be spotted first in Theresians' changing understanding of prayer. In the first few years Theresians moved from a conception of themselves as conduits, seeking to efface themselves to offer prayer for others, toward a view of prayer as a means of self-definition and empowerment that did not require suffering and self-sacrifice.

We have already seen in the vocation crisis literature how Catholic laywomen's prayer was often perceived. Laywomen were praised most for prayer that emphasized their own submission. Indeed, it was thought that Catholic women excelled at this form of prayer because of their natural passivity and receptiveness; they modeled submission to God's will for those in the culture less suited to surrender—namely, men. Prayer rooted in the suffering and, at its most extreme, the victimhood of women, was also a strong theme in mid-twentieth century devotional culture. According to historian Paula Kane, "Catholic girls and women were especially encouraged to embrace the ideal of redemption through submission, since it had become a commonplace in Catholic circles to describe suffering as women's 'natural' role."[17]

This is a tricky business, though, because while a modern reader might decry this as sexism, pure and simple, laywomen ironically recognized this very submission as a source of power (and in fact they were encouraged to do so). That power was derived in proportion to the woman's degree of self-sacrifice. The more she suffered to offer the prayer, the more selfless her act, the more powerful she became. Examples given in the vocation crisis articles illustrate this concept. Women who prayed specifically for their own loss—that is, the prayer that their children be received into religious life—were regarded as having the most powerful prayer (for example, the woman whose ten children became priests or religious, or the woman who practically dictated the outcome of her three pregnancies). Thus laywomen gained power by presenting themselves as powerless.

In its earliest days, the Theresians demonstrated how rooted they were in this worldview. First, it cannot be forgotten that the group's patroness was Saint Thérèse of Lisieux, the "Little Flower," whose cult was particularly preoccupied with suffering.[18] Knowing this adds clarity to Elwood Voss's first "Theresian Prayer." The preference for suffering explains why Voss wanted laywomen to pray to be stepped on and over. From correspondence in the Theresian collection, we learn that Voss originally wanted the prayer to stress victimhood even more. He sent an earlier draft to Bishop Charles Buswell, the new bishop of Pueblo, for his approval. Voss received the bishop's *nihil obstat*, but only after Buswell suggested he remove language emphasizing "the crippled body," that is the idea that women should offer up their physical suffering to increase vocations.

At least one Theresian unit followed Voss's lead. Cynthia Bordelon, for example, recommended recruiting the elderly and bedridden to pray for vocations, "as it gives them a great sense of satisfaction to be able to offer all their sufferings for the Church's great need." At the first national conference in 1964, Theresians were also told that "costly" prayer would be most effective, that is, mortification and fasting. Voss declared that vocations "are bought at the price of hours spent in the shadow of the sanctuary lamp." Theresian leaders argued in the earliest days that prayer should be viewed as an essential sacrifice if the apostolate was to bear fruit.[19]

Theresian prayer was rooted in devotional culture in other significant ways. Every Theresian committed herself to a weekly "holy hour," a time of prayer and meditation often in the presence of the Blessed Sacrament. In fact, once a laywoman joined the Theresians, the only concrete requirement was that she maintain her holy hour. Theresian unit newsletters, particularly at the high school level, often exhorted their membership to pray. "Don't let spring fever cause you to neglect your weekly Holy Hour and monthly Mass Day," the Shrine High School Theresian newsletter reminded its membership. "I hope *you* realize the importance of your commitment and that you are faithful to your holy hour," the president of the Santa Monica High School Theresians wrote.[20]

Although Theresian prayer seems of a piece with the devotional worldview of the 1940s and 1950s, signs point to change, even in the group's early years. For example, although Theresians' use of the term *zeal* to describe their approach to prayer sounds, at first glance, like devotionalism, it in fact suggests a subtle change. The word comes up often, in official documents, correspondence, and speeches. Prayer wasn't a duty so much as an "act of zeal." And Theresians did not typically connect zeal with suffering; the terms coexisted in Theresian ideology for a few years but were not combined. *Zeal* expressed not only Theresians' devotion to the cause but also revealed the joy and fulfillment Theresians derived from prayer. Prayer for them was not dour, or an act of unseen sacrifice; the joy of it was celebrated as a defining characteristic. Their delight in prayer—not their suffering—gave them their identity.

It also empowered them. At the first National Sisters Vocation Conference in 1964, Mrs. Charles H. Lovette described for the assembled sisters the Theresian way of life: "To me, being a Theresian is really a call from God because we, as lay women and girls, can have an invitation to work with Him as surely as Religious can. It is a call to be of this world, to work in it and to meet it head-on. Just because we are of the laity, we need not be deprived of a spiritual career." I, too, have a call from God, she tells the room. She then asserts her difference by naming her work as "of this world," which she dynamically meets "head-on." But the key here is her assertion of the right to a "spiritual career." She continues, "Every woman and girl who has been called to share in this work enjoys *a higher state of life* and consequently should be filled with gratitude." With this remark she announces that lay-women, women who choose a lay vocation, are not consigned to a lower rung on the spiritual ladder. Think again of Lucy, Ellen, and Fran from Sister Mary Yolanda's reflection on vocation in 1959. Lovette denies implications that the Ellens and Frans of this world are limited and unworthy. In fact, she says, "it is the purpose of every Theresian member to instill in the hearts of people everywhere a fervent desire for a deeper spirituality."[21]

Lovette's talk is a first sign of the shift. To this point, their prayer had been other-directed, focused on increasing vocations to a field that was not their own. But Lovette points the Theresians toward a new end, spreading the "fervent desire for a deeper spirituality." Such a desire is the opposite of self-effacement; it is the desire to spread their own identity—an identity not based on their own fundamental inferiority—to others. Prayer becomes a means of self-assertion. In time, as we shall see, Theresian prayer transitioned much more drastically, becoming both more communal and more inner-directed simultaneously. The nature of their prayer would change, but the fact of it would not. Theresians had found what gave them purpose.

The final aspect of the Theresian program that hints at laywomen's changing identity is "self-education." Elwood Voss claimed in this period that every Theresian unit had a dual purpose: to work for sisterhood voca-tions and to focus on self-education. For at least the first four years, "self-education" primarily meant laywomen educating themselves about the lives of religious so that they could better promote the sisterhoods in their own communities. From talks given by lay Theresians at early annual confer-ences, it is clear that members absorbed multiple tropes from the vocation crisis, including the belief that parents obstructed vocations; self-education was used at first to dispel misconceptions and obstacles at home.

But within a few years, self-education took a different, more fruitful turn in Theresian units. Instead of focusing mainly on the failings of parents, Theresians put their energies into interacting with and getting to know sis-ters, both as individuals and as communities. The idea at first was that igno-rance of sisters' lives, and the distance placed between sisters and laity, bred misinformation and distrust, leading to obstruction by parents. To counter this, units invited sisters to speak on their spirituality, their paths to their vocations, or their particular work. High school students went on field trips to convents, learned about the daily life of a woman religious, and observed sisters in their jobs at hospitals or schools. Laywomen sat on panels with sisters, sharing their different perspectives on a girl's call to religious life and how it might be both affirmed and tested.

Self-education in this form had unanticipated consequences, occurring as it did just as documents began disseminating from the Second Vatican Council. What was meant as a means of fixing an older problem—selfish mothers—transformed into something else entirely when the forces of change in the American church began coming together in Theresian units. In this moment when lay Theresians chose to engage on a more personal, open level with women religious against the backdrop of Vatican II, they found themselves in contact with one of the most powerful instruments of renewal and reform in the American Church: the "new nuns."

THE ELEMENTS OF CHANGE

Theresian units promoted many types of activities in the early 1960s to achieve their purposes. They sponsored speakers, hosted lunches, led holy hours, and organized panels to recruit teenaged girls. The most popular activities at all unit levels, however, were those that brought women religious and laywomen together. Among the most successful in the mid-1960s were the "Jericho meetings" that, as the name suggests, were designed to make the walls between sisters and laywomen "come tumbling down." Although they took a variety of forms, these were usually unstructured gatherings where sisters and laywomen (including high school girls) could sit and talk informally. Sometimes these were couched in terms of giving the poor sisters some recreation (campfires! hayrides!), but usually the purpose was to bring sisters and laywomen together for the sole purpose of interaction.

A Houston unit invented the Jericho meeting, and it quickly spread across the country. In other words, this initiative came from women themselves, not from the Theresian administration. I stress this because it is clear that interaction between the two groups—their meeting on equal terms—was a deeply felt need among sisters and laywomen alike. Theresians began to lose some of their reverential tone for women religious, or at least the stereotypical talk of glowing nuns. One laywoman noted that the "conspiracy of gentility, politeness and adulation" was beginning to lift. At the same time, sister Theresians' rhetoric shifted as well, showing a new respect for and curiosity about the laywomen in their midst. Theresian promotional

Promotional image of lay and religious Theresians meeting together in the early 1960s. (Courtesy of the Women and Leadership Archives, Loyola University Chicago)

materials highlighted sisters and young laywomen conversing comfortably. Both suddenly seemed to recognize that they had unnecessarily, and harmfully, been kept apart.[22]

The first task was moving beyond stereotypes. In 1964, Mrs. John Downs said candidly that laywomen and sisters knew little of each other: "Very few laywomen in the 'old days' knew Sisters as individuals," she noted, "but only as Sisters who acted like Sisters were expected to act." They only saw what they had been schooled to see. Sisters recognized this too. "I feel very much that they expect us to show joy in the type of life we are living," Sister Kathleen Mary, SL, poignantly confessed in a conference talk. But, she asked, how often do we look into the faces of our fellow women religious and see sadness? "Sometimes there's not much joy evident."[23]

Some began to ask who was to blame for the misunderstandings that divided the two groups. Virginia Siegle believed that sisters must make personal contact with laypeople for their work to make an impact. "Has she succeeded in years gone by?" she asked. "I say no. She has failed to make that personal vital contact.... she has not let her lay counterpart see the real 'her.'" Siegle blamed this failure on rules that were too strict and the burden of paperwork which took up too much of sisters' time. Laywomen did not get off scot-free in this assessment, either. Siegle assigned them the most blame for not wanting to know sisters, for not reaching out. Proving that old themes persisted, she argued that laywomen were "too interested in material goods. They wanted that new car, a nice comfortable home for their children. They weren't interested in what was being hidden from them." It is a mark of where these women were in their relationship to feminism in the mid-1960s that sisters and laywomen only blamed themselves and each other; no one was yet able to articulate, let alone criticize, the larger masculine systems that worked to keep Catholic women divided.[24]

Although they may not have been able to converse about the patriarchy at this stage, both sisters and laywomen now began to acknowledge the inequalities inherent to the relationship. Sister Elena, CSC, remarked in 1966, "If Vatican II has made anything clear it is that there is no second class citizenship in the Church." The two vocations are complementary, she argued, "not *better than* one or the other." Another woman religious wanted a stronger relationship with laywomen, "hopefully without perpetuating the kind of subservience of one to the other." Laywomen, too, mentioned this subservience. A priest Theresian recalled a letter written by "one irate laywoman," who claimed that no vocation campaign would have a chance of success until "she gets invited to have coffee with Sisters over the kitchen table." In this laywoman's world, meeting at the kitchen table was the mark of respect and equality. It meant that sisters would sit down with her as equals over the table, in a space that symbolized her authority.[25]

Yet the dominant tone in this period was not anger but joy. These women genuinely enjoyed sharing each other's company, learning that they were more alike than not. Laywomen were "in constant hope of getting to know sisters better," Mrs. Charles Lovette said. Speaking of these middle years of the decade, Kathy Cribari, a single Theresian in her twenties, recalled how she "liked the kick" she got out of getting to know the sisters. She "relish[ed] the joy of discovering that they were people! Not only did they have real bodies, with legs (which I seriously doubted in my elementary school), but they were living in the same world we were in." Sister Annina Morgan thought she knew what laywomen were saying to sisters: "BE REAL! BE WARM! BE HUMAN! BE LOVING! BE CONCERNED! BE—A WOMAN!!! and if you *are* all these things, then I truly get your message—I meet Christ in you."[26]

So here was one major element in place; the move on both sides by laywomen and women religious to cross the divide and view themselves as equals had a major influence on how laywomen would reenvision their vocations. A second major factor was, of course, the Second Vatican Council itself. How were the Theresians affected as an organization, born as it was in the Council years? How did Theresians view the changes brought by Vatican II?

Preconciliar mindsets did not flip like a switch; the old and the new coexisted for quite some time. Yes, the first meeting of the Theresians took place in January 1962, just a few months before the first Council sessions that began that fall. But in the years of the Council (1962–65), the Theresians were still deeply committed to a very pre–Vatican II purpose: fostering sisterhood vocations. The 1965 National Sisterhood Vocation Conference—focused on the theme "Theresians and Renewal"—is a prime example of this. To begin, Mrs. Raber Taylor's conference talk, "Theresian Influence," is a complicated mix of pre- and postconciliar thinking. As quoted earlier, she demonstrates in this talk a commitment to female essentialism, referring to woman's "inborn" talent for nurturing. Later, she displays a strong Marian devotion, saying "we look to the Morning Star, the Mother of God, glorified and assumed bodily into heaven."

Yet she also believed the Theresians were "modern" and eager to "absorb something new and valuable." According to Taylor, since Pope John XXIII and Pope Paul VI "called forth the Ecumenical Council in Rome, it is not enough for any one Christian woman to cultivate exclusively the garden of her own soul." But the actions Taylor believed women should take were familiar: "The Theresian Movement, born to the age of renewal, accepts the challenge and the task with zeal and growing competence. We must foster Sisterhood vocation. This is the role we play." In 1965, Taylor saw "renewal" as simply adding zeal to an old commitment. So, too, did speaker Dan Maio, who believed that the Council's most important development was "the activation and mobilization of the laity." Nevertheless, Maio continued to believe that "our personal obligation to 'build up the Body of Christ' makes it imperative that we concern ourselves actively, in whatever way possible, in the work of fostering and developing vocations."[27]

Regardless of how they interpreted their new role, excitement about change was undeniable. As Father William Steele, a consultant to the national office, proclaimed in 1966, "A meaningful worship—and a meaningful vocation—this is the quest of the Church in Vatican II. Let us all join in the pursuit. It's a great time to be alive!" Nowhere in the papers do Theresians express concern or unease about the transformation just beginning. Confusion, yes, but not fear.[28]

The 1964 national conference booklet is instructive. The organizers included a few pages on "American Lay Women" that used the metaphor of the old and new world to explain Theresians' understanding of renewal.

Their position is made clear immediately when the author refers to lay Theresians as "pioneers" with a new world to navigate: "We know the formulations of the past are now inadequate. In part we have outlived them. In part we have fulfilled them. In part they no longer apply, and because of so many changes, they are not in focus. The methods of yesterday relied almost completely on the home-school-parish vocation spirit brought here from the countries of the Old World. That spirit has been gradually disappearing. The Theresians try to rediscover it and to create a new vocation atmosphere in the surroundings of modern life as it is lived in this day." This is not a hard rejection of the past but a desire to move forward holding on to the best of what they have known.[29]

Perhaps it is not surprising, then, that the Council did not immediately cause Theresians to change their purpose. Of all the themes to emerge from the Council—opening up to the modern world, liturgical reform, ecumenism, and subsidiarity, just to name a few—the one the Theresians spoke of the most was reform of the role of the laity. "The Christian today . . . cannot count it a privilege to be on the fringe of the Church's life," one speaker noted in 1964. "The Holy Pontiffs of our day have repeatedly said that 'this is the hour of the layman.'" When the *Decree on the Apostolate of the Laity* was promulgated in late 1965, Theresians heard that they now had a legitimate purpose apart from the work of the clergy. They were called in their own right, by virtue of their baptism, to take a vital role in promoting God's kingdom on earth. The church validated their worth as distinct and separate from the clergy, and empowered them.

The Theresians, already full of zeal, stood ready. In their minds, they had already taken steps to develop an apostolate of their own in service of the church. In time—namely, by 1969—the Theresians would take the Decree to its logical conclusion, coming to believe that Vatican II freed laywomen to develop and promote a vocation of their own unconnected with women religious. But the first step was simply stepping away from a pre–Vatican II mindset of Catholic Action, the midcentury program that enlisted laypeople to help implement the bishops' agendas.[30]

Reflecting on the recent past in 1971, Mrs. Charles Strubbe spoke of this transition, remarking that Catholic Action was "the first big breakthrough" for laywomen. "At last we were recognized!" She recalled that in Catholic Action laywomen "had no particular worries" because the bishops told them what to do and how to do it. "But we know very well that in the last ten or fifteen years the role of the laity has been examined in a very different light. We know that we don't have to look to anyone. . . . Each one of us, from the pope on down to the tiny, newly baptized baby, each one of us receives the permission to act, to give, to love, from the first encounter with Christ which we have in Baptism." Although she welcomed the changes wholeheartedly, she admitted how difficult they were to make. Catholic Action made them feel "so safe," she said. "Now this being on your own is much harder than the old way."[31]

It appears that the sister Theresians were the most instrumental in helping lay Theresians understand the implications of Vatican II in their own lives, and accept the new ways of thinking that would eventually transform their organization. Although the majority of Theresians were laywomen, women religious played an outsized role both in Theresian units and in national governance. Elwood Voss noted that "nearly every unit we have has been begun by a sister." Women religious also were heavily represented on the Theresian "Board of Consultants," whose annual meeting often drove policy changes. Sister Patricia Mullen became highly influential in the Theresian national office as "Continuous Renewal Program Director" and publication editor starting in 1968, and later as the organization's executive director from 1981 to 1990. (The Theresians did not have a laywoman as executive director until the mid-1990s.) Finally, as we have seen, women religious were featured prominently as conference speakers throughout the period under study.[32]

The sisters who influenced the lay Theresians so strongly appear overwhelmingly to have been "new nuns." In the early 1960s progressive sisters received this moniker from the American Catholic press, which largely viewed them as the harbingers of renewal in the United States. In fact, the term describes them well. Sisters had quietly begun renewing their approaches to both formation and professional life through the national Sister Formation Conference (SFC) in the 1950s, and had also begun the process of revisiting their congregational charisms and histories with an eye to modernization. Seen as theologically and culturally progressive, the new nuns exemplified a church struggling to open to the modern world. A new nun embraced change, projected enthusiasm for her role in an emerging church, and advocated major changes in the everyday lives of women religious from simplifying religious habits to pursuing unorthodox apostolates to increasing interaction with the laity.[33]

Theresians welcomed the insight of new nuns in the first decade of the Vatican II transition. The Long Beach unit newsletter mentioned that the unit's spiritual moderator was a woman religious and that sisters moderated the group's meetings. "These holy women have exposed us to many spiritual and theological realities that have enriched our church, ourselves, and our need to grow in grace," the editor noted. Another laywoman, Cathy Achatz, thought that the new nun and the lay Theresian were an ideal match: "As the 'emerging nun' desires to communicate and be in tune with today's world and as the changing role of the nun confuses and puzzles many of our lay people—Theresian groups can provide a meeting ground for a better understanding on the part of both."[34]

While a great deal of communication was taking place on the unit level, particularly from women religious to laywomen, most of these exchanges are unavailable to us, as unit records are spotty at best. However, we do have a number of talks delivered by women religious at Theresian national and regional conferences in the mid-1960s, particularly in 1966, which provide an idea of what the "emerging sister" had to say to "the emerging laywoman," to use the parlance of the day. When reading these talks, a researcher is immediately struck by the disparity between the addresses of women religious and those of laywomen. Sisters spoke with authority, and their texts were based on specific premises rooted in modern theology and the conciliar documents. It is not surprising that laywomen did not display this depth of knowledge; very few laywomen in the United States had received a substantial theological education in the mid-1960s.[35]

Sister Elena, CSC, addressed the need to bring modern theology not only to sisters, but to the people they served (and to the older and younger laywomen involved in increasing sisterhood vocations). In a talk not to laywomen but to other sister Theresians she stressed that vocation and formation directors, and by extension all women religious, needed a much deeper theological understanding of religious life, as well as a formation that was "scriptural, sacramental, psychologically sound . . . and related to the development of women in our times." Such training would allow sisters "to provide a biblical-liturgical formation for the persons with whom we come in contact." Sister Elena hoped sisters would embrace their own "biblical-sacramental spirituality, so that these attitudes are communicated in everything we do and say." Her ultimate goal was communicating the new way of approaching vocation, in fact, the new way of being Catholic, to the laity.[36]

The sisters who spoke to Theresians in the years just after the close of the Council addressed a variety of topics—"religious and lay cooperation in the light of Vatican II," "the modern girl," "vocation principles," "a need for youth in the vocation apostolate"—but the same ideas kept emerging. The most obvious, but still to the laywomen the most striking, was that *they* were called. To these women constantly on the lookout for girls destined to be nuns, speakers said repeatedly, "There is no type." Stop wasting your time trying to identify the girl who fits the stereotype of a nun, they said. If you do, you will miss the larger message of Vatican II. Instead, teach your girls—and yourselves—that all of you are called.

Sister Thomas Aquinas's 1966 talk on Vatican II stated the laity's new role as clearly as she possibly could: "Laymen are not being called to the apostolic works because there is a shortage of religious to do the work that needs to be done, but because it is their vocation, stemming from Baptism and Confirmation, to do so. The Decree on the Lay Apostolate is clear. The laity derive the right and obligation to the apostolate from their very union with Christ as head."[37] Several sisters made the same point using *Lumen Gentium*: "Chapter five of the Constitution on the church . . . insists that *all Christians* are called to the perfection of charity." Another woman religious remarked, "One cannot read the Constitution on the Church, for instance, without being struck by the repeated emphasis on the unity and charity of all those who have been baptized into the Body of Christ."[38]

But the most passionate voice raised for the laywoman's vocation was that of Sister Mary Margaret. "For us today to limit our vision about God's call to a vocation to be a Sister would be an insult to God and an insult to what it means to be a Christian," she argued. Sister Mary Margaret defined vocation—everyone's vocation—in terms of inclusion, love, and freedom (not "higher callings" and selfishness). "God's call to you and to me is not a static thing. . . . Vocation is the constant call of God's love, and only in this context can we fully appreciate His careful respect for His person-creature's freedom." She looked out at the lay Theresians and said, "It is a call that must be listened to by all—by you in particular. . . . The Pentecost of NOW bids us all to a deep and serious reflection."[39]

The talks from the sisters also provided further arguments for the idea that sisters and laywomen belonged on common ground. Each of us is a *person*, Sister Annina Morgan told the national conference audience in 1968, "who through our Baptism has become a Daughter of God the Father, and a vibrant member of the people of God." Moreover, she continued, "each of us is a WOMAN." But only by living authentic and relevant lives could sisters hope to convince laywomen that "religious life is not only a partnership with their own womanhood, but even a choice of life-to-be-lived for themselves."

The new nuns, then, assisted lay Theresians in processing both the documents and the spirit of the Council. Their emphasis encouraged laywomen to accept that they might have a vocation distinctly their own, but in a way that sought to strengthen the bonds between the two groups. In a time when the church was experiencing great stress, even crisis, and laywomen were beginning to reject the concept of subservience to women religious, it is remarkable that the Theresians would survive the period. It is even more notable that they did so with their commitment to each other intact.

THE CHANGE OF PURPOSE

Finding common ground helped sisters open up to the world and laywomen contemplate a new take on vocation. The Theresians were having an impact, if not the one they initially intended. Look a little closer in the late 1960s, though, and it appears the Theresian organization was showing signs of strain. One indication of trouble originated from the very women who did so much to assist laywomen in these years, the new nuns. In letters to Voss, and especially in the minutes of the annual meetings of the National Board of Consultants, Theresian leaders expressed concern that women religious were losing interest in the Theresians. Father Steele, the founder of a Theresian unit and member of the National Board of Consultants, spoke for many when he privately warned Voss that "younger sisters of the progressive type seem puzzled by a group of lay people devoted to promoting their vocation."[40]

Moreover, women religious who had been the backbone of the high school units (the majority of all units) were abandoning them in large numbers. In 1969, fifty letters were sent out to high school units, but only six replied. "Speakers are becoming increasingly difficult to procure," Sister Elise Marie noted, "and the students are less and less inclined to be interested." Another consultant, Father Wilson, believed that sisters were no longer interested in "vocation-getting clubs." "Sharp sisters want nothing to do with Theresians," he concluded.[41]

At the same time, leaders also raised the opposite concern, that religious were *too* involved in Theresian governance. In 1967 Elwood Voss warned that there were simply too many priest and women religious speaking at the national conference, although the schedule was not adjusted. By 1970, the problem was even worse. Of eight formal talks at the national conference— ironically themed "Woman to Woman"—three were delivered by priests, four by women religious, and only one by a laywoman. In that same year, the national consultants had a long debate over whether sisters should finally be allowed to join the Theresians as official members (to this point they had organized units, served as spiritual moderators, and participated but were not allowed membership status). Some believed the mutual respect created in

Womanhood Is Sisterhood

the Theresians demanded such equality, although others feared sisters' dominance enough that they called for a rule barring them from holding office.[42]

The large and highly publicized number of defections from the sisterhoods around this time was also beginning to cause stress among lay Theresians. In 1965, 765 women religious left their orders; by 1975, the height of the crisis, that number jumped to 4,337. The loss of sisters was confusing to many laywomen, whose purpose was to channel women to the sisterhoods. Should laywomen continue to do so when so many sisters themselves appeared to be rejecting their vocations? Claiming the issue was leading to a loss of membership, a lay leader in Canada expressed concern about "the devastating effect, emotionally, of the appalling numbers of religious defections, many of them sons and daughters of original dedicated members." Another lay Theresian spoke plainly on this subject to Elwood Voss, labeling the defections as the devil's work. Yet she was compassionate toward these women religious, as were most laywomen who commented on the subject. "I feel we need to pray for those who are betwixt and between, and who are terribly confused," she said. "Thanks be to God, there are so many more, who have no misgivings."[43]

Women religious were not the only confused Theresians. Several oblique comments surfaced in the late 1960s suggesting that the organization might be outgrowing its purpose in the age of renewal. Sara McCarthy wrote to Elwood Voss in August 1969 to resign her position on the Executive Board. She had many reasons for this, including her frustration with Voss's managerial style, but the comment that jumps off the page is about the purpose itself. She stated that having to explain the purpose of the Theresians to outsiders was becoming "embarrassing." Another asked if unit meetings were clear enough that "visitors can get a real sense of just *what* the Theresian Apostolate is?" There was little doubt about the purpose just a few years earlier. One sentence on laywomen supporting sisterhood vocations would have made everything clear. The fact that the purpose was muddy in the late 1960s shows that at least some Theresian units had already begun to move away from the promotion of sisterhood vocation. It is worth noting, of course, that the sisters *themselves* encouraged this in the process of helping laywomen understand their call to vocation in the context of the Council.[44]

The drastic change of purpose noted at the start of this chapter did not result from long consultation and hand-wringing. On the contrary, it seemed to come out of nowhere, surprising no one more than Elwood Voss. In the first days of September 1969, Voss typed up a proposed agenda for the annual Executive Board meeting to take place before the national conference in October. He proposed a slight revision to the "Theresian Purpose," changing "foster Sisterhood vocations" to "lay women dedicated to the apostolate for religious women." His reasoning was that "fostering" implied that a vocation had to exist before a Theresian met a young woman. But overall, the purpose was the same: laywomen dedicated to the sisters' apostolate.[45]

Two days earlier, long-time Theresian consultant Father William Steele wrote a revolutionary letter to Voss. It is likely that his letter and Voss's memo crossed in the mail. In this letter, Steele outlined why he believed a substantive change of purpose was warranted. The most compelling reason was that the old purpose was sputtering out. He argued that "the idea of one group of people in the Church devoting themselves to another group's vocation seems to be declining in appeal both ways. . . . this is particularly true of the more avant garde type in both groups." Steele envisioned a group still focused on vocation but centered on "a mutual endeavor involving exchange and mutual enrichment." His proposed draft shifted the organization toward seeking "a deeper understanding of the vocation of the Christian woman in the church today," as well as highlighting the need to "keep up with the renewal of the Church."[46]

Voss was so taken with the idea, so thoroughly convinced by Steele's reasoning, that he abandoned his own minor change to the purpose and put an entirely new purpose up for a vote at the Executive Board meeting the next month. The board was well primed for the change; the new purpose passed 10 votes to 0. Here, then, was the new "Theresian Purpose" of 1969: "The Theresians of America is an organization of Catholic lay women who are dedicated to a deeper appreciation of the vocation of the Christian woman . . . as it is lived in the religious and lay states in the world today." Most obviously, the purpose explicitly moves away from any reference to sisterhood vocations. The new purpose affirmed the shifts in emphasis from the mid-1960s onward, under which laywomen came to embrace an empowered spirituality, place themselves on equal footing with women religious, and accept a new role as laity given to them by the Second Vatican Council.[47]

We will explore the transition in depth, but it should be noted that Voss indulged in some revisionist history very shortly after the document passed. By 1970, he claimed that the change was "the result of widespread experimentation and a considerable amount of diligent study." Voss also went to great pains to make it appear that laywomen were the force behind the change. No doubt individual lay Theresians were ready for this shift, as evidenced by the unanimous support of the Executive Board, which was stacked with laywomen, but the change did not originate with laywomen; it was engineered by two priests.[48]

Womanhood Is Sisterhood

Elwood Voss and others claimed that the new purpose was widely accepted, and quickly. This appears to be true, but again, there are hints of dissension. Someone at the Board of Consultants meeting in spring 1970 argued that the annual conference needed a speaker "to keep us from polarizing," although William Steele professed in a separate document a few months later that "the polarization so evident in our Church today is not found in the Theresians." The 1970 consultants meeting minutes also contain the remark that "Chicago reacted strongly against [the new purpose]," yet few other documents betray any trouble. The 1985 internal history of the organization is more forthcoming, however. Speaking of "growing pains" in the early 1970s, *The Theresian Story* notes that "a few of the large, original groups disbanded early in the decade because, admittedly, they could not accept the restatement or broadening of the purpose of Theresians."[49]

What seemed to resonate most with Theresians who supported the new purpose was the sense of possibility. William Steele saw these women as "looking toward their mutual vocation as Christian women and asking, 'What would you have us do, Lord?'" after which he added: "Beautiful." The Theresian president, Mrs. Raber Taylor, spoke of "the limitless boundaries [that] exist within ourselves as the Spirit hovers over us" and "the great untouched horizons for us to tackle." An early institutional history likened Theresians in this period to "astronauts, whose history is parallel."[50]

Lay Theresians especially embraced the call to mutual understanding and support between laywomen and women religious. They did so not only because they liked interacting with sisters (which they had done for years at this point) but because the new emphasis encouraged a new sense of self-worth. The young lay Theresian Kathy Cribari made this point quite clearly in a 1971 *Theresian* article: "I liked the old Theresians and the nuns who wore long black gowns and the many hours I spent memorizing answers to the catechism questions like 'who made you?' (God made me, if anyone is interested.) But you know what else? I like the new nuns. . . . I like the new Theresians, too. Because now they're mine. They're out to foster people like me—Christian women—just as much as they support sisters (who are also Christian women, remember? You should. They dress just like you do.)" Note her use of the word *foster*, significant for its prominence in the original purpose. Now laywomen themselves could be "fostered" instead of just fostering others. She went on to remark that laywomen "at one time didn't realize we even had vocations," an observation made numerous times in this period. Cribari is also the writer who provides the highly relevant epigraph to this chapter: "Now the Theresians are an edifice built on womanhood—not

just sisterhood. (Except 'womanhood' is 'sisterhood,' how 'bout that?)"
She playfully juggles two meanings of the word *sister*, suggesting equality,
mutual affection, and trust between these two groups once so distant from
one another.[51]

In the first year of the new purpose, Mrs. Betty Barrett articulated what
this new "sisterhood" relationship might look like. "We can help each other
with our growing pains," she said, "as we make better use of our talents and
potential." A lovely example of this occurred at the 1970 national conference, which featured a "clothing workshop." The Theresians of Houston, the
conference's host, decided that all members would benefit from a demon-
stration of home sewing techniques, patterns, and suitable outfits, as "how
to be tastefully and appropriately dressed for any occasion at a minimum
of expense was becoming a growing problem for all of us women—lay and
religious alike." But the fashion show was chiefly designed to help sisters who
were "experimenting with secular dress and modified habits." Lay and sister
Theresians constructed their own knit separates and modeled them for the
attendees. Keeping a sense of humor about the whole thing, the organizers
added that "for those who had elected to remain in conservative habit we
hoped it would prove entertaining." Tragically, no images of the event have
survived.[52]

THE "VOCATION OF CHRISTIAN WOMANHOOD" AND FEMINISM

Any allusions to feminism are rare in the Theresian records prior to 1971. That
in itself is remarkable given what a hot topic feminism was in the ten years
after the group's founding. The group's trajectory toward female empowerment suggests that Theresians internalized some of its teachings in this
period, but they certainly did not credit it. One of the lone exceptions was a
remarkable talk given by Mrs. Joseph Zavadil at the New Mexico State Convention in 1966. Zavadil proved knowledgeable of developments in the world
of Catholic feminism in her talk, "The Emerging Role of Laywomen in the
Church." She spoke of Gertrud Heinzelman and her petitions to Vatican II on
women's equality, recent articles by feminists in the Catholic press, and the
limited role of female auditors at the Council. She was well-versed in the new
field of Catholic feminist theology as well, speaking cogently about the myth
of the eternal feminine, the importance of Galatians 3:28, and the limitations
of theologian Karl Rahner's dualistic thinking on men and women. She even
went so far as to champion Betty Friedan's *The Feminine Mystique* (something

many Catholic feminists were reluctant to do since the book was perceived to have an anti-Catholic bias).[53]

Moreover, her talk reflected another theme that runs through this monograph, the idea that many laywomen were wrestling with feminism and Vatican II simultaneously, and each was helping women (whether or not they were self-identified feminists) to draw conclusions about the other. She was trying to point out that the definition of the laity and the old version of Catholic womanhood simply could not fit together. "It seems to me that this new call to the laity is the real reason why the old concepts of women are so particularly inadequate at this time in the life of the Church in the world," she argued. "Because, I think they work directly to keep women, as my friends, apathetic, defensively feminine or openly antagonistic." Zavadil believed the basic problem was "this apparent contradiction between the Church's traditional teaching on the nature and role of women, and the call of a fuller life in the Church." Yet Zavadil made a point of telling her audience that she had surveyed her friends on the issue of women's rights in the church and received little positive response. This was no different from the Theresians, where she would appear to be an outlier.[54]

I did not find another explicitly feminist voice until three years later in 1969, when the feminist Sister Margaret Ellen Traxler, SSND, addressed the national conference. She hit hard the theme that women religious were now ready to join laywomen in the struggle for equality: "Sisters will join the universal Sisterhood of women in the modern world, struggling to achieve human rights of all women." Moreover, she hoped laywomen would help women religious achieve "self-determination." Traxler urged that women be made aware of their "second-class citizenship."[55] These two speakers aside, the absence of evidence strongly suggests that Theresians did not, as a group, wish to address feminist issues. This hypothesis is confirmed by a very brief statement in the ever-useful 1970 Board of Consultants meeting minutes. After someone suggested inviting the prominent Catholic feminist Sidney Callahan to speak, this person insisted that "Theresians can't ignore the feminist movement," as if to suggest they had been doing so purposefully for some time.

Because feminism was so much in the air at the time of the change of purpose, it is instructive to place this major change within that context. Theresians, like other ordinary Catholic laywomen, were trying to make sense of changes for women and changes for Catholics concurrently. Theresians talk infrequently of feminism as a movement before the mid-1970s, but this does not indicate a lack of engagement with its concepts. If we follow the Theresians from 1961 to 1970 we can see that their self-perception as laywomen changed fairly drastically at the same time that second-wave feminism was beginning to have an impact in the United States. They started with a mindset of inferiority, weighed down by prayer lives that demanded complete submission to be successful, dedicated to assisting other women they believed to be their superiors. By 1970 the lay Theresians had placed themselves on an equal plane with the women to whom they once deferred. Moreover, they made their own concerns, their own call, the centerpiece of their mission. If we count female empowerment as a fruit of feminism, then the Theresians seemed to be beginning to feel its effects. But we must delve into the Theresians' relationship with feminism in detail to truly understand its influence (and lack of influence) over these Catholic laywomen. Theirs is the most convoluted—and fascinating—relationship with feminism of all the groups studied in this book.

Directly after the change of purpose occurred, something odd begins to appear in the Theresian records. Seemingly out of nowhere their magazine, the *Theresian*, and the national conferences began to feature talks and articles attempting to define womanhood. This in itself is not surprising; the national office had just placed the focus squarely on laywoman's vocation. Naturally, the Theresians would try to develop a definition of this concept for their membership. After all, any group wanting to delve into the issue of laywomen's role had some major questions to address: What did these vocations look like? What limits did laywomen face in pursuing them? How would laywomen's relationship to laymen change? How did laywomen fit into the overall picture of Church practice and governance?

What is extremely odd, though, is the direction this questioning took. Feminism was at its most visible in the early 1970s, and Catholic feminism was both ascendant and well-covered in the Catholic press. Catholic feminists and those in sympathy with them had been attempting to answer questions about laywomen's vocation since 1963. But the Theresians did not turn to Catholic feminism as a resource to puzzle out the answers to these questions; instead, they actively rejected it, turning instead to the ideology of essentialism and complementarity. This is surprising for two reasons. First, the Theresians cultivated a persona for themselves as reformers in the spirit of Vatican II. Why would a group of leaders that spoke frequently, with pride, about their progressive outlook turn so obviously to the past for their gender ideology? Second, consider the other organizations in this study. The NCCW and WUCWO rarely employed undiluted essentialism after 1965, and even when they did other voices counterbalanced it. Laywomen were filling the pages of *Marriage* magazine with lively debates that challenged complementarity and essentialism as early as 1966. But the Theresians chose to revive a much more "traditional" definition of Catholic womanhood firmly rooted in essentialism just as the other communities were leaving it behind or at the very least tempering it. (Only the Catholic Daughters and the Daughters of Isabella, much more conservative organizations than the Theresians, still regularly spoke of gender in these terms). It is as if the leaders were at a loss now that they had jumped into this new way, but, distrustful of feminism, they had to look further back to find commentary on womanhood that they considered authoritative.

We witness their fumbling in the early days after the change of purpose; the Theresian leadership could not seem to articulate what the "vocation of the Christian laywoman" was. In 1970 Voss said the Theresians were going to "focus attention on the apostolate of women dedicated to encouraging those who are dedicated to the service of mankind." What does that even mean? Is it that some laywomen have an apostolate to the service of mankind and other laywomen have an apostolate to serve those who serve others? Or is it a holdover from the old purpose, with laywomen serving those who did the actual work? Consultant Father Mullaney tried his hand at a definition: "Theresians is an organization of women heading to a dynamic Cristocentric appreciation, of the love choice of the woman as it is lived today." Again, what does the "the love choice of the Christian woman" mean? Kathy Cribari thought she understood what the new Theresian was. "In this age, femaleness is difficult to spot and to keep," she argued, "so she who remains, now, as the idea of womanhood, is much more a woman than any other generations of women ever were." Their convoluted language itself suggests they were chasing their tails. Moreover, they seem to place more emphasis on defining "woman" than on defining "vocation."[56]

If we are to understand why at a moment of "progress" the Theresians looked to traditionalist sources, it helps to take a second look at the new purpose itself. Elwood Voss tried to make the purpose appear as a complete break from the past, because he valued the changes occurring in the church and he wanted to affirm laywomen's empowerment. But the phrasing betrays an ironic contradiction that demonstrates continuity with the old way of thinking. Voss and William Steele believed they were turning the world upside down by placing "the vocation of the Christian woman" at the Theresians' center. But they still used the singular *vocation* and *woman*; they were not yet able to express laywomen's fundamental diversity.

By the late 1960s, feminists had largely succeeded in eliminating the singular *woman* from their writings when discussing all women, thus denying that all were naturally endowed with the same characteristics. This shift in language is an indicator of whether or not an individual in this time period was working from within a feminist worldview, and Voss does not seem to have been. His comments on the historic 1969 conference for the organization's 1972 history "Women of Vision" confirm this. He noted that "the Theresian apostolate is deepening from the apostolate of the religious vocation to the apostolate of the vocation of the Christian woman—be it housewife, mother, or sister." Even by 1972 his working definition of "laywoman" was decidedly narrow.[57]

An essentialist approach to the laywoman's role dominated from 1970 to 1975. It must be emphasized that this was a deliberate choice on the part of the leadership, since these speakers and writers were chosen by the national administrators, the Board of Consultants, or the Executive Board. In some cases, speeches were reprinted in the *Theresian*; if the administration disapproved of the talk as given, they need not have reproduced it. Theresian leaders used their best means of communication to disseminate this worldview.

Numerous articles, particularly in the first few years after the new purpose, attempted to define "woman" by describing her fundamental characteristics, an approach common in the 1950s. Authors noted her inherent generosity, her motherhood, and her ability to nurture. Others waxed poetic about her sensitivity to those around her, calling on men and women to "treasure the feeling and perceptiveness that is uniquely woman's." Woman used this perceptiveness to foster Christianity through personal contact, "mov[ing] toward graciousness, the distinction of the Christian woman." This last author believed that woman enters her vocation fullest when she is "cultured, competent, apostolic, and Christian." Not surprisingly, these characteristics coincide nicely with those expected of a middle-class Christian housewife and hostess.[58]

The Theresian authors and speakers also called upon the ideology of the "eternal woman" or "eternal feminine," to define laywomen's vocation. The eternal woman was a widespread concept in the United States in the 1950s, and persisted well into the 1960s, although to see it this late in a self-proclaimed progressive organization is surprising. In this way of thinking, woman is valued most for both her specific role in redemption and the fact that this role is eternal or unchanging. Woman in this view is inherently passive or submissive, demonstrating to all humans—especially men, who are so focused on action—the importance of putting God's will before one's own. For this reason, women were taught to emulate the Blessed Mother, whose "fiat" or selfless "yes" to God allowed Christ to come into the world and redeem it from sin. Woman's role was considered to be timeless, the anchor that would keep humanity focused on God and not self. The eternal woman ideology also served as one theological basis for complementarity, the belief that men and women are by nature different and the two distinct roles must be preserved for the good of the home, society, and the church.[59]

After the Executive Board adopted the new purpose, eternal woman rhetoric began to appear in earnest (it rarely appeared among the Theresians when one would expect to find it, in the period before 1965). Nor was this rhetoric tempered with ideas about equality. Take, for example, this quote published a few months after the change of purpose: "A man expresses his love for others by doing and making, a woman primarily by being and serving." The following summer Father Robert Wilson claimed that "masculinity is activity, creative activity; femininity is potentiality." A laywoman, Dr. E. Dawne Jubb, claimed that "it is of her essence that she dedicate herself . . . as to a service in the spirit of 'Thy Will Be Done.'"[60]

Perhaps the most glaring example came from Father Bernard Mullaney in 1971. To Mullaney, "a woman stands before her God, radiant in that triune splendor, gazing at him, begging, loving, demanding, even counseling, 'till Christ turns and says, 'Woman, what would you have me do?' And she turns to the men in her life and says, 'Do whatever he tells you.' And man is born again." This passage references the gospel story of the wedding at Cana, where Mary prods her son to work a miracle, then directs the household servants to follow his instructions. Mullaney's interpretation views Mary as a conduit, an active/passive figure who stimulates the leadership of others and uses it to bring the men in her life to God. A few years later Mullaney reinforced this point by claiming that a laywoman should value her role as housewife because it gives her husband "extension into a world he could never feel or touch or live or love without your invitation." Note that these examples come from a laywoman, a sister, and two priests. A rank-and-file member of the Theresians could easily believe that this view represented the leadership's best, unified thinking.[61]

The best example of the clash between progressive Catholicism and traditionalist views of gender is a pair of liturgies celebrated at the 1971 Board of Consultants meeting. The masses are very much in the experimental mode of the early 1970s, so much so that they border on parody. To find them in the Theresian files was a shock and demonstrates how the board, at least, viewed itself as part of the progressive spirit of the times. The two masses featured nonscriptural readings and a Sanctus from *Jesus Christ Superstar*. One homily on the wedding at Cana declared that "Mary was a sweetie!" and expressed the view that "maybe we don't rejoice enough! Maybe there ought to be more wine! Maybe all of life should be a kind of picnic—party!" The creeds were written as free-verse poems: "To believe in such a God who made music and rainbows and waterfalls and colored leaves and strawberries is more than I need to make believing more than making believe." The previous day's creed included the line, "To believe in God / is to get high / on love enough / to look down / at your loneliness and / forget it forever."[62]

But their take on gender roles was not quite so progressive. One of the first readings was a mash-up of Genesis 2 and Judith 8–11, the theme of which was that woman was created as man's helpmate. Man thought she was "beautiful and charming to see." The woman said, "Your servant strives to be a devout woman; she honors the God of heaven day and night." He replies, "You are as beautiful as you are eloquent." At the second mass, women received roses to remind them "that as a woman of the Theresians she is committed to live a life of loveliness, of scattering flowers into the lives of those who touch her along the way." The first day's original responsorial psalm, though, makes the most enigmatic statement on gender roles. The verses included the prayer that "woman was born to give life," and "the life of woman is one of giving and one of redeeming." The congregation was to respond, "If woman would fulfill her mission she must always be in some sense a mystery to man." The response suggests that women must remain essentially different from men to fulfill their purpose from God (and, therefore, that men need not try very hard to understand them).[63]

Finally, an aversion to feminism was not merely implied. Some speakers condemned the women's movement specifically. The 1971 conference keynote speaker was Mrs. Rita Metyko, who began her talk by identifying herself as simply a "housewife, a mother, and a Theresian." She decried the state of affairs in the country as a whole, noting that "35,000 housewives ran away from home last year, a phenomena [sic] we used to equate with adolescence." As if her message was not clear enough, she ended her talk by calling her fellow Theresians "a group of *truly* liberated women, free to be and to give the best of themselves."[64]

But the strongest indictment of feminism was delivered in a second talk at the 1971 conference "Woman in the Age of Aquarius" by a laywoman ob-gyn, E. Dawne Jubb. She encapsulated the eternal feminine outlook perfectly, claiming that "the loving generosity of woman is the catalyst for man's creativity and much of the source of its inspiration, while her holy passivity . . . is the necessary complement for his unbridled activism, his insatiable curiosity, and his spirit of conquest." Jubb then identified feminists as the biggest threat to the eternal feminine: "Those who try to repudiate this spirit of submission as lessening their dignity, or in an effort to assert themselves as women 'of strong muscles,' lose something and succeed only in exchanging charm for harshness. A false emancipation in this regard will not signify progress but retrogression." Jubb took aim at feminists' sexual politics as well, blasting them for promoting sexual liberation and contraception. "How can any girl or woman who barters her genital function on the pleasure market . . . ever experience human fulfillment?" she asked. Earlier in the talk she argued that God gave women a menstrual cycle to remind all women, even those who were single, that motherhood was their most essential function. At the end, she asked passionately, "How can abortion—the killing of her *own* child, in her *own* womb, inside her *own* body—ever possibly improve in *any* aspect the health of a girl or woman whose very essence is geared to creating and sustaining life as reflected in her anatomy, physiology, and psychology?"[65]

One explanation for the turn to essentialism is a rise in references to "crisis" or evil in the world. This, too, is consistent with eternal woman rhetoric. Several speakers explicitly linked the promotion of female essentialism to the desire to save the world from impending crisis. Such fears were evident in the Catholic Daughters and the Daughters of Isabella at this time; in the early 1970s Catholic laywomen were encouraged to believe that their commitment to home, family, and womanliness could stave off impending doom in society and the church (riots, assassination, protests, immorality, drug abuse, birth control and abortion, underground masses, the defection of priests and nuns, etc.). "Woman's exquisite sensitivity enables her to bring understanding to people afflicted today by alienation, dissension, meaninglessness," an article from a 1970 *Theresian* claimed. "The very depth of today's needs requires the quality of response for which woman has been so richly gifted." Historical precedent indicates it is not unusual for a culture in transition to emphasize rigid gender roles as a means of maintaining stability.[66]

Another explanation is that the Theresian leaders simply were not ready to jettison their deeply entrenched view of the Catholic laywoman wholesale. Seeking laywomen's empowerment seemingly did not imply the need to seek laywomen's *equality* in the minds of most Theresians. This is yet another example of how complex the dissemination of feminist ideas was in the 1960s. Like the NCCW leadership, the Theresians took from feminism what they wanted without affirming any connection to the ideology. Unlike for the NCCW, however, I have little evidence that the Theresian leadership engaged with feminism seriously in the process of selecting what they might accept or reject.

Female empowerment was a huge step forward for these laywomen, as was the desire to claim their own vocations, and equality with sisters. But the move toward empowerment was not accompanied by any serious study of the sexist structures that denied women's self-determination in the first place. Theresians rarely said anything about their relationship with men, only their position vis-à-vis sisters. Unlike the authors in *Marriage,* the Theresians did not challenge a social preference for women's domesticity that, coupled with Catholic teachings on female submission, locked Catholic laywomen into the dichotomy of housewife/mother and woman religious. Nor did they discuss in any methodical way the problems inherent in a church that wished to empower the "layman" while ignoring the strictures that made such a role change unlikely for laywomen. Instead, they turned back to a ready-made body of literature that appeared authoritative, doctrinally sound, and most important, untainted by an ideology that was making them nervous.

Dissenting voices do pop up in these years, such as the brave soul who in 1971 encouraged Voss to establish an official Theresian reading list. "I suggest the magazine *Ms.,*" she wrote. "It's great. Some of the older women might feel that it's a little much, but at least it would make them think." In late 1972, a Theresian symposium in Denver attracted a crowd of 800 . . . and some blowback when the organizers snuck in too much talk about liberation. "We got much publicity from it and quite a backlash of the Women's Lib image," Kathy S. wrote in a letter to Elwood Voss. "Some of the members and some of the older generation that attended thought we were too liberal or that our speakers were rather." Their speaker list included feminist politician Pat Schroeder. As if to confirm this backlash, *The Theresian News* tried to distance itself from what occurred: "The talk titled 'Oppression, What is It?': *Not a discussion on oppression of women,* but an *effort to make women aware of causes of oppression* in other areas of the world."[67]

The young laywoman Kathy Cribari also revealed an openness to feminism in 1971 (the same year as Dr. Jubb's talk above). Her comments are worth quoting at length:

Change is not a trauma now, it's a fact. We're swarmed with things like women's liberation, free sex, religious revolution. And these current topics came about just as violently, just as drastically (just as slowly, just as surely) with just as much commotion (and just as much complacency) as resulted from Vatican II when "Hic est enim corpus meum" turned into "This is my body." . . . And just because some of us turn out to be the family-hearth-type woman, that doesn't mean some of us can't join the Kate Millett types and light bonfires for female freedom. (And it doesn't mean some of us can't enjoy the warmth of the flame without striking the match.)

Tellingly, she compares her process of accepting feminism with her own gradual acceptance of the changes brought by Vatican II. Her phrasing points beautifully to the paradox at the heart of these changes. We can perceive them as both violent and drastic, and slow and sure at the same time. Just as Catholic historians have indicated, the changes were jarring but not necessarily a "trauma." The ground had been prepared for them long before. So, too, with feminism, Cribari says. She also wanted to make the point explicitly that a diversity of opinions on feminism existed within the Theresians, and one of those positions included enjoying the fruits of other women's activism without claiming feminism as your own.[68]

As if the abrupt turn to essentialism in 1970 was not surprising enough, in 1976 the Theresian leadership turned sharply once again, this time embracing feminism (specifically Catholic feminism) wholeheartedly. Like the change of purpose in 1969, the shift seems to come out of left field, although I suspect it began earlier than the records indicate. In 1976, then associate director Sister Patricia Mullen sent a memo to the Board of Consultants about the upcoming national conference. In this memo Mullen admits to reading "everything I could get my hands on relating to women and church and women and society," which might have something to do with her transition to feminism. Her reading list included the Leadership Conference of Women Religious (LCWR) pamphlet for International Women's Year, a decidedly feminist document, and in Mullen's word, "tremendous." On the strength of her reading, she chose the theme "Women and the Church" for 1976. She acknowledged that "the majority of [Theresians] are in the initial stages of consciousness." Nevertheless, she believed "our program must be designed in such a way that we reach out to these women and provide a sensitive but firm consciousness-raising program." She cautioned against coming on too strong, fearing losing "the faith of those who are just beginning." Mullen understood that "some of us will have to go elsewhere for greater depth of consciousness and action to suit ourselves, but we do have an obligation to nurture the spark we have lit for others."[69]

I call this the "reveal" of Mullen as a feminist, but only because it's the first indication in the record. The document itself indicates that her audience was fully aware of her position, and Mullen assumes the Board of Consultants is in agreement. She does not explain feminist terminology such as "consciousness-raising" and includes them when she mentions that she and others will have to supplement their Theresian membership to get the depth of feminism they require, since she did not want to jeopardize the organization by moving too quickly for the constituency. A few months earlier, Mrs. Maelsel Yelenick produced a "Theresian Position Paper" for the spring 1976 meeting of the Board of Consultants. Here we find Catholic feminism in full flower. On complementarity she wrote, "Such a condition of inflexible external rules and cultural bindings is totally incompatible with the radical call to freedom, fulfillment and maturity found in the Gospel." A more direct condemnation could not be found. For the first time in the 1970s, we also have a record of a Theresian discussing the inequality of women in the church, saying that women's "present tension" was due to "the struggle of women to escape the subordinate and inferior work to which she [sic] has been assigned by society and the Church."[70]

The 1976 conference itself shows the extent of the Theresians' transition to feminism. A top priority, according to Mullen, was "a consciousness-raising experience for each participant." Elwood Voss's opening address was designed "to stimulate some thinking on the subject of full participation of women in the Christian ministries," a surprising theme to be sure, since this is most certainly a reference to allowing women into the priesthood. If we had doubts about Voss's feminist commitment, the next line would erase them: "The centuries long twilight of a male-dominated Church has almost ended and that sun is rapidly setting. The full participation of women in the Church is now dawning and the signs of brightness are rapidly appearing on the horizon."[71]

Voss tried to ease this transition by praising Theresians for their leadership and initiative. "You have been in the forefront in the past," he reminded them. "You took initiative in breaking down the walls that separated women who were in religious communities from yourselves." Now, he said, "once again you are being challenged." He quoted Yelenick's position paper, saying that "women should insist on shared responsibility in influencing the course of the Church and the world." In a sign that even the most die-hard essentialists had been converted, Voss quotes Father Bernard Mullaney as saying, "Let's not blow it. All we need to do is quote Church documents." From a man who once asked Theresians, "What is woman?" and then attempted to explain femininity to them, this was a pretty big leap. It is telling, too, that the Theresians now believed that the Council could be used to support a feminist worldview.[72]

The Theresians' gender politics, while instructive, were not central to their identity. This was true in the debates over the position of laywomen vis-à-vis women religious in the mid-1960s, and it continued to be true as the Theresians worked out the meaning of "the vocation of Christian womanhood" over time. In both cases, spirituality (much more than feminist consciousness) proved to be the site of the Theresians' most creative thinking and deepest interest. At the turn of the 1970s, Theresian spirituality changed again by necessity. They had confidence in their own power, but what were they praying *for* if they had turned away from promoting sisterhood vocations? On what would their Holy Hour focus? The answer is complicated, because prayer itself is not one-dimensional or easily explained. Theresians continued to pray for those in need, for the troubled world and church. But increasingly they seemed to be praying for themselves and for each other. In this way, their prayer was paradoxically both more intensely personal and deliberately communal.

At the same time as the change of purpose, William Steele and Elwood Voss attempted to articulate the Theresians' shifting experience of prayer. First, both priests wanted the Theresians to view themselves as "communities," not as Catholic women's organizations. Steele envisioned the Theresians as "an inter-parochial experience" akin to a "floating parish." He refers here to the "underground church" movement of the late 1960s and early 1970s, where American Catholics experimented with small, sometimes illicit, prayer communities that gathered to celebrate liturgies outside of traditional parish structures.[73] This later morphed into the home mass trend of the 1970s and can also be connected to the emergence of charismatic prayer groups in the United States at the same time. Although Steele's immediate point of reference is the underground church, this concept of small or base communities is also linked to liberation theology then ascendant (although the Theresians were not using this language). Voss approved of the idea that Theresian units should function as "small Christian communities." He predicted that in the future Theresian units would be much smaller, and there would be more of them.[74]

From within these small communities, individual Theresians were encouraged to believe that the deepening of spirituality was an end in and of itself. Prayer need not be focused on a specific goal; rather, the transformation of self through prayer became central. In a flier for the 1970 national conference, the organizers claimed the conference was designed to help women "explore and share together . . . the best that the Christian woman of the 70s has to give for her own growth and in service to mankind." How striking that they put the individual Theresian's personal growth first. William Steele hoped the Theresians would see themselves as seekers. "To search is part of the pilgrimage of God's people," he wrote. "A pilgrim people is a people on the go, ever searching, ever discovering, ever hoping. . . . This is our basic vocation. . . . to search and explore life for its deepest mysteries in Christ." Theresians were now being told that their vocation was striving for spiritual depth. It should be noted that this development places the Theresians squarely within larger trends brewing in American culture at the turn of the 1970s. Historians have variously referred to this period as the "me decade" or "the Culture of Narcissism." The turn toward the self, manifested through the search for meaningful spirituality, has been well-documented and it is not surprising to see these laywomen affected by these trends.[75]

These are not full-blown narcissists by any stretch of the imagination, however. As of the early 1970s they were very much engaged with the world and its concerns, as well as the rapidly changing situation in the church itself. The Theresians added a new component to their program at middecade. As of the early 1970s, the four basic goals of the Theresians were encompassed under four dimensions: Spiritual, Educational, Vocation, and Community. Laywomen lobbied hard for the addition of "Ministry," to accommodate those units that wanted to focus on a particular service (to the poor, the mentally ill, etc.). It should be noted that they specifically chose the word *ministry* instead of *apostolate*, a direct reflection of their emerging feminism.[76]

Moreover, one of the most fascinating aspects of their transitioning prayer lives was a new emphasis on mutual support. The Long Beach unit's newsletter reveals how prayer bonded Theresians to each other. One Theresian wrote, "You are my sister, you who came before me, prayed that I would come. I became a Theresian because of the prayers of other Theresians. My spirit delights in the knowing that I may kneel when another Theresian kneels, as if we knelt together, yet we are miles apart. . . . May my hour of prayer warm you, strengthen you, comfort you, delight you as yours has given me energy and the awareness of the gifts of grace I have received from sources outside myself. Theresian sister, I love you most—because of our One Hour of Prayer." Another laywoman and founder of the Denver Theresians, Jo Taylor, looked back on her history with the organization in 1976 and concluded, "With the advent of the Theresians of America lay women were drawn together to pray for other women." A talk by Patricia Mullen at the 1976 conference suggests that these small Theresian communities came to see themselves as prayerful support groups. It used to be that Theresians "didn't get too personal, air our dirty linen," she said. "Today we do discuss these aspects of our lives, and best of all, we do discuss prayer in our own lives."[77]

I would be remiss if I didn't make a connection to consciousness-raising groups as well. After all, it was Patricia Mullen who in the same year hoped to give each Theresian a consciousness-raising experience. By the mid-1970s feminism joined the mix of influences on these women, adding a dose of cultural feminism to their self-perception. Sister Jane Abell's 1978 conference talk "Women in Support of Women" makes the connection explicit: "Tomorrow in our workshops we will be listening for each other's experienced pain, searching for human symbols with which to communicate, confronting societal structures that dominate and exploit . . . asking how we can join with other women for greater impact."[78]

But while feminism made its mark, it did not turn Theresians into activists. At their heart they remained focused on spiritual development and love of neighbor. Increasingly the word that drifts to the surface is *love*. Their job was to show "the light of Christ's love as radiated by Christian women," laywoman Betty Barrett remarked. According to Mrs. Raber Taylor, the act of being Theresian "plummet[s] us into the great and vast vacuums of love and spirit that exist all around us."[79]

It is fitting to end this chapter with the anonymous voice of a laywoman. According to one rank-and-file member in 1979, "In 14 years in the same community, I feel I have grown spiritually, I have been stimulated and educated; I have come to a real awareness and appreciation of my role and worth as a Christian woman . . . and most of all I have experienced love. This is an ongoing process and I don't ever want it to stop." Having joined the Theresians in 1965, she must have seen incredible changes over time. Yet she still recognized the Theresians of 1979 as linked to those of 1965, despite the drastic shifts in self-understanding. What's more, she valued what these changes brought her: stimulation, education, appreciation of her role and worth, and sisterhood.[80]

The Theresians demonstrate for us, year by year, what was required for a Catholic laywoman to "come of age" in the postconciliar period. Obviously not every laywoman, or laywoman's organization, followed this path; the Theresians were unique, but they are important precisely because they worked out the problems of laywomen's vocation so publicly. Laywomen could not step forward to claim leadership in the church without first

THERESIAN
INTERNATIONAL
CONFERENCE

WOMEN
IN SUPPORT
OF
WOMEN
reaching out with
Gospel Values

SPONSORED
BY:
THE
THERESIANS
OF
AMERICA

DENVER, HILTON HOTEL
OCTOBER 27, 28, 29, 1978

The flier for the 1978 conference illustrates the
Theresians' shift to a feminist outlook.
(Courtesy of the Women and Leadership Archives, Loyola University Chicago)

confronting their own sense of vocational inferiority in relation to women religious. They could not accept their own spiritual strength without first rejecting the idea of their inherent selfishness. Most important, they had to learn the basic idea that they, too, had vocations, and could be at the center of their own prayer lives. Their ultimate vision of their vocations is still quite "feminine" (the emphasis on love and mutual support especially), but they discovered that their gender identity need not be linked to complementarity or essentialism for them to find fulfillment. We also learn that laywomen, women religious, and priests could work in constructive, supportive partnership to encourage the process of laywomen's coming of age in the midst of massive upheaval and renewal. The Theresians are no paragon, of feminism or anything else, and I have no wish to imply that they are. But they do show us the limits placed on laywomen by the church and its culture, and the ability of Catholic women to confront them while staying true to an ever-changing purpose.

Catholic (Non)Feminism

Is the NCCW leadership content to sit outside new
structures, ignoring uneven or unequal representation of
women in them, or sometimes no representation at all? As
women, are we secure enough to take our place, our rightful
place, as an essential segment of the people of God?

Margaret Mealey, 1970

As I began researching my first book on Catholic feminism, I knew very little
of the history of the American Catholic feminist movement or, indeed, Catholic women in the 1960s and 1970s. Quite early in my research I stumbled
across a 1966 article about women and the Second Vatican Council. Its title,
"The Buried Talents Symposium," suggested that I might find some Catholic
feminists in its pages, and I was not disappointed. The article featured the
perspectives of a number of prominent Catholic women including Margaret
Mealey, identified as the executive director of the National Council of Catholic Women (NCCW). Mealey's comments were striking: "By the action and
pronouncements of Vatican II, women have been given their wings. But too
many pastors and bishops are reluctant to let them fly. If the Church is to be
relevant in the world, it must pay serious attention to the status of its women.
Catholic women are growing tired of being ignored in this most important
area of their lives, but they are still ready to step forward and assume an adult
role in the Church with intelligence and grace when it is offered. It is not yet
too late—but it is surely high time." Perhaps I can be forgiven for assuming
that Mealey was a Catholic feminist; her support of Catholic women moving
out of traditional roles is clear, as is her criticism of the hierarchy.[1]

As I moved forward with my research, however, I discovered that
Margaret Mealey was not part of the Catholic feminist movement, nor

was the NCCW considered a feminist organization. In fact, according to self-identified Catholic feminists, the NCCW was an antifeminist organization, dedicated to blocking the Equal Rights Amendment (ERA), curtailing abortion rights, and dominating any commission called by the bishops on the question of women's place in the church. Feminists' comments on the NCCW always seemed punctuated by a rolling of the eyes at best or, at worst, flashes of angry frustration at the organization's perceived backwardness. For example, the always outspoken feminist Sister Margaret Ellen Traxler once ripped into the leaders of the NCCW, accusing them not only of being mired in the "parochial company of the Altar Society" but also of possessing a "neanderthal self-image as women."[2] Taking them at their word, I classified the NCCW as a foe of the movement and turned my attention elsewhere.

I am not alone in my assumptions about Mealey and the National Council of Catholic Women. Historians consistently assume a monolithic antifeminism within the organization based almost entirely on the group's opposition to the ERA. Scholars also assign a fundamental passivity to these laywomen, claiming that they acted solely as agents of the hierarchy's agenda. It is worth noting that the scholars making these arguments were themselves Catholic feminists active in the 1970s. For example, in an article celebrating the feminism of priest-sociologist Joseph Fichter, the sociologist Ruth Wallace notes Fichter's dismissive comments on the NCCW's anti-ERA vote in 1973, quoting him as saying that it "probably reflected the sexist attitudes of their priests and bishops." In other words, the women were both backward and held in thrall by the hierarchy. Historian Mary Jo Weaver also dismissed the NCCW out of hand in her influential book *New Catholic Women* (1985), arguing that the "NCCW has consistently reflected the American Catholic experience, espousing causes dear to the hearts of the American hierarchy: their strong opposition to communism and feminism and their support of Radio Free Europe and the Hatch amendment against abortion follow the lead of the bishops exactly." But this analysis cannot explain the mystery of Margaret Mealey's statements in "The Buried Talents Symposium."[3]

If the NCCW was solidly and consistently antifeminist at the behest of the bishops, why would its leader make such boldly provocative statements, in a public Catholic forum, challenging Catholic gender roles and the men who enforced them? Why would an antifeminist write so eloquently not only of Catholic women's oppression at the hands of the church, but of her belief that Vatican II offered women freedom? These questions led me to the archives, where I encountered the complexity of moderate laywomen's discourse on women, church, and identity for the first time. There are no simple answers here, only the voices of women engaged in thoughtful debate, wrestling with the ideas and opportunities afforded them by American Catholic life in the era of Vatican II and women's liberation. Here I found my first inkling of the laywoman project.

What they were *not* was a tool of the hierarchy. Labeling the NCCW as a mouthpiece for the National Council of Catholic Bishops (NCCB) conceals both the monumental task it set for itself in the decade following the Council, and the complex conversation on gender identity that it eagerly fostered at a time when the vast majority of the nation's bishops would have greatly preferred silence on the subject. What they *were* is more complicated, because they defy simple classification.

The papers of the NCCW reveal that Margaret Mealey and many women in the NCCW's leadership—its committee chairs, conference speakers, magazine and newsletter editors, board of directors and staff—did call for women's rights, leadership, and autonomy, not just in 1966 but through the early 1970s. While they did not self-identify as feminists, labeling them anti-feminist is simply inaccurate and disguises the amorphous state of feminism in this period. Accepting only the perspectives of self-identified feminists on this issue helps conceal the willingness of moderate and even conservative women to espouse feminist ideas before the definition of "feminist" hardened into something they could no longer support. The NCCW's experience gives nuance to a historical narrative that regularly assumes that opponents of feminists' most cherished goals must have opposed feminism in its entirety.[4]

During the 1960s, the NCCW's leadership transformed its organization in response to conciliar principles as they interpreted them. As they did so, they invited the membership to consider what laywomen could be and accomplish, and encouraged them to evolve into new kinds of Catholic women. NCCW leaders coaxed the rank and file to venture out of the parish hall, the altar society, and the Christmas bazaar, and seek the leadership and opportunities promised by "the spirit" of Vatican II. At the same time, they gave women the vocabulary to challenge a hierarchy that hoped to keep gender roles unchanged even as the modern church moved on. These changes may not have been drastic, but clearly the NCCW was inclined to embrace change, not forestall it. Like the Theresians, but on a much larger scale, they used the dual influences of the women's movement and Vatican II to fling open the doors to a larger world of adult responsibility, committed leadership, and engaged spirituality. This call to empowerment was not prompted by the desire to pursue a larger conservative political agenda, despite the group's official opposition to the ERA and abortion rights.[5] It also had its limits, clearly visible when contrasted with the more progressive World Union of Catholic Women's Organizations, of which it was a member. Rather, it appears to have been an attempt to create a new, viable, responsive approach to Catholic womanhood, as the ground shifted beneath its feet.[6]

GROWING UP AND TURNING OUTWARD

The National Council of Catholic Women was founded under the auspices of the American bishops in 1920, its stated purpose being "to give Catholic women of the country a common voice and an instrument for united action."[7] At midcentury, the NCCW functioned as an umbrella organization for thousands of parish- and diocesan-based women's groups, as well as many national laywomen's organizations, and claimed to represent all laywomen in the United States. In 1960, affiliates numbered 13,000. Those affiliates were as diverse as the range of American Catholic women. However, while women of color did rise to leadership in local affiliates, the leadership at the national level (responsible for policy, agenda, and messaging) was overwhelmingly white.[8]

Margaret Mealey (1912–2006) guided the organization through the transitional years at midcentury, serving as executive director of the NCCW from 1949 to 1977. Due to her prominence in the NCCW, Mealey was often asked to represent Catholic laywomen nationally and internationally. She served on Paul VI's Pontifical Commission on the Council of the Laity and observed at Vatican II. She also served on John F. Kennedy's Presidential Commission on the Status of Women and the Citizen Advisory Councils of three different presidents. Through Mealey's influential voice, NCCW women staked a claim for themselves in the broader world.

Through biennial conferences and numerous publications, the national organization provided a forum for laywomen to organize, discuss their priorities, highlight their service to the church on the local and national levels, and foster laywomen's leadership. Through the 1950s, loyalty to the nation's bishops and their policy positions was absolute, at least in the NCCW's published and archived written materials. Its leadership usually spoke in reverent tones when referring to the Catholic hierarchy.

As the Second Vatican Council neared, the NCCW looked much as it had in the 1950s. Publications were largely geared toward the promotion of parish-centered events and fund-raising, and the NCCW continued to

NCCW officers at the 1963 national convention. The group appears to be overwhelmingly white. Margaret Mealey is in the front row, fourth from the right. (Courtesy of the National Council of Catholic Women)

pursue a socially conservative agenda. For example, a Family and Parent Education Committee panel at the 1960 conference described its purpose as affirming that the "home was a worthy career for women," and instilling "respect for large families." The committee also set out "to fight the evils of artificial birth control, abortion, divorce and free love." The same conference passed a resolution supporting modesty: "The dignity of the individual woman demands that the Catholic women exert their influence in the fashion world to overcome styles which offend modesty and jeopardize virtue."[9]

Bishops and clergymen were common keynote speakers at NCCW conferences and other programs, and they had an obvious relish for speaking to such dedicated Catholic laywomen, but their comments, meant no doubt to be supportive, could quickly veer into condescension. "My dear Catholic women," the Very Rev. Alexander Sigur told attendees of the 1960 conference, "you are really fortunate to be invited by Almighty God to join Him through the Popes and the Bishops, in the establishment of the Kingdom of Christ on earth. . . . I really congratulate you." Similarly, the Most Rev. John Spence gushed in 1964 that the NCCW's president, a council visitor, had been given "a place of honor close to [the pope's] throne."[10]

Catholic (Non)Feminism

NCCW leaders from Washington, D.C., a much more diverse group, participate in the regional Study Days in 1967 in Pennsylvania. (Courtesy of the National Council of Catholic Women)

Such clerical speakers mixed their praise for the women's service with pronouncements on their essential nature. In the same address, Sigur insisted that "women must see to life, their essential domain. . . . Women must see to home and family, where they are the queens." In 1963, the Rev. Leo W. Duprey, OP, told a group of NCCW leaders that "Woman's nature represents those psychological endowments which are more or less static and without conscious motivation." The following year, Spence expounded on the theme "Woman's Particular Role" in the context of the Council. Outlining the new role of the laity, he nevertheless concluded that "perhaps what the Church needs today is more Indians. She may have enough chiefs." He encouraged the assembled women to be "privates, corporals or sergeants in the Army of Christ." Of course, the women themselves also spoke the language of essentialism. A 1963 NCCW fact sheet, "The Nature of Woman," warned that "struggles of woman for freedom have led her deeper and deeper into a state of conditions which continually frustrate her nature and her mission."[11]

Such sentiments were not unusual in Catholic circles in the early 1960s, but what is so remarkable is how quickly they disappeared; the NCCW's leadership was ready to make a change. By 1964, such overblown essentialist rhetoric—that is, the assertion that men and women have essential traits and are fundamentally different and complementary—was largely absent from NCCW publications and conference proceedings. What the membership heard instead was a new kind of talk about Catholic women, which was homegrown and clearly inspired by Vatican II. The NCCW's leadership approached the Council with great enthusiasm. Their positive response to Vatican II is all the more striking when you compare it to that of two other national Catholic laywomen's groups: the Catholic Daughters of America and the Daughters of Isabella. As we shall see in chapter 4, these traditional, fraternal organizations had a much more guarded, and at times oppositional, approach to the Council, compared to the NCCW's embrace of renewal.

First, there was acknowledgement that Catholic women needed to get onboard with the changes early or miss their chance. In a 1965 editorial, Margaret O'Connell urged women to "*make ourselves ready. We can so conduct our lives and prepare our minds that when the moment of change and opportunity reaches to the parish level—as it most certainly will—we shall be ready to act and to fulfill what is required of us. We must not be caught napping when the moment comes—lest we awaken to find that the moment has gone by.*"[12]

Others wrote not just of coming changes to parish or liturgy but of more profound implications. In a talk on the new liturgy at the 1964 convention, Mary Perkins Ryan, a significant figure in the liturgical movement, spoke eloquently of the transformation Vatican II could make in the lives of women: "No wonder the changes in the liturgy disturb many Catholics—for they constitute a call to conversion. . . . But once we realize that this is basically what the Church in our times is asking of us—to make Christ the real center of our interests; to make living His life the central drive of our lives . . . surely every serious Catholic will say 'Amen.'" Here we see enthusiasm mixed with a commitment to deepening women's spirituality through the Council.[13]

For the most part, NCCW leaders were not theologians and did not attempt close readings of Council texts for the membership. They did, however, encourage members to read the documents on their own or in groups, and the 1966 conference "The New Pentecost" was dedicated to understanding the larger implications of the Council for laywomen. Overall, the NCCW's posture toward Vatican II was one of openness. In the NCCW, then, we find support for historian Mark Massa's argument that American Catholics stood ready to embrace the changes brought by the Council. In *The American Catholic Revolution: How the Sixties Changed the Church Forever*, Massa explains that American Catholics were particularly open to the central ideological shift of the Council, the acknowledgement of historical change: "Certainly Catholic Christians in the United States, where historical

Catholic (Non)Feminism

consciousness had won the day in so many parts of the culture . . . were ready when what Garry Wills termed the 'dirty little secret,' that the Church itself changes, was let out of the bag. . . . they had been waiting for precisely that little secret for some time."[14] The rapidity with which the NCCW leadership embraced changes brought by the Council, and shortly thereafter began to question its own subservience to the hierarchy, suggests that these women rejected the fundamental immutability of the church. "There is no doubt but that ten years ago, we were all oriented to the past," the chair of the Church Communities Commission wrote in 1968. "The future, if it seemed to hold anything new and different, would just have to be reformed and conformed to the sacred past, we thought, and our programming reflected that, too. . . . Today we know this is not sufficient."[15] Not until the mid-1970s do we find evidence that some members regretted the loss of the certainty that comes from unchanging tradition.

In the 1960s, on the contrary, the NCCW saw itself as a key player in spreading its excitement about change by spearheading the education of laywomen about the Council. In her 1966 Report to the Board, executive director Margaret Mealey wrote, "These are exciting times for the Church, for its members, and for its organizations. Careful thought must be given as to how we can best assist the membership in attuning itself to the Council Documents. . . . This is our challenge! We will pursue it."[16] Margaret Mary Kelly offered more practical suggestions to parish leaders in the organization's primary publication, *Word*. She urged local chapters to read the constitutions paragraph by paragraph, and to create "a favorable climate—for understanding and acceptance of the Council's conclusions." She warned that the bishops' efforts would meet with failure "unless *we*, with sincerity and willingness, make the Council's reforms and renewals our own."[17]

If the NCCW did nothing but champion the Council, one could argue that they were still operating in a preconciliar mode by simply rubber-stamping the bishops' agenda. However, we begin to see signs in the mid-1960s that they were using Vatican II explicitly to question and challenge both their traditional role in the church and their relationship to the hierarchy. Both were in line with the kinds of questions secular liberal feminists were asking in the same period. First, the documents show that the NCCW's leadership believed the Council to be an invitation to reevaluate "woman's nature." For example, they interpreted the Council as a call to Catholic women to stop focusing exclusively on traditional forms of parish-level service. Discussing the NCCW's revamped organizational structure in 1967, the editor of *Word* said bluntly that the new approach would have no "relation to such activities as pot luck suppers, parish picnics, fashion shows, and the laundering of altar linens . . . and readers who look to *Word* for guidance and direction in these activities will continue to look in vain."[18] The older forms of service were referred to as the "little clique" and "the cozy sewing circle." As one commission chair insisted, "The new Catholic woman, God bless her, is a bridge between the Church and the World." It is worth comparing these statements to a 1962 address by John Tracy Ellis in which he called on the women of the NCCW to "withstand the world's contagion."[19] In just five years, the NCCW had largely abandoned the idea that Catholic women should flock to the parish to protect themselves from external threats.

Many reports and articles sought to provide an alternative to the old insular model of Catholic womanhood, one that called for openness and turning outward. At the 1964 conference, the chair of the Spiritual Development Committee, Mary Perkins Ryan, declared that "Catholic women need to see that the changes in the liturgy, the new shape and spirit in religious instruction, the new emphasis on our duties with regard to racial and social justice, the present developments of the Church's teaching about married love, the new emphasis on ecumenism, are all inter-related. They all open out to us and make available to us a more complete, more whole-hearted, more vital Christian life, the life to which we all are called." Two years later, the national Organization and Development chair insisted that if members claimed their first duty was to their home and family, the job of the local Organization and Development chair was to "convince such women that they are placing too much emphasis on only one part of the truth." Such a statement is a striking contrast to the 1960 conference, at which women were asked to protect home and family. Ryan urged chairs to "raise the sights of the members, and to encourage them to reach out from their 'little world' into the 'big world.'" To put this idea into practice, in 1965 the NCCW started the Women in Community Service program, a national service project with the goal of placing working-class women in job-training programs. Significantly, the NCCW partnered with Church Women United, the National Council of Jewish Women, and the National Council of Negro Women, inviting the membership into ecumenical and interracial community action. The NCCW insisted that laywomen's call to service must be larger than the home and parish hall.[20]

A second theme was the exhortation to the membership to grow up and assume adult responsibility in the church. As early as 1960, this theme emerged in the staidest of contexts: the Committee on Libraries and Literature, long preoccupied with indecency. The committee chair declared,

Catholic (Non)Feminism

"Let us make this our 'coming of age year,' first by raising our own reading standards and then by tactfully trying to bring others to a more adult Catholic life through reading." Ten years later, Margaret Mealey echoed the theme, but with a greater sense of urgency. "In this day and age," she asked the membership in 1970, "are we equipped to leap from our own dependency to realistic maturity?" This message was delivered frequently to both laymen and laywomen in the years surrounding the Council, but it held special meaning for laywomen who had traditionally been expected to surrender to the will, not just of the church, but of their husbands as well. Margaret Mary Kelly neatly encapsulated the change in one *long* word: "The attitude of sit-with-hands-folded-until-someone-tells-me-(preferably in words of one syllable)-what-to-do-is-definitely-not-it."[21]

NCCW leaders tried to parlay this new sense of adulthood into concrete leadership opportunities. The membership was urged to get on the new parish councils and finance committees, and participate in the liturgy to the extent that they were allowed to do so, although there was certainly some naivete about how successful women might be at this. "We can go home and get ready to get elected," one optimistic committee chair claimed at the 1966 national conference. "You know there will be a place for us," she went on. "The decrees have said so."[22]

This desire for responsibility also took the form of pointed comments about laywomen's fawning attitude toward their pastors, since challenging the ultimate authority of the clergy was a third theme in the attempt to redefine woman's role. In advising organizations on ecumenical programming, one leader commented that she was tired of seeing "Father Smith will speak" in diocesan newspapers. "It doesn't seem to matter what Father Smith will speak on," she said. "If it comes from Father, it is bound to be religious." "Isn't it amazing," the editor of *Word* commented in 1968, "to realize that women, who . . . are teachers, lawyers, nurses, doctors, secretaries and manage the great institution called home . . . become simpering idiots in their communication and understanding with the parish priest?" An image from a 1967 regional meeting shows how the NCCW tried to put these ideas into practice. A group of laywomen and a priest appear to be intently discussing an important issue. Everyone, including the priest, is listening carefully to one of the laywomen. Significantly, the priest is one among several, and not at the head of the table.[23]

By the mid-1960s, then, NCCW women were becoming more attuned to the need to step outside their traditional roles, turn outward toward the world, and claim the right to leadership in the church. They were also

A small-group discussion at the 1967 NCCW Study Days in Yakima,
Washington, included, but did not appear to be dominated by, a priest.
(Courtesy of the National Council of Catholic Women)

prepared to criticize clergy and challenge Catholic Tradition (with a capital
"T") publicly. Since this looks, on the surface at least, like the stirrings of
feminist consciousness, we must ask how influenced the NCCW was by
feminism, then in its ascendency.[24]

THE NCCW AND THE FEMINIST MOVEMENT

Let's return, for a moment, to the original question driving this research: If
Margaret Mealey and the other leaders of the NCCW were antifeminist, as
self-identified Catholic feminists claimed, why did they speak so eloquently
about the power of the Council to liberate and empower women? This
mystery proves how fruitless it is to employ such terms as *feminist* and *antifeminist,* or even *moderate* or *conservative,* to analyze a period in which such
concepts were in flux.[25] It is not just that people are themselves complex and
defy easy labeling. While this is true, we must also consider that the women
in this story were living in a time before such ideas hardened into labels.
When Mealey made her comments about women and Vatican II in 1966,
the feminist movement was just developing in its newest incarnation and
had not yet radicalized, the Right was regrouping and soon to surge, the Left
was fracturing, and the Catholic Church was emerging from the close of the
Council ripe for redefinition and experimentation.

Catholic (Non)Feminism

Before exploring the limits of these labels and the exact nature of NCCW feminism, a little background is in order. Historians of feminism's midcentury resurgence date the beginning of the movement to around 1963, the year Betty Friedan published her best seller *The Feminine Mystique*. Friedan's book did not cause the resurgence single-handedly—it had its origins not only in white middle-class suburban women's discontent, but also in the civil rights movement, the labor movement, and the New Left—but it provides a handy starting point since the book helped bring the movement its initial broad base of popular support, particularly in the middle class.

The Catholic feminist movement also began in 1963, but its origins were firmly rooted in the Second Vatican Council; the first Catholic feminist writers were equally inspired and infuriated by the clash between what they perceived as the Council's ideological promise of change for women and its near exclusion of women from the Council sessions. The Catholic feminist movement began its organizational phase in 1970, and by 1975 included major organizations of women religious such as the Leadership Conference of Women Religious and the National Coalition of American Nuns. While many women religious flocked to the movement as their lives changed immeasurably in the wake of the Council, laywomen were less visible in Catholic feminism and were certainly underrepresented given their numbers in the Catholic population.[26]

The NCCW showed a remarkable openness to feminism in the latter half of the 1960s. This matches with the tone of Catholic feminism (and indeed the larger feminist movement) at that time, when the movement was ascendant and women across the country were hearing their first feminist ideas and finding themselves nodding in agreement. The radical wing of the larger feminist movement, and its counterpart in the Catholic movement, did not emerge until 1968. The national media seized upon radicalism, highlighted its more outrageous manifestations, and painted all feminists with the same brush, causing many women who espoused more moderate ideas about equal rights to distance themselves from the term *feminist*.[27]

The media is not entirely to blame for this distancing. Radical feminists were quick to dismiss (and antagonize) women whose beliefs began and ended with straightforward liberal feminist goals such as equal pay for equal work or ending job discrimination. Around the turn of the 1970s, moreover, liberal feminists embraced two controversial goals as markers that defined a woman as a feminist: support of the Equal Rights Amendment and support of abortion rights. Regardless of what brought about the hardening of the definition of *feminist*, it caused many early supporters of women's rights like Margaret Mealey to opt out. By the early to mid-1970s the brief window when "feminism" seemed fluid was now closed. In retrospect, we label Sister Margaret Ellen Traxler "feminist" and Margaret Mealey "antifeminist" because the former self-identified and supported ideas that we now associate with early Catholic feminists (such as the ERA, the ordination of women, and public protest), and the latter opposed the ERA, did not advocate women entering the priesthood, and would never do anything so impolitic as to stage a rally in front of the headquarters of the National Conference of Catholic Bishops. But we can also see that in this time of extreme fluctuation, self-identified Catholic feminists on the political left and in the thick of the promise of renewal were actively trying to define and police the label *feminist*. To Margaret Ellen Traxler you were either on the side of the angels, or you were on the side of Phyllis Schlafly; there was no in-between.

In reality, however, many women who served as the NCCW's leaders—that is, its executive director, its presidents, the chairs of its commissions, the members of its board, and the editors of its publications—freely used the language of the women's movement to advocate for a change in women's status in the Catholic Church and their roles at the national, diocesan, and parish levels, as well as in liturgy. Moreover, they used feminist rhetoric to argue for the survival of the NCCW as an autonomous women's organization. However, Mealey and the NCCW clearly were not feminist *enough* to meet the emerging standard that would earn one the title of feminist, not least because they still occasionally used the rhetoric of essentialism, arguing for women's essential difference. Their ideas also lacked feminist theological underpinnings recognizing women's fundamental oppression. You would think that their call to preserve an autonomous national organization for laywomen would strike a chord, since women's autonomy and leadership was a goal these women shared, but in the eyes of self-identified feminists, the NCCW remained too backward on issues such as the ERA and abortion to earn them a place in the sisterhood. Mealey participated in the hardening of the labels by opting not to claim the title feminist for herself and her organization, despite her continued quiet—and ideologically complex—advocacy for women's rights in the church and society.[28]

So what did feminism look like in the context of the NCCW? At first, it looks very much like mild liberal Catholic feminism from a white perspective. The first thing that strikes a researcher in the NCCW papers of this period is the sheer number of articles on feminist issues, and openly feminist articles in the NCCW's primary magazine, *Word*. In 1967, the NCCW hired a young editor fresh from the recently launched, and quite liberal, *National*

Catholic Reporter, hoping to use their own magazine as a more provocative platform to push their membership forward.[29] It featured many articles on social justice issues, including women's rights. An NCCW member could read about the emerging female theologians, feminist biblical exegesis, or the first Catholic feminist monograph, *The Illusion of Eve,* all with a positive spin. Sarcastic comments on the editorial pages about blatant discrimination against women in the church were not uncommon. In 1967, the magazine even featured a very even-handed roundtable on Catholics and abortion rights, leaving readers with the surprising suggestion that intelligent Catholic women could differ on the subject.[30]

NCCW conferences and periodicals featured numerous self-identified feminist contributors from the 1960s through the mid-1970s. These included Sidney Callahan, author of *The Illusion of Eve;* Sally Cunneen, author of the sociological study *Sex: Female; Religion: Catholic;* and Frances McGillicuddy, founder of the American section of the Saint Joan's International Alliance, the first Catholic feminist organization in the United States. The most important of these contributors, though, was Arlene Swidler, editor of the *Journal of Ecumenical Studies.* Swidler was a woman who not only served the NCCW faithfully but also had her hand in nearly every Catholic feminist group in the 1960s and early 1970s, including the radical ones. She first appears in the proceedings of the 1968 conference as the only married woman listed under her own name (as opposed to "Mrs. Leonard Swidler," the style followed by all the other married women presenters), so presumably she made a special request to be identified by her given name.

Swidler wrote impassioned articles about embracing Vatican II as chair of the Church Communities Commission, and she encouraged members to "Make Theology Your Business" in *Word.* By 1970 it was clear that she was an ardent feminist, and yet the NCCW still named her editor of *Word* in that year. One of the first things she did as editor was to publish an article on the brand new movement to ordain Catholic women as deacons. An inset beside the article gave directions to local leaders on how to plan a program on Women and the Church, including extending an invitation to an ordained Protestant woman minister or deacon to speak to their affiliate. While she did not hold the post long, she did not cut ties with the organization. In 1975, when the NCCW unveiled a new magazine, *Catholic Woman,* its cover story featured Arlene Swidler on feminist liturgies, a subject that could not have been fathomed just ten years earlier.[31]

Despite these prominent Catholic feminists who made occasional appearances, the NCCW's publications rarely featured blazingly feminist rhetoric; even Arlene Swidler toned down her feminism for her audience. What we find, then, in NCCW publications and conferences as a whole during this time period is a mild, but still recognizable form of feminism, tempered so as not to appear too radical. A prime example of this appears in a 1971 article titled "Children, Church,—and Lib" by Theodora Briggs Sweeney, who opened with this provocative sentence: "Traditional Marian piety has affected the Catholic woman's self-image badly." The author further claimed that the male-dominated society was harmful to girls and boys, as well as to priests, who were kept from "reaching their full human potential." She discussed the ideas of several prominent Catholic feminist writers, including the theologian Rosemary Ruether, and concluded that "after listening to these women, it seems as if we have reached a point from which there is no turning back." Yet she felt the need to add the caveat, "While there are, of course, the radical, bra-burning man-haters, none of the women quoted here would fall into this category." Her moderate bona fides established, she felt free to end with a quotation from Catholic feminists' favorite scripture verse: Galatians 3:28 ("In Christ . . . there are no distinctions between Jew and Greek, slave and free, male and female, but all of you are one in Christ Jesus.")[32]

A second example of tempered feminist rhetoric comes from a 1966 conference talk by Mrs. John Paddenburg. She related a disturbing story about a mass held as part of the meeting for a women's organization at which she and another woman were asked to bring up the offertory gifts. As they reached the foot of the sanctuary and prepared to hand the gifts to the bishop presider, the priest acting as the master of ceremonies stepped in behind them and hissed in a loud voice, "Don't you women dare put your feet in that sanctuary." Reflecting upon this incident she commented, "You think, 'when are we going to have our chance?'" But she went on to say, "I would request that you remember that time heals all wounds. This might be good to bear in mind in case our feminine feathers get ruffled. . . . So please don't be impatient."[33]

NCCW feminists also wrestled with female essentialism and complementarity well beyond the time when self-identified Catholic feminists had rejected such concepts. While some might maintain that this made them less "feminist," I would instead argue that their persistent engagement with the essentialism of their Catholic past was a natural response to the barrage of changes coming at them from multiple quarters. Such prolonged processing made the nature of their feminism more complex and resistant to easy labeling.

When we discuss essentialism, it is vital to remember how much change these women were experiencing in so short a time. These changes manifested in concrete ways (women experienced the Mass in a fundamentally different, more participatory way) and more amorphous ways (women were asked to question their identities, how they expressed their spirituality, and their vocations). In a world in which everything seemed to be in flux, these women were now being told—by their own leaders—that what they had been taught was their very essence was no longer true. No wonder Mrs. Louis Sweterlitsch went out of her way to assure the gathered members at the 1968 conference that "we are still the same women, the same persons, part of the same people of God. . . . we find the same women with the same loving hearts yearning to serve God with love and to reflect God's love to our fellow men."[34]

It remained a tricky proposition, for those with an affinity for feminism but unwilling to make a complete break with the past, to determine what exactly of the old identity to discard and what to keep. Some tried to reject essentialism, others to downplay it. Still others tentatively embraced essentialism as proof of why women needed their own autonomous organizations; without them, women's special talents and leadership styles would be lost. A full range of these approaches can be seen in the papers of the NCCW between 1964 and 1975. What is clear, however, is that very few leaders in the NCCW after 1964 espoused or disseminated pure essentialist ideas, as they so commonly did prior to that year. Whatever their approach to the question of women's difference and complementarity, feminism had left its mark.

Some writers had no trouble rejecting the notion of female difference outright, on the grounds that it was both untrue and harmful to women. One of the most eloquent denials of essentialism came in 1967 from Lillian O'Connor, a major figure in Catholic women's organizations on the international level to whom we will return later in this chapter. In a *Word* article she described the old identity, focusing not on the trope that "woman's place is in the home" but on the persistent stereotype that women focus on the details to the detriment of larger ideas, and as a result come to doubt their own abilities in the larger world: "Confused by the clamor of society . . . we generally have been content to let the world plunge on, steeling ourselves against every challenge, refusing to see the whole picture, busying ourselves with details until details themselves loom larger than ideas. . . . Always the focus has been on the unimportant." She concluded that women were tired of being revered only if they limited themselves. The needs of the world were too great to perpetuate women's doubts about their own abilities. "As Catholic women no choice is given to us," Mrs. Louis H. Sweterlitsch wrote in 1968. "We must take up the leadership role." If leadership was an imperative, so was change more generally. The editor of *Word*, Joanne Moran, remarked in 1969, "Never before has the individual woman had more freedom to choose the manner in which she wishes to respond to change, and in so doing, to choose the type of person she wishes to become." She can be open and constructive, Moran argued, or she can follow "the more comfortable . . . course and passively drift along the surface of life."[35]

Moran is a prime example of how NCCW leaders wrestled with essentialism. The following year, she wrote an editorial introduction to a special issue of *Word* focused on the role of women. She began with a clear feminist statement: "Remember that every individual, regardless of race, sex, or religion, has a right to equality of opportunity, a right to develop her potential to the fullest. . . . This principle is at the core of the various women's liberation movements whether radical left or middle establishment." After criticizing "women's lib" for its style ("It is true that many of our brethren could approach the subject in a less distasteful and more sophisticated way"), she went on to state a very curious hybrid affirmation/denial of women's difference. "The intelligent woman seldom permits herself to be categorized," she wrote. "In fact, she has the 'knack' for performing all the roles traditionally and erroneously assigned to the list of 'masculine' traits while still retaining her femininity and charm." She added that "if women's liberation is to succeed, its members should note that the badly needed demasculinization of our institutions does not mean the masculinization of themselves." So a woman was the same in that she had the same traits as men, but she was different in that she had a unique feminine nature (and charm!) that she must retain. Members might be forgiven if they emerged from this editorial more confused about feminism and women's identity than when they started reading it.[36]

NCCW leaders, then, could reject essentialism in the name of feminism or affirm feminism and difference in the same breath. Some made a claim for women's difference outright, without the connotations of subservience and self-denial so common before Vatican II and the resurgence of feminism. Their arguments reflected the idea that women had a unique way of doing business, which made the existence of women leaders and women's organizations essential in the modern world. Women tended to be "both synthetic and practical," one committee chair claimed. A report on the importance of women's organizations concluded that they preserve "those qualities of organizational life which are uniquely feminine," such as nurturing women leaders and paying attention to people who were without power. While the author cautioned women against being "duped" into thinking they must give all to their families, he also warned the NCCW against going to the other "extreme" advocated by liberal feminists—namely, integrating with men.[37]

In 1968, the NCCW Board of Directors made an official statement on "the Identity of NCCW as a Woman's Organization," in which essentialist rhetoric flowed freely. The board argued that "the way women work," must be highlighted and preserved, including such traits as the tendency to nurture growing things, following projects through to completion, valuing committee work, and being committed to climbing the organizational leadership ladder. Most important, women nurtured other women's potential and focused on community concerns. By the same token, the more unsavory side of "the way women work"—manipulation—emerged in an article by Margaret Mary Kelly titled "Cooperation with Vatican II." "And remember," she wrote, "in this as in all things to use the 'feminine method'; not charging into the rectory with crusader banners flying, but the gentle (and persistent reminder)—'Father, do you think maybe if . . . ,' 'as you mentioned recently, Father' (even if he didn't, he probably meant to!)." Under patriarchy, manipulation had always been the resort of those without power, particularly women, but even in a world where the NCCW had opened itself to feminist principles, old habits were hard to break.[38]

If we look at the NCCW's feminist development over the course of the 1960s, we see one final characteristic, a strong link between the NCCW's nascent feminism and the Second Vatican Council. The NCCW did not emerge from the Council making openly frustrated or political statements about discrimination, as the self-identified Catholic feminists did in the last few sessions of the Council. Rather, NCCW leaders interpreted Vatican II as an invitation to do and be more, to stretch themselves as Christians and laity; in time this led to new assertions of women's leadership and authority, and eventually a handful of stronger statements of feminist beliefs.

At first, the leadership simply attempted to explain to the membership what profound changes the Council had wrought in the laity's orientation. "Why this new emphasis on our understanding the texts and rites?" Mary Perkins Ryan, an NCCW leader and professional catechist, asked at the 1964 convention. "Because the Church is realizing afresh in our time that God calls all her members, not just the priests and religious, to know Him with the personal knowing that means sharing of thoughts and plans, of life and action—as intimate friends know one another, as husband and wife know one another." Ryan explains Vatican II in language appropriate to married women, language devoid of exhortations to service or appeals to women's special nature. Learn the new liturgy, Ryan says, and you will find intimacy with Christ akin to your most deeply felt relationships. You will grow and you will be called, she assured them.[39]

The expanded vision of the laity's role was not the purview of laymen alone, and NCCW leaders seemed sensitive to the fact that the term *laymen*, meant to include all laity, would soon be interpreted as men only if women were slow to assert their rightful place in the new church. In 1964, Margaret Mary Kelly reminded the membership that Cardinal Leo Jozef Suenens, an outspoken supporter of women auditors at the Council, included lay-*women* in the laity. "Never underestimate the power of a woman . . . to create that climate of *involvement*," she remarked. Kelly noted that the men were working hard, "but the Council is not the work of men alone." This assertion was not mere rhetoric. Margaret Mealey, herself an official observer at the Council, was told by an unnamed archbishop that Council reforms could not hope to be successful unless laywomen's organizations took ownership of implementation.[40]

As we have already seen, the NCCW determined that a core message of its implementation initiative was that the new Catholic laywomen needed to break out of their insularity, their hyperfocus on parish-level service, to engage with the larger world. That language carried a good dose of female empowerment, if not yet outright feminism. The church in America needs women with a "willingness to share their talents," read a proposed conference resolution from the Church Communities Commission in 1966. But not to staff the doughnut table: "Through a study of the documents of Vatican II and the encyclicals of recent Popes we will strive to equip ourselves for responsible action in the intellectual and apostolic renewal called for by the Council." Then board president Rosemary Kilch made a similar point in an editorial just before the same conference: "The stated purpose of the NCCW 1966 convention is to provide the opportunity for our Catholic women to orientate themselves to their new and enlarged role." Get ready, ladies, the NCCW seemed to say. This is our time to become something new, to be significant.[41]

Finally, a handful of authors in *Word* explicitly linked their own full-blown feminism to their interpretation of Vatican II. Not surprisingly, one of these women was Arlene Swidler. In her 1969 article "Make Theology Your Business," she conveyed an infectious excitement for both feminism and the emerging church. To the women of the NCCW she said, if you are "excited by all the new ideas and the opportunities for service in the Catholic Church, you probably find yourself day-dreaming about what it would be like to get really involved in theology: to teach the stimulating new theology, to be a college chaplain, to work in ecumenism professionally." Were rank-and-file NCCW members really daydreaming about theology? Maybe, maybe not, but Swidler treated them as the mature, educated adults she wanted them to be, assuming that they were eager to immerse themselves in the ideas behind church renewal. More important, she argued that NCCW women could make theology a career, using her article to profile numerous women theologians employed by the Catholic Church in a variety of positions. Swidler also chose to express her feminism through her enthusiasm for Vatican II. The Council, she suggested, had broken the stained glass ceiling (or at least raised it higher): "The walls are breaking down, women are being given a chance to work to capacity, women's talents are both needed and wanted."[42]

A second article, also about women theologians, appeared a year earlier, and although its feminism was much more overt, it too linked feminism to the Council. "Today the time has come for women to take their stand as theologians," doctoral candidate in theology Helena Malinowski wrote in the first paragraph. She then approvingly outlined the explicitly feminist writings of Mary Daly and Rosemary Ruether, the most prominent female Catholic theologians at the time. She also hailed the work of the National Organization for Women's recently convened Task Force on Women and Religion. Malinowski noted that these feminists "have looked to the prophetic Church to be 'God's avant-garde,' to be the context in which new, diversified and liberating images of woman may arise." She also went on to co-opt Pope John XXIII's most famous image to explain her excitement about Catholic feminism. "Thus the windows have been opened and the light has pierced through," she said, "and with the light has rushed in the wind of change."[43]

The key to understanding the NCCW's approach to feminism is a remarkable report written by Margaret Mealey for the organization's fiftieth anniversary in 1970. Published for the membership in *Word*, the report defined a mild, pragmatic form of feminism that reflected both the leadership's desire for justice and its aversion to self-identified feminist activity. What we learn from this document is that the NCCW supported justice for women while rejecting organized feminism; that NCCW leaders considered Vatican II and women's rights to be strongly linked; and, perhaps most significant, that the NCCW viewed the confluence of Vatican II and women's rights as a means of securing women's leadership and autonomy at a time when the continued existence of separate women's organizations was under threat.[44]

First, the report makes a clear statement about the NCCW's relationship to feminism. "There can be no differentiation between male and female," Mealey wrote, "no unequal consideration and treatment, no relegation to demeaning roles." However, as we have seen with other leaders in the NCCW, she made an effort to distance herself from the people she thought of as feminists: "Certainly such drastic action as the revolution being staged by some secular and 'Catholic' organizations of women, the women's liberation front, and other militant groups, to draw attention to their treatment as second-class citizens is not the way chosen by all to highlight inequities." Note that she does not take issue with their beliefs, only their approach. She went on to say, "Because we acknowledge [that equal dignity has] long been denied, NCCW is deeply committed to the goal of helping women achieve their full stature, in justice and with an equal measure of dignity."[45]

As was true of much NCCW literature from the mid-1960s to the early 1970s, Mealey explicitly linked feminism and Vatican II reforms, arguing that "Vatican II recognized women as persons possessing full dignity, and as having inherent rights to develop and perfect their natural and supernatural qualities. The documents state that no longer need woman's identity as a person be submerged because of her role as wife and mother. Her whole person must be developed to the fullest, so she may make the unique contribution she was meant to make, in the community and in the world, as well as in her family and in her parish." It could be argued that Mealey made such a connection to defend her position against those in the church who might object to feminist beliefs, but I believe that the link served a larger purpose.

Mealey tried to use the language of both Vatican II and feminism to achieve her ultimate goal of autonomy for Catholic women's organizations at a moment when their continued viability was in doubt. By 1970, the NCCW was hemorrhaging members, losing 1,100 affiliated organizations in 1969 alone. In an unrelated development, the NCCW was faced with the possibility of merging with the National Council of Catholic Men (NCCM), a contentious (and short-lived) experiment that ended in 1973. Many in the leadership of the National Conference of Catholic Bishops and the United States Catholic Conference could not see the purpose of retaining separate organizations for men and women at a time when new possibilities for mixed lay organizations were emerging.[46] The bishops were also aware that support for traditional Catholic women's organizations was on the decline. Mealey had strong doubts about the merger, first because the NCCM did not function on the same scale as the NCCW. The former existed primarily as an advocacy group and did not have a large or active membership. But mainly, Mealey feared that her constituency would lose the confidence in women's ability to lead that she had worked so diligently to inspire in them.

In her report to the board in 1968 she spoke against the merger in these terms: "It is difficult to avoid sounding defensive in this area," she said, "but it . . . gives concern to us because the women, themselves, do not see their own potential, and are easily influenced by some plan presented by a priest moderator or recommended by a bishop. We ask for deep and thoughtful study, therefore. We are devoted to the task of keeping women's organizations individually identified so that the potential of women may be developed; that women may be in the policy-making levels; and that women themselves will aspire to accepting this responsibility." She feared not only that the NCCW's authority and purpose would be lost if it were forced to merge with the NCCM but that NCCW members would automatically defer leadership to laymen.

Mealey's 1970 report must be read in the context of these two problems: loss of membership and the threat of merger. It begins with a discussion of the upcoming national conference, the theme of which was "Celebrate Life! Choose Life!" This was a reference, not to abortion, but to the very existence of the organization.[47] As Mealey noted quite frankly, "In this climate of change, and in this transitional period, NCCW's organizational strength has suffered." Listen, then, to how she interweaves feminism, the vital, continued importance of women's leadership, and the Council's mandate to open the church to the world: "Are we significantly equipped to bring the Church to the world? . . . Can women's organizations adjust to the new pattern? Is the NCCW leadership content to sit outside new structures, ignoring uneven or unequal representation of women in them, or sometimes no representation at all? As women, are we secure enough to take our place, our rightful place, as an essential segment of the people of God?" Mealey consciously used the Council and feminism as arguments to save the organization to which she had dedicated nearly her entire professional life.[48]

Were NCCW leaders—under Mealey's direction—thus stealth feminists flying under everyone's radar? Not exactly. Mealey wrote a second version of her report, this time for the Board of Directors, in which she tweaked her definition of NCCW feminism significantly: "Women must be encouraged, not to pursue equal rights, as such, but to take their place in society, as persons with dignity . . . with an opportunity to contribute what has been not only their experience but the particular temperament and complementary nature which women bring to the whole of society." It is unclear to me why Mealey spoke of complementarity in one document and seemed to reject it in the other. She may have been trying to appeal to a more conservative segment of the board with the second report, but it is more likely that this was the nature of Mealey's pragmatic feminism (or at least how she chose to interpret that feminism for the organization). The most important object for her was promoting and preserving women's leadership and autonomy. To gain it she would argue either position.[49]

We can view her approaches not as inconsistent but as logical responses to the situation she faced. She strongly believed that separate women's organizations brought something unique to the table. Unfortunately, they had been stymied in the past by discrimination within the church. The women's movement provided the impetus to challenge that discrimination, which Mealey embraced, but the women's movement also insisted that all-female organizations like the NCCW—with its parliamentary procedure, white gloves, and bishop keynote speakers—were out-of-date and on the way out. Despite the NCCW's efforts to reform itself for the new postconciliar world, it could not make changes fast enough to attract the young women of the rising generation, for fear of alienating its core constituencies. Meanwhile, the Holy See—and by extension, the NCCB which sponsored the NCCW—was becoming increasingly wary if not openly hostile to anything that smacked of feminism by the mid-1970s. By mixing moderate feminist statements, denials of "militant" activism, and comforting reassurance about women's nature, Mealey seemed to be trying to strike a balance that would allow the work of the NCCW to continue.

CATHOLIC WOMEN'S IDENTITY AND THE WORLD UNION OF CATHOLIC WOMEN'S ORGANIZATIONS

Margaret Mealey and the NCCW were participants in a larger discourse on women, feminism, and the church at this time that extended beyond the national organization to the world stage. The NCCW was one of the most active national affiliates of the World Union of Catholic Women's Organizations (WUCWO), which was itself fostering similar conversations on Catholic women's identities and responsibilities. Through WUCWO, the NCCW had access to a set of ideas that offered new perspectives and additional options for resolving the group's tensions over gender identity in a changing Catholic and political landscape. That it did not take these options again demonstrates the variety of positions available to moderate laywomen as they negotiated their own gender identities.

WUCWO was founded as the International Union of Catholic Women's Leagues in 1910. An umbrella organization for national Catholic women's groups, WUCWO by 1961 had affiliates from sixty-one nations and claimed to represent 36 million Catholic women.[50] Originally founded to promote unity among Catholic women worldwide, WUCWO became increasingly involved in advocacy and policymaking. The group was the first Catholic nongovernmental organization to be granted consultative status at the United Nations, and its leadership took full advantage. From the 1940s to the early 1960s, WUCWO placed staff, funded by the National Catholic Welfare Conference (NCWC), full-time at the United Nations, where they were influential in the development of projects to promote human rights, including the International Declaration on Human Rights. These staff members—namely, Catherine Schaefer and Alba Zizzamia—were also closely linked with the NCCW.[51]

In the era of Schaefer's greatest influence, from the mid-1940s through the early 1960s, WUCWO was also known to be a strong advocate for women's rights, particularly in developing nations. The international organization focused especially on citizenship and voting rights for women, educational parity for girls, and ending sexual exploitation. Not surprisingly, these mid-century WUCWO (and NCWC) representatives at the United Nations joined their enthusiasm for women's rights to accepted Catholic teaching on gender roles. Schaefer and Zizzamia "continued to couple the status of women scrupulously to Catholic principles on marriage, children, and the family," but they also helped establish WUCWO's reputation as an organization that was eager to stand and fight for women.[52]

WUCWO was based in Europe, and its leadership from the beginning was dominated by Western women, although by the 1960s efforts were being made to diversify and shift the group's perspective after considerable pushback from Catholic women in the global South. WUCWO's transition in this area is fascinating in its own right, as the group negotiated development work amid the remnants of colonial privilege. For our purposes, however, we'll keep the focus on another kind of transition occurring within the organization. Like the NCCW, WUCWO was testing its strength in the postconciliar era, shifting its orientation away from Catholic Action—which empowered laypeople to enact the hierarchy's agenda—and embracing its own outlook and agenda. As a vital part of that shift, the organization's leadership began

Margaret Mealey participates in WUCWO Study Days, Paris, 1963.
(Courtesy of the National Council of Catholic Women)

a project not unlike those undertaken by the other groups in this book: the project of redefining Catholic womanhood and new possibilities for laywomen in light of Vatican II.

Because my ultimate interest is less in WUCWO itself and more in the ocean of ideas in which the NCCW was swimming, my focus now turns to the papers of the American Lillian O'Connor (1904–87), an expert in international development and WUCWO board member who served as vice president from 1970 to 1974 and treasurer from 1974 to 1979. O'Connor was deeply embedded in WUCWO, attending nearly every conference and session of study days in her tenure, and helping to plan many of them. Her correspondence was voluminous, linking her to WUCWO officials and delegates around the world. Moreover, she had very strong ties to the NCCW. As we have already seen, she published in *Word* on numerous occasions. She was also friends with Margaret Mealey, and O'Connor's correspondence reveals a close bond of long-standing. There is no doubt that Mealey, so influential in shaping NCCW policy, would have been aware of how the winds were blowing at WUCWO.

WUCWO's changing views on Catholic women paralleled those of the NCCW through the end of the 1960s, although WUCWO began with a stronger sense that their organization needed to change in order to adapt to laywomen's new apostolate. In November 1966, the leadership held

Catholic (Non)Feminism

"International Study Days" in preparation for the WUCWO World Congress in Rome in 1967, and made their focus a renewal of WUCWO itself. "For the past few years, WUCWO has felt the need of change to keep pace with modern times and also with renewal in the Church, as inspired by the Vatican Council," the official report remarked. "We considered that the freedom of women is a condition to all human freedom, and that here we would find our universal solidarity."[53]

WUCWO explicitly stated its intention in 1967 to rethink Catholic womanhood as part of its aggiornamento, showing their analysis, in part, to be an exercise in self-awareness: "It is true that with an unprecedented effort, women are trying to take stock of themselves: to look at themselves through their own eyes, to diagnose their own nature." Starting in 1967, a common theme in WUCWO's proceedings and study papers— presumably a fruit of this analysis—was a concern about women's fundamental passivity. The 1967 World Congress brimmed with enthusiasm for change and for action; WUCWO leaders were fully aware that their constituents needed to challenge this aspect of "woman's nature" if they were to seize new opportunities in church and society. As one of the officers mused in preparation for the Congress, "How can WUCWO help women both to keep their own personalities intact and to fully develop them in this new context of living, not only to avoid a merely *passive endurance* of all these new social pressures, but to make a positive contribution and actively to participate in building this new world?" WUCWO will not help you escape the times, ladies, it seemed to say. You are, and must be, in and of the world.[54]

Lillian O'Connor's speech at the Congress (reprinted in *Word*) *was* uncompromising on this subject: "What has brought us to this last quarter of the 20th century, still arrayed in the swaddling clothes of earlier times? Still unsure of our own identity as persons, insecure, full of self-distrust, unable to exult in being what we are? . . . Ideas which come from women are still rejected, scorned, and woman has turned back to the old comfortable corner, discouraged, apathetic, seeking security in familiar routines, refusing to accept the challenge of life in the 20th century, withholding her contribution to the world of ideas and to her fellowmen." One hears in this echoes of Margaret Mealey in "The Buried Talents Symposium" from the previous year. Both women were full of anticipation that Vatican II would provide Catholic women with liberation in some form, yet both felt stymied. Mealey blamed the hierarchy, O'Connor Catholic women themselves; both eagerly hoped to give women their wings.[55]

Knowing the preoccupation of the Theresians in this same period, it is also useful to track WUCWO's perception of Catholic women's vocation and how it changed over time. María del Pilar Bellosillo addressed the 1967 World Congress on the theme "WUCWO after Vatican Council II," but the speech was really a meditation on vocation in the context of Vatican II. Citing *Lumen Gentium*, she explained that the church "becomes more clearly aware of *what she is* and of *her vocation*, and each member of the Church receives new light on his place, vocation and participation in the overall mission of the Church." Her feminine pronouns clearly reference the church, but the emphasis she places on them nods playfully to women's new role. From *Gaudium et Spes*, she took the church's purpose as being "to form new men, artisans of a new humanity." But Bellosillo was careful to define "new men" inclusively: "Men and women co-responsible for the overall mission of the Church." She ended her speech with the then ubiquitous quote from Pope Paul VI, proclaiming, "But the hour is coming, in fact has come, when the vocation of woman is being achieved in its fullness."[56]

Jumping ahead three years to 1970, one sees an organization that continued to embrace these ideas about renewal and vocation, but with an added intensity. Now president general, Bellosillo gave an opening speech to the WUCWO Assembly of Delegates in 1970, liberally marked with emphatic underlinings. It must be a "*total* aggiornamento," she said. "All the materials which form the building must be altered. The house must be knocked down and rebuilt. It is a renewal which concerns *the very life* of the institution." She repeated the need for men and women to be copartners and coartisans in the work of the church but added a more specific focus: "When we consider women's status in the world, we feel that the advancement of women should be our main aim." She went on to call for "more radical social change" to achieve "the *liberation* of man." But she wasn't done yet. "We feel," she said, "and this is what we propose—that our commitment to the Church's mission should become a reality through Education and Faith, and through our work to improve the status of women in the Church." And with that, the leaders of WUCWO revealed their intention to pursue justice for women—for themselves—in the Roman Catholic Church.[57]

It is here that the NCCW and WUCWO diverge. In Margaret Mealey's fiftieth anniversary executive director's report, also written in 1970, she worked hard to express a form of feminism that would not alarm or offend, taking care to criticize self-identified Catholic feminists who confronted the church directly, providing a more essentialist version of the document for her more conservative board and a more progressive version for her membership. WUCWO, less controlled perhaps (at this stage at least) by ecclesial oversight, felt no need to pull punches, and it was less and less circumspect as the 1970s progressed.

Like Mealey, Bellosillo was closely attuned to her own organization. Her opening remarks at the 1970 Assembly of Delegates emerged from the responses to a working paper she circulated prior to the meeting. WUCWO leadership confirmed its desire to focus on women's passivity and women's rights. In her report on the working paper, "Aims and Programme," Bellosillo hinted at WUCWO's new Catholic feminist orientation: "The primary point here is the urgent need to arouse women and make them aware of what they are. What [th]is means is the true liberation of women. Sometimes Catholic circles are the most closed-in and yet it is in Revelation, in the Gospel, that Christian women discover the full greatness of their dignity, and where they are called on to advance toward their complete fulfillment." In other words, Catholicism may seem like the last place to find liberation, but Catholic women know the possibilities embedded in their faith. Lest one interpret this as false feminism, the canard that the church liberated women by affirming their true identity as mothers and wives, one need only read on in the document: "Women seemed to be defined by a function: motherhood, and not by their own real being (human person)." Bellosillo outlined two aims: to "improve the status of women in the Church" and "to help women participate more fully in the Church as a community of Faith." Women were coresponsible in the church's mission, but to fully be so they "must pass through the institutional church." This left the women of WUCWO no choice but to challenge the institution itself.

In this WUCWO separated itself from the NCCW ideologically, but it put further space between the two organizations by taking concrete action on its principles. WUCWO attempted to intervene with the Pontifical Commission for the Revision of Canon Law, issuing a memorandum with "demands" "based on the request for recognition, in Church law, of the fundamental rights of women as human persons, both in fulfilling their human status and in their family, civic, social and Church life." The organization also requested a theological study on women and the priesthood, not "because WUCWO is interested in the access of women to the priesthood" but because women's unfitness for priesthood was repeatedly used as evidence for denying women's fundamental personhood. Feeling the need to justify WUCWO's new line of activism she interjected, "If we have done this, it is because Vatican II urges us to go forward." Once again, Catholic laywomen drew a direct line between their feminism and the principles of the Second Vatican Council.[58]

For Lillian O'Connor, the first few years of the 1970s reveal her emergence as a solid proponent of feminism within WUCWO. The letters she received from all over the world in this era take for granted her feminist sympathies as friends shared with her stories of women's frustrated attempts to push the boundaries of liturgical participation in their dioceses, for example. A silly poem, jotted down at a conference to honor various participants, immortalizes O'Connor with these lines: "Lillian O'Connor—World V.P. / Of varied Catholic Unity / She's for women to be free / And the one for you to see." O'Connor also appears to have been a proponent of using prayer and liturgy to forward feminist goals and express a Catholic feminist identity. She saved the handout from a liturgy celebrated for WUCWO Prayer Day in 1972 ("Sharing of a Shalom Meal") that had many hallmarks of Catholic feminist liturgies in the early 1970s, from the invocation of female historical figures to the use of scriptural readings about justice.[59]

She also wrote a lengthy prayer for the WUCWO day of prayer in 1973, which she sent to both Margaret Mealey and María del Pilar Bellosillo for comment. She used the prayer to highlight women's individuality: "We pray for all women everywhere, for each other, for our own individual self, each one in her own identity." She prayed for courage to "overcome the confusions and conflicts" that kept women from assuming their roles as "co-fashioners of a renewed and compassionate humanity." She feared that these conflicts "doom countless individuals, each endowed with gifts from your hands, to fruitless lives of insecurity and apathy: joyless, hobbled."

After asking for God's abundant gifts upon women everywhere, she prayed specifically, that not just feminists but also women generally might engage in appropriate forms of activism that would not detract from the cause: "Oh, God, giver of every perfect gift, grant that our sisters who seek to plead for changes in outmoded customs which formerly restrained our whole sex, may spread understanding and respect for our true human dignity, leaving aside the non-essentials which lend themselves to exploitation by those who are hostile or merely amused, thus invalidating the whole meaning of our ordeal." As O'Connor remarked in a rationale for the prayer, "attention-getting behavior has important psychological results and values" but only if the movement didn't lose focus on the main goals, and only if the behavior didn't cause too much adverse publicity. The main goal for O'Connor (and for WUCWO) was always "seeking our place as co-sponsors of a new humanity."[60]

As for Margaret Mealey, when asked for comment on the prayer she responded to O'Connor with a one sentence note: "Lillian dear, it is beautiful." Her note suggests that she shared O'Connor's viewpoint, or was at least open to it. It also helps explain points of tension concerning feminism on the NCCW board at this time. Mealey's extremely moderate, unnamed feminism had room for those who did embrace Catholic feminism more willingly, and that may have spooked the NCCW board at a time when they were being courted by anti-ERA activists.[61]

Celebrated as International Women's Year (IWY), 1975 marked an important turning point for most women's organizations, but especially the NCCW and WUCWO. As we shall see, IWY proved divisive for the NCCW, revealing a split over essentialism in the organization; it also marked a turn away from feminism and toward a more conservative agenda. In marked contrast, WUCWO decided to include questions about women's position in the church in its agenda for IWY. The year was most significant, however, in that it ushered in "the Decade of the Woman," and WUCWO was determined to play a role on that stage. Subsequently, WUCWO became more outwardly feminist, more aggressive in its opposition to church sexism, and more willing to downplay its differences with secular feminist groups in order to forward a global agenda for women's rights.[62]

NCCW MEMBERSHIP AND ANTIFEMINIST BACKLASH

The NCCW's ties with WUCWO were close enough that one could imagine the two groups working together on their projects of determining a future for Catholic laywomen. Yet Margaret Mealey proved more cautious in her leadership, and the two groups diverged ideologically by the mid-1970s. The reasons why extend beyond Mealey.

It had become clear by the turn of the 1970s that certain sectors of the group's leadership had become too progressive for many in the rank and file. The membership's views can be difficult to gauge due to a lack of sources, as much more information flowed from the leadership to the membership than the reverse, but feedback from members does indicate a definite strain of antifeminism. Such responses may simply reflect differences of opinion in the membership, not surprising since antifeminist sentiment was quite common in the early 1970s. They might also indicate discomfort with a leadership that seemed dominated by educated lay elites who after the Council tended to follow an agenda more oriented toward social justice. As the editors of *Catholics in the Vatican II Era* remind us, "Historians of the Council may not have paid enough attention to the ways that conciliar mandates built on and even endorsed emergent structures of class, cultural capital, and privilege that were rapidly dividing Catholics into different strata in various places in the era." The NCCW's membership, long consisting of a mix of middle- and working-class laywomen, may have resented their leaders' attempts to push them in a direction the leadership deemed necessary.[63]

The first indication of a lack of enthusiasm about the new programming initiatives began in the mid-to-late 1960s. The NCCW leadership often noted that the membership needed prodding to embrace reform and that no one seemed to be responding to their efforts. *Word* editor Margaret O'Connell described "the uncomfortable feeling, probably akin to what an all-night radio announcer must occasionally feel, that . . . there is nobody 'out there' listening."[64] It did not help, of course, that NCCW leaders' perception of their members as unsophisticated and difficult to prod forward undoubtedly filtered down to the membership.

For example, a 1970 letter to the editor of *Word* complained about a change of format that emphasized substantive articles on justice and theological issues over "Program Pictures," which chronicled the doings of local affiliates. "Our Catholic women are hungry for growth at this time but let's keep the food *within their reach!*" the writer argued. The editor responded condescendingly. "Learning always involves a *reaching* or striving toward something before it is grasped," she explained. "WORD operates on the premise that our women *care enough* to exert the energy toward perpetual growth as persons. . . . a format filled with program pictures is not the answer." Perhaps more charitably, a local organizer observed that "our women are not terribly sophisticated, but they are truly the 'salt of the earth' and I sometimes think that perhaps part of our problem is that we have not challenged them enough."[65]

Responses from the rank and file in the form of letters to the editor indicate that many women had been challenged quite enough, thank you very much, and did not care for the results. A 1969 letter to the editor was frank: "About the nature of woman—our job is not out fighting poverty but rather in our homes preparing our husbands and our children with the means to reach heaven." Later that year another letter simmered with anger: "Please send *Word* to Mrs. _____. It's too liberal for me to take. . . . Fr. Beckman's article on revision of Canon Law so women can work as priests, etc. should not be published by NCCW. *Word*, I hope, will someday have something to help us spread *God's* message, not someone's political ideas." "I'm ashamed to show it to any women," another member wrote.[66]

Catholic (Non)Feminism

Conference evaluations also provide a rare window into the opinions of women in the pews. The 1968 national conference elicited some strong responses. "God help the poor affiliations who have to listen to these reports," one woman wrote, "provided their representatives can find something that won't shock. . . . Let the laity stick to their knitting and let the appointed clergymen run their end of the business." "Rather than clear the air for definite guidelines," another commented, "our women are more confused than when they left home." A third conference attendee's comments tell us that the NCCW was trying to innovate in the area of liturgy as well, and this member was not pleased: "One such hand clapping Mass would have been more than enough." Such comments were balanced by positive responses, but in the few places where we see the membership allowed a significant voice, many express opposition to the changes they were being asked to make, in both politics and personal identity.[67]

The membership is not the only place where we find a strain of antifeminism within the organization. The Board of Directors' opposition to the ERA in the 1970s was interpreted by many outside the organization as an antifeminist position. From 1956 onward, the NCCW consistently opposed the ERA, on the grounds that it would eliminate special protections for women, although by the 1970s the leadership protested that its opposition was not indicative of hostility to women's rights. A report from the 1972 general assembly illuminates this issue. During a question-and-answer session with then president Bernice Zilly, several members apparently questioned the NCCW's official position on the ERA. Zilly replied that the women should just read the copy of "a superb article on the ERA" recommended by Bishop Harrison found in their conference packet. "It will be helpful for anyone who has to stand up and give the reasons why the NCCW has taken this stand and our position to this particular amendment," she added. She did not leave the subject, however, before insisting "we must keep stressing the fact that this is just an amendment, because we are not opposed to equal rights for women."[68]

In hindsight, one can see why the NCCW members were confused about the organization's position on the ERA and what they should do about it. The NCCW's Board of Directors made strong position statements against the ERA, yet its president tempered this position while speaking to its members. We also know that Mealey produced one document for the board that espoused essentialism, yet omitted this section in her version for the membership. It would appear, then, that the organization was divided on the issues of the ERA and feminism in the first half of the 1970s.

Further evidence of this division comes in 1974, when a tantalizing entry appears in the board minutes: "Motion made and seconded that a letter of commendation and encouragement be sent to Mrs. Phyllis Schlafly for the work she has done in her opposition to ERA." The motion was followed in the minutes by this note: "The committee felt that some of [Mrs. Schlafly's] statements were inaccurate and the motion failed."[69] That same year, the Executive Committee was also split over the matter of International Women's Year. At the 1974 conference, the Executive Committee wrote a draft statement in support of IWY, which contained clear essentialist language: "The National Council of Catholic Women endorses in general the theme of International Women's Year, which is 'equality, development and peace,' and will cooperate in the program of activities proposed by the Economic and Social Council to implement the principles proclaimed in the United Nations General Assembly to evaluate the status of women throughout the world . . . the NCCW believes that the greatest contribution most women can make to development is to fulfill their role as wives and mothers." But when the resolution was brought to the general assembly for a vote, the language had been changed substantially: "While strongly supporting the need to elevate the status of women throughout the world, NCCW believes that equality, development and peace are best achieved when women pursue their individual roles in the home and society with honesty and integrity." The statement added that women should seek holiness in "whatever role they perceive as their particular call from God."[70]

The effect of these divisions, both among the leadership and the membership, was that the NCCW did not emerge as a potent organizational force pursuing "feminist" or "conservative" women's goals in the 1970s or the 1980s. While the NCCW opposed the ERA, the membership was not urged to fight the amendment in any organized way, and it was not a major part of the NCCW agenda. If the membership had been encouraged to take to the streets (or the halls of Congress) against the amendment, some evidence of this would appear in the publications or program initiatives, but it does not.

This finding is significant because the NCCW, if it was indeed as conservative as Catholic feminists believed, would have been in a prime position to take advantage of the growth of conservative political women's organizations at this time, especially fellow Catholic Phyllis Schlafly's Eagle Forum. In fact, there is evidence that the NCCW participated in Schlafly's "pro-family" rally protesting the feminist-led 1977 National Women's Conference in Houston, and scholars continue to link the NCCW with "the

New Right."[71] This characterization of the NCCW, even in the late 1970s into the early 1980s when it had turned more conservative, is still inaccurate. The NCCW was clearly internally conflicted, and unprepared to name emerging issues of the culture wars such as the ERA and opposition to abortion rights as its raison d'être. Beyond the archival evidence, we should also consider the organization's decreased membership and prominence. The NCCW was in a position to ride the wave of the growing "Moral Majority" coalition if it wanted to, but it did not, even as membership continued to fall.[72]

Instead, members were treated to a slate of mixed messages in 1975, reflecting the organization's ongoing confusion over women's roles and its lack of a concrete agenda on women in the church. There is some evidence that the organization's leadership—and membership—had swung more firmly to the right by 1975. For example, a resolution from the 1975 conference is a patchwork of feminist but ultimately firmly essentialist ideas. The first line alone would have been confusing for anyone with even a cursory knowledge of feminist theology: "Whereas, men and women were created to complement each other, 'male and female He created them,' and firmly believing in Paul's statement that there is no distinction between 'Jew and Greek, male and female.' . . . be it resolved that the NCCW fully respond to Christ's expectations of the ministries of women in the life of His Church, recognizing their special talents and abilities."

The resolution's authors here mixed the notion of complementarity with the two Bible passages used most often by feminists to claim that men and women were not created differently to complement each other. The authors then affirmed the limits on women's ministries (most likely a response to the first Women's Ordination Conference to be held later that same month), yet they also claimed that they would "continue to inaugurate programs that will strengthen women's positions in the Church." A member reading this resolution, and thinking back to the article on feminist liturgies in the first issue of the organization's new magazine that same year, might wonder what message she was supposed to take to heart. One can hear the desperate desire for direction in a resolution to "reaffirm Mary" introduced at the 1974 general assembly: "Mrs. Rita Burke reminded the assembly that Mary never lost her way. Maybe some of us did in the last difficult years, but Mary never did."

From the mid-1970s onward, the NCCW became more likely to support church teaching on gender than to question it. Not coincidentally, the image of the NCCW as obstructionists on feminist issues became cemented in the minds of historians not long after. Although the Theresians and the NCCW ended up in very different places on the feminist spectrum by the 1980s, how their history has been recounted is similar. In both cases, the years of the mid- to late 1960s have been conveniently forgotten, effectively eliding the work of the laywoman project.

It is fair to ask what the leaders of the NCCW accomplished, as we draw this narrative to a close in years of confusion and rising hostility toward even the mild feminism that the leadership espoused in the immediate postconciliar period. Did the end of the NCCW's laywoman project mean that its leaders and membership returned to an essentialist outlook? The balance of the group's leadership seems to have leaned that way, certainly, by the mid-1970s. But overall, the numbers suggest women in the pew had other ideas. Catholic laywomen were increasingly choosing not to join the NCCW by the mid-1970s, and it rapidly diminished in reach, power, and authority. There are many reasons why Catholic women may have made this choice—chief among them increased rates of paid employment—but laywomen who had been offered new understandings of gender and frameworks for their own service in the church by the NCCW itself in the 1960s may have more easily said no to the NCCW as it turned more conservative in the 1970s.

Margaret Mealey's desire to promote justice, equality, leadership, and new roles for Catholic women was expressed consistently in the NCCW in the immediate postconciliar era, and it had a lasting impact. She and the leadership of the National Council of Catholic Women believed in the power of the Second Vatican Council to transform their church. They embraced what they considered to be the promise of renewal: an energizing force that would call all Catholics to a world outside their comfortable parishes and their everyday experience. They craved a challenge that would move them beyond complacency to a new, revitalized, spirituality. Yet Mealey believed that promise would go unfulfilled without a change in the identity of Catholic women.

Mealey therefore turned to a moderate form of feminism—one that self-identified feminists were reluctant to acknowledge—to liberate Catholic laywomen and promote their leadership so that they might respond to that call for renewal. In the midst of the women's movement then insurgent, and the excitement following the Council, the NCCW created a new vision for Catholic womanhood, using the language and ideology, if not the identity, of feminism.

3

Complementarity and Intimate Life

No wonder the trends of the sixties blurred the Catholic woman's
self-concept and left her validly disturbed about her role. Was
her life of service to her husband, her large family, her parish
and church organizations no longer enough for a fulfilling life?

Antoinette Bosco, "What's Really Happened to Women?" (1971)

The quotation that opens this chapter, with its pointed central question,
came from an article published in *Marriage*, a magazine for Catholic couples.
It was accompanied by a photo of Betty Friedan flanked by protestors, one of
whom carried a sign that read, "Unpaid Slave Laborers! Tell him what to do
with the broom!!" Yet the brief bio for Antoinette Bosco, the piece's author,
could not have seemed in greater contrast: "Mrs. Bosco, mother of six, is the
staff feature writer for the *Long Island Catholic*." The inflammatory photo
had very little to do with the article, but what lay within was much more
intriguing—and rarer—than a seemingly staid Catholic woman espousing
feminism, even in a mainstream Catholic magazine. What Bosco offers is a
reflection on laywomen and women's liberation over the course of the 1960s
from the perspective of a moderate Catholic laywoman with feminist lean-
ings if not a feminist identification.[1]

Her main argument was that "the jarring noise" of "women's lib," as she
termed it, was "drowning out the other, the quiet-revolution that was nurtured among the female 51 percent of the United States' population during
the sixties." She could, in fact, have been describing the laywoman project
directly for *Marriage*'s readers. "The quiet revolution is the one to watch,"
she insisted, "for it starts—not with the flamboyant demands of Women's
Liberation—but in the very depth of woman and her evolving vision of who

she is. . . . Sometimes vocal in their protests, sometimes unaware that they were in revolution, American women made the sixties the decade for persistently demanding a new image of woman in the modern world."[2]

Lest we imagine that Bosco was simply reporting on what was happening around her in the secular world as a detached observer, most of the article was concerned with her own community of Catholic women, whom she identified as participants in this quiet revolution. Laywomen were in the process of reassessing every aspect of their identities from working outside the home ("'Working mother' was almost synonymous with every form of social evil existing," she recalled) to their sexuality ("Changing attitudes about women's sexual role were bound to result from the popularity of a pill that placed a woman in control sexually") to motherhood ("The declining birth rate and the new emphasis on a woman having status because of who she is and not on the fact that she's somebody's mother, has indicated a coming 'deglorification' of motherhood and large families") and, finally, to their identities as Catholic women in an unjust church ("Another area notoriously closed for women leaders is religion, with virtually no administrative or theological positions open to women in the Church. Yet, the question of ordaining women must be faced").[3]

The editors chose as the header for the body of the article, "Many of the changes create confusion for the Catholic woman," but this was not in keeping with the spirit of the piece. Antoinette Bosco was not confused, and, despite the magnitude of the changes they were facing, she did not think the majority of her fellow laywomen need be confused either. While she conceded that some of these shifts in identity were disconcerting, even "disturbing," she clearly thought the developments of the previous decade were fruitful and must continue. According to Bosco, the 1960s showed that Catholic laywomen knew exactly how to process these changes and become something new, through what her article termed "a personal look at women by women."[4]

This chapter documents the transformations in identity that Antoinette Bosco describes through a deep dive into *Marriage* magazine from the early 1960s through the mid-1970s. Unlike the first two chapters in this book, this chapter turns the focus away from women's organizations to a different kind of community of laywomen in order to investigate changes to laywomen's self-conception. *Marriage*, a publication more than usually preoccupied with changing gender roles (to put it mildly), could not stop talking about Catholic women and how they were changing in the face of the modern world and church. Its editors could very easily have handed the conversation to those entrusted with such issues in the past: clergy, male Catholic theologians and social science professionals, and a handful of female freelance writers affirming the virtues of complementarity.

Instead, they became supporters of the laywoman project—at times perhaps unwittingly—by fostering lively, protracted conversations about every aspect of Catholic women's lives, most especially in the intimate areas of home, spousal relationships, work, and bedroom, subjects that the Catholic women's organizations in this study rarely discussed. While both men and women participated in these conversations, I have largely focused on the voices of laywomen, so abundant in this forum. Bosco could have been speaking about *Marriage* itself when she bore witness to the revolution so quiet she felt the need to document it in 1971 in case her readers had not noticed it had taken place.

The changes may have been gradual enough that readers had missed them, but a systematic analysis of the magazine's articles on gender identity does indicate change over time, just as Bosco claimed, and shows that these changes were of laywomen's own making. Laywomen had ideas to explore on many subjects relating to their own gender identity, but the common theme is a steady erosion of the foundations of the teachings of complementarity. In 1961 complementarity was unquestioningly accepted in the magazine; by 1975 this was no longer the case. What was once fixed, unchanging, and sacred—and furthermore, offered as consistent justification for denying self-determination, opportunity, or authority to laywomen—was now openly challenged in all of its manifestations. In *Marriage*, the laywoman project set its sights on Catholic homes and the marriages within them, calling into question the worldviews that formed laywomen at midcentury and continued to confine them.

BACKGROUND AND METHODOLOGY

Marriage magazine was a monthly periodical published by the Benedictines of St. Meinrad Abbey, Indiana, under the auspices of Abbey Press starting in 1959. The magazine seemed designed to appeal to educated white Catholic couples negotiating the tricky questions confronting middle-class Catholics in the "modern world." In its earliest years, readers could find in its pages articles on suburban parish life, the Second Vatican Council and its implications for marriage, and excerpts from the works of major European theologians.

They might just as likely find an article on parenting teenagers, a comic piece about the chaotic daily life of a housewife, or a debate on the question of limiting family size.

Marriage reflects a desire both to inform a readership that felt empowered by the lay action movements of the postwar years and to create a forum for debate where laypeople, male and female, could speak openly on a variety of topics of concern. The editorial team also hoped to reach young people preparing for marriage or who were newly married, and train them to this particular idea of active citizenship in the Catholic community. While *Marriage* had no formal ties to movements such as Cana or the Christian Family Movement (CFM) it is fair to say that the magazine shared a similar outlook at its founding and sought the same audience. Throughout the years in this study, *Marriage* occasionally checked in with each movement, generally reporting favorably on developments in both for its readership. While the magazine carried a whiff of CFM about it, the connection should not be overstated. *Marriage* viewed itself as its own creation, and its readership did not seem to identify firmly with any one movement (or indeed, with any movement at all). *Marriage's* circulation was modest, but it did see an increase over the course of the 1960s. As of 1963, circulation stood at 65,000; it reached 80,000 by 1968.[5]

The magazine underwent a few notable changes over the course of the 1960s and early 1970s. For example, the magazine gradually moved from clerical to lay leadership, appointing a lay editor for the first time in 1966. This transition would prove permanent. In that same time period, featured experts on a variety of topics shifted from predominantly clergy to predominantly lay. Over time, the fields from which these experts came gradually transitioned from theology to the social sciences, especially psychology and sociology. Further changes are reflected in the magazine's subtitle. What began its life as *The Magazine of Catholic Family Living* had become by 1966 *The Magazine for Husband and Wife*, signaling a change in direction and a warning, perhaps, that Catholic moms and dads best keep it off the coffee table from here on out. Not coincidentally, perhaps, 1966 is also the year that *Marriage* ceased to include discussions of rhythm as a viable form of family planning for Catholic couples and turned toward new conversations about Catholic marital sexuality.[6]

On its surface, *Marriage* may seem an unlikely vehicle for investigating how the American Catholic community debated questions of women's identity in the context of their intimate lives, particularly if one's focus is laywomen's agency. From the beginning the positions of editor and managing editor were filled by men. Although Catholic laywomen did work as associate editors and served on the advisory editorial board, they never had editorial control of the magazine. *Marriage* also published its fair share of aggressively essentialist articles as well as blatant antifeminism that explicitly called for women's submission. Why turn to such a publication to reconstruct a debate about women and their sense of themselves within their families and relationships?

As is evident in the previous chapters in this book, the women's organizations in this study largely steered away from issues related to married women's home lives in the 1960s—at least publicly—so their records are not helpful in this area. They discussed their changing ideas of Catholic womanhood as they related to vocation, renewal, authority and hierarchy, prayer, liturgical change, and women's place in the church. For the most part, however, they did not sustain conversations about more personal matters, such as spousal relationships, women's domestic lives, and sexuality. If we want to know more about Catholic women at home, we need to leave the conferences, board meetings, and newsletters behind.

Curiously, one can't look to the Catholic feminist movement, in its ascendency in the same period, for answers in this area either. Women religious and Catholic theologians (often one and the same), who were dominant in the movement's leadership had different preoccupations in this period, and they were unlikely to raise domestic issues as most pressing. Moreover, lay Catholic feminists seemed to ignore these topics because, for them, the questions were already settled. Self-identified feminist laywomen took for granted that they were all in agreement on questions such as egalitarian marriage, a woman's right to work outside the home, or the importance of artificial contraception, and as a result these issues simply did not arise.

So who did talk about shifts in gender identity in the context of domestic life and family relationships? As it turns out, these conversations were raging in *Marriage*, a community of mainly moderate to moderately conservative lay Catholics. These editors, contributors, and letter writers, male and female, had come of age in a postwar Catholic world that liked its laypeople active and informed, and its women at home leading the family rosary. Here is where we have ample evidence of the conflicts that arose when the rising confidence of lay action in the Vatican II era ran headlong into the destabilizing ideas of the women's movement. These folks seemed determined to puzzle out the implications of this collision.

One does not need to look long or hard to find evidence that gender was a major preoccupation in this community. This study encompasses the years 1961 to 1975. From those years, I pulled a total of 571 articles, editorials, and sets of letters to the editor for analysis.[7] Of these, there were fifty-eight articles and editorials published whose primary purpose was to discuss gender roles, generally for women. That's a stunning average of one every three months over fifteen years. In this same period, *Marriage* published an additional 143 articles and editorials that in some way made an argument about gender roles for Catholic men and women, arguments, incidentally, that both affirmed and challenged the status quo. It is not an overstatement to note that the topic of changing gender roles in Catholic life was ubiquitous in *Marriage*.

But what can we learn of women's self-perceptions if *Marriage* was controlled by men? The first answer is that the magazine is replete with laywomen's voices, laywomen who felt empowered to make claims, build arguments, and share their opinions with the world even when their views contradicted either accepted Catholic teaching or the growing voices in support of liberation. In my sample, ninety different laywomen appeared under their own byline, or in a few cases, shared a byline with a male coauthor. Yet these were not the only women's voices to appear in *Marriage*. An additional 137 women had their views published under the heading "Reader Reaction," the magazine's section for letters to the editor. Women were even less guarded in their views in this format than paid contributors, and the editors allowed these opinions to be published without commentary (except when they perceived an unwarranted attack on another author). In its effort to respond to and include the voices of women, especially female readers, *Marriage* was in step with other women's magazines at midcentury. Though perceived to be static entities that merely perpetuated prevailing notions of domesticity, women's magazines of the era did attempt to foster communities of women readers and writers who expressed opposing positions on questions of family life.[8]

As I have noted, however, *Marriage* was male-dominated. We must treat women's words with care in such contexts. We do not know how much they curtailed their own thinking so as to meet gendered expectations, for example. We also don't know how many women were unable to express their ideas because they were denied access by male gatekeepers. Throughout, we must pay careful attention to how the editors framed debates, chose topics and authors, and manipulated the presentation of women and their concerns.

My point, however, is that if we only look to female-run forums free from male authority to understand female perceptions of gender identity in the Vatican II era, we will leave out huge swaths of the Catholic community. Laywomen chose to raise these issues in a space not entirely under their own

Complementarity and Intimate Life

control, in part because few spaces where laywomen are entirely in control exist in the Catholic Church. Not surprisingly, historians haven't looked for discussions of women's liberation in spaces such as *Marriage* because our assumption is that they would never have taken place there. As a result, we have missed how widespread conversations about Catholic gender identity (and challenges to accepted teaching) actually were, and how openly non-feminist Catholic laywomen expressed themselves about issues relating to their own liberation even in the most unexpected places.

COMPLEMENTARITY

As I outlined in the introduction, we know that laypeople in the American church were feeling empowered to challenge authority and accepted practice at midcentury. The signs of this were abundant: in voices raised in explicit challenge to the ban on artificial contraception (and in the sheer numbers of Catholic women using birth control), in surging interest in liturgical renewal and declining participation in confession and devotions, in groups promoting racial justice, and in flourishing lay apostolates such as CFM and Cana that encouraged lay leadership and minimized clerical control.[9]

Yet while the more modern lay apostolates beginning in the 1940s seemed to contribute to a steady pushback against ecclesial authority from laypeople, this move coincided with a particularly strong wave of teaching on gender complementarity that served to undercut laywomen's growing empowerment as it strengthened laymen's authority. As historian Colleen McDannell notes, "During the 1940s and 1950s Catholic culture reassert[ed] the patriarchal nature of Catholicism as a balance to suburban domestic life." This was also the peak of the eternal woman, a popular quasi-theological construct designed to highlight the importance of female submission at a time when Catholic leaders feared the effects of secularization and affluence on Catholic families. Before delving into the conversations in *Marriage* that reflected changes in laywomen's gender identity, it is worth investigating understandings of complementarity that were dominant in the lay apostolates that constituted the magazine's target audience at its inception.[10]

Catholic teaching on gender roles was clearly and frequently stated for the benefit of Catholic couples. The essential twentieth-century starting point is *Casti Connubii* (1930), Pope Pius XI's oft-quoted encyclical on Christian marriage written to outline the church's opposition to artificial contraception and abortion. While it has been discussed primarily in that context, it also outlines expectations for male and female roles within the family in response to feminism. The encyclical goes out of its way to say that the point of marriage is not merely procreation but the "mutual molding of husband and wife, [the] determined effort to perfect each other." But soon after, Pius XI notes that within this mutuality there is an "order of love," marked by "the primacy of the husband with regard to the wife and children, the ready subjection of the wife and her willing obedience."[11]

To clarify, he says that "this subjection does not deny or take away the liberty which fully belongs to the woman both in view of her dignity as a human person, and in view of her most noble office as wife and mother and companion." However, "it forbids that exaggerated liberty which cares not for the good of the family; it forbids that in this body which is the family, the heart be separated from the head to the great detriment of the whole body and the proximate danger of ruin. For if the man is the head, the woman is the heart, and as he occupies the chief place in ruling, so she may and ought to claim for herself the chief place in love." Later, in warning of grave threats to the family, he singled out "false teachers who try . . . to do away with the honorable and trusting obedience which the woman owes to the man." Seemingly referencing feminists, he claimed they went so far as to assert that "such a subjection of one party to the other is unworthy of human dignity." They proclaimed her free of childbearing ("not an emancipation but a crime"), free to "follow her own bent and devote herself to business and even public affairs," and free to work "without the knowledge and against the wish of her husband."[12]

Here the encyclical asserts this can only be false emancipation, unlike the "rational and exalted liberty which belongs to the noble office of a Christian woman and wife." Moreover, "unnatural equality with the husband is to the detriment of the woman herself, for if the woman descends from her truly regal throne to which she has been raised . . . she will soon be reduced to the old state of slavery." To the church, "rational liberty" was complementarity, the belief that men and women were simultaneously equal and different, bound by their natural God-given traits to enact particular roles in the world with equal dignity, if not equal power: "In such things undoubtedly both parties enjoy the same rights and are bound by the same obligations; in other things there must be a certain inequality and due accommodation, which is demanded by the good of the family and the right ordering and unity and stability of home life."[13]

By midcentury, the teaching on complementarity had shifted away somewhat from the emphasis on the hierarchy within the complementary relationship, which frankly identified the female as subordinate. Instead, newer expressions after World War II took pains to stress women's essential equality that could coexist alongside her difference. As religious studies scholar Aline H. Kalbian points out, however, complementarity remains hierarchical, "not so much in the sense that one party submits to the other but rather that the designated role for the female gender is one that is inherently more repressive; they often define the female primarily in terms of her role as complement to the male, as his helper." Complementarity does not merely define gender, it also dictates the appropriate form of relationship that can exist between the sexes. Ultimately, the Catholic Church relies heavily on the complementary relationship and the teaching that each sex is imbued with specific God-given traits, to uphold its "sense of order," not only in the family but across each facet of Catholic life.[14]

Casti Connubii was widely cited in the postwar years as evidence in support of complementarity in general and Catholic women's submission to authority specifically. It must be noted that CFM, though quick to support lay autonomy, promoted such ideology into the first half of the 1960s. The April 1959 issue of Act, the CFM newsletter, featured a reprint of a CFM conference address by Fr. Richard Hopkins titled "Role of Husband and Wife." Hopkins quoted liberally from the sections of Casti Connubii cited above to make his point that if lay Catholics were going to be witnesses to the world they hoped to engage, they needed to do so as the strongest Christian families possible. He described the Christian family as "a mystical body of Christ in miniature. The husband and the father is the head of the body and represents Christ. The wife and mother is the body itself and represents the Church." Yes, submission can seem off-putting to modern sensibilities, he conceded, but "the old traditional subordination on the part of the wife had its uses . . . in holding the family together." Hopkins did acknowledge the times, however, advising that "in our present society where women are more highly educated, ordinary prudence would seem to indicate the need of a delicate and tactful exercise of the power of family headship by the husband."[15]

The lay editors of Act chose to amplify these remarks by reprinting them. And lest we think this an isolated occurrence, in 1962 a laywoman wrote a piece for Act called "Woman's Role in Next Year's Program." Wanting to contribute, but fearful of women stepping out of the domestic role even in such an action-oriented ministry as CFM, she concluded that "as she is the 'heart of the home,' so must the wife seek ways to be the 'heart' of the social apostolate." After all, "if the heart cares, the head will try harder to think of what to do and how to do it." Although historian Sara Dwyer-McNulty has argued that laywomen did quietly challenge gender norms through lay action in this period, she noted that CFM wives "had to make sure they did not appear as the voice behind the couple—even if they knew that they were."[16]

The Cana Movement, administered by clergy but largely staffed by married lay volunteers, did even more to spread the word, enthusiastically, about appropriate gender roles to the young engaged and married couples of the postwar years. Cana facilitators "emphasized a constant review of gender roles that they maintained were 'natural' to men and women because many Catholic couples had been 'infected' by the secular trends of the day." In *The Basic Cana Manual* (1963), used to structure pre-Cana marriage preparation classes, Walter Imbiorski was direct. "Men and women are different," he wrote. "They are equal in the sight of God, but in marriage they assume different roles, and man in this structured institution is head of woman."[17]

It is in this environment that *Marriage* emerged, and for the first half of the 1960s the magazine largely reflected dominant Catholic teaching on gender roles. One does not have to look hard for these ideas in *Marriage*. In the seventy-three articles and editorials that discussed gender in the years 1961 through 1966 (after which challenges to these ideas began in earnest), fifty-seven (78 percent) affirmed complementarity and/or gender essentialism. Written by laywomen and laymen, sisters and priests, doctors, theologians, professors, and husbands and wives, they reasserted in a variety of forms what Catholic men and especially Catholic women were to be and do. A smattering of representative articles will show the multitude of ways that readers could encounter the same message in the magazine.

In *Casti Connubii*, Pius XI elected not to spell out in detail the traits that marked men's and women's essential differences, but that did not stop the writers in *Marriage*, who regularly delineated what it meant in practical terms to be a "complementary" Catholic couple. "Men are more 'fact-minded,' whereas women are more 'intuition-minded,'" G. C. Nabors, MD, claimed in the article "Making Rhythm Work, part I." "Measuring the body temperature is a fact-finding issue and therefore more easily evaluated by men. The whole idea is so involved with the most delicate of female emotions and intuitions that it is easy to understand why they have difficulty in evaluating the relationship of a temperature graph to the fertile span." J. Cain, in writing his "Valentine for a Wife," also expounded on a wife's limitations: "A wife can be methodical and tidy when it comes to kitchen drawers, but when it comes to reason, her mind is adrift with dreams and tag ends of ideals." Concurring, Mrs. Robert Jarmusch wrote that suburban couples are balanced since wives focus on "coping with emotions," while husbands "deal with intangibles and ideas."[18]

Clergy also weighed in regularly, throwing the weight of their spiritual and temporal stature behind advice designed to shape intimate relationships and domestic arrangements well outside their personal experience. Aurelius Boberek, OSB, tried to explain "God's Image in Woman" in 1962, hoping to discourage women from competing with men by praising their most important qualities: "Like God Himself, a woman sees more deeply into the meaning of things, not with the cold calculation of logic but with the wisdom of her heart." Her vocation "is more in being than in doing. She is not expected to be great. But she is expected to give to man the love, courage, and understanding that inspire him to do great things." Two months later, the Dominican priest Augustine Rock wrote a lengthy article about the relationship between fathers and daughters. Like Boberek, he concluded that boys are made for doing things in the world, but girls are for love. "He will be proud of her, but a man is more interested in being proud of his sons. His daughters he would rather cherish than be proud of."[19]

Women religious appeared far less frequently in the pages of *Marriage*, surprisingly, since they were such a strong factor in the education of the lay Theresians in the same time period. In the first half of the 1960s they were likely to affirm a traditional view of gender, as in the article "Femininity Can Be Taught," by Sister Mary Eva, OSB. It described a course on Catholic womanhood taught at Brescia College, a co-ed liberal arts college in Owensboro, Kentucky. According to its designers, "The purpose of this course is to re-emphasize with hardheaded realism the psychological, biological, spiritual and equal (though not identical) role of woman in relation to man in society." Their curriculum asked, "*What* is a woman? *Why* is a woman? And *how*?" The course was taught in a special pink room with art depicting a woman "kneeling in submissiveness to the Dove, the Holy Spirit, whence flow her virtues, gifts, and fruits. . . . A woman is made to the image of the Holy Spirit of Love. She is made to receive love and to give it back. By using the Gifts of the Holy Spirit, she acquires the Fruits—the gentle, home virtues of charity, joy, peace, patience, long-suffering, modesty, chastity. . . . These help her fulfill the "*Why* of her existence: A helpmate to man."[20]

Authors wrote about every possible trait said to be linked to woman's nature: submissiveness, receptivity, self-sacrifice, intuition, love, care, generosity, contemplation and mysticism, and above all, motherhood. They wrote with humor, with defensiveness, with patience, and at times with blatant condescension. They chose different characteristics to emphasize but in the first half of the 1960s, few were inclined to challenge the twin ideas that gender was fixed and that men and women were designed, in their natures, to complement each other in their domestic choices, with woman staying at home and man acting as provider. Laywoman Mary Maino spoke for many when she said in 1961, "When God made the two sexes, He made them different in order that they might fulfill their unique roles, and He gave them emotional and intellectual responses to fit them for the role. . . . In either case, personal fulfillment means living according to one's nature and destiny."[21]

Play your role and you will be happy, readers were told, but there were warnings for those who might begin to question. Regular feature writers Richard and Margery Frisbie put readers on notice two months earlier: "The biological and emotional divergences between the sexes are basically unchangeable and no mere alteration of our culture pattern will ever reverse them." The Frisbies were defensive for good reason, just as Pius XI had been in 1930; they were responding to changing expectations for couples at midcentury—particularly the increasing number of women working outside the home—and they hoped to use Catholic teaching on gender to stop these changes. In the first half of the 1960s, very few challenges to complementarity were mounted in the pages of *Marriage*, but there are small indicators that the Catholic community, male and female, was preparing to shift its thinking.[22]

The first of these is a series of articles claiming that gender was more fluid than had been previously admitted. It wasn't only that these ideas ran in *Marriage*; they seemed to be particularly supported by the editorial staff. "There is no such thing as a pure male or pure female; we are all mixtures, a polarity of maleness and femaleness," C. Q. Mattingly, managing editor, proclaimed in a book review in 1965. Moreover, for the 1963 article "The Role of Man and Woman in Marriage," the editors chose the tagline: "No man is 100% masculine, no woman entirely feminine." Finally, in 1964 the editors ran two lengthy articles condensed from recent work by the Jesuit theologian Karl Rahner. Near the top of the first article, Rahner states, "Let us first agree that no one sex is better than the other, and no one can possibly act in an exclusively masculine or feminine way as a free person obligated to realize moral values in his or her acts."

Ultimately, the messages these articles offered were conventional. All three articles undercut their basic premises by continuing to assign specific traits to men and women. In the case of Mattingly, he merely argued that male traits had become too dominant and needed to be balanced by female traits, which men could adopt. The editors negated their tagline in the 1964 article with their own title which allowed only one "role" for the singular man and woman in marriage (even though the article itself was more open to change). And Rahner, after arguing against the rigidity of gender roles, went on to rail against the feminization of the church for eight pages. Nonetheless, these authors were taking a small step toward undermining one of the basic principles of complementarity.[23]

A pair of articles by Mary Maino from 1961 also illustrate mixed messages on fixed gender roles. Titled "Gifts of the Mind," and "Getting to Know You," they offered information and advice to young couples thinking about (and perhaps struggling with) gender role expectations in the early 1960s. The first, while still quite gendered, pointedly notes that women were conditioned to believe they are intuitive, and men were conditioned to be logical. Similarly, college women were taught to use their brains in a logical fashion but were told they were sacrificing their intelligence to become housewives, and it became a self-fulfilling prophecy. Marriage requires intelligence, she argued, and not any special female intelligence either. "In marriage, particularly, men and women need to see one another not as men or as women but as persons," she wrote, "made by God with an intellect that hungers after the things that are of God." But her second article demonstrates how confusing it was to read *Marriage* on gender in the early 1960s. Just after declaring that couples should view each other as individual people, ungendered, her second piece delineated the traits of male and female and the importance of Catholic women staying within their natural role.[24]

Lastly, a handful of articles in the first half of the decade represent a more familiar indicator of discontent about the implications of fixed gender roles: the cry of the unhappy Catholic housewife. The most well-known of this genre is "Happy Little Wives and Mothers," a moving piece by Katherine Byrne that appeared in the influential Catholic weekly magazine *America* in 1956. In that same vein came "The Motherhood Wilderness" (1961) and "Prayers for the Reluctant Housewife" (1966), the authors of which ultimately acknowledged the rightness of Catholic housewifery but spent the majority of their column inches venting their myriad frustrations and revealing their sadness.

Robin Worthington recommended that housewives know what type of prayer will work best for them, because they would not survive housewifery without it. If the prayer begins with asking God to make you perky and cheerful and you can't stomach it, move on, she advised. If it starts, "The next hour or two is going to be perfectly vile," that's the prayer for you. "Let's say you're a Reluctant Housewife," she wrote. "Full or part time housewife. Full or part time reluctant (we all have our days). We won't go into *why* you're reluctant. You've met theories enough already. The psalmist summed up the classic reason centuries ago: Lord, 'I am shut in. I cannot escape.'" Anne Topatimlis's

"The Motherhood Wilderness" was an epic recitation of her daily ordeals, ending with a plea that Byrne and Worthington would recognize: "When these pressures reach their boiling point comes the cry 'I've got to get out of here!... [but] we cannot go, whether we want to or not."[25]

The year 1967 marks a change in *Marriage* on questions of complementarity and laywomen's gender identity. Of the 106 articles and editorials in the study published between 1967 and 1975 (whose primary or secondary purpose was to discuss gender), 62 affirmed traditional roles (58 percent—a drop from 78 percent in the first half of the 1960s). What happens, then, is clearly not a sudden shift to feminism if the majority of articles still supported the status quo. Yet something definitely changed in these years, as more and more writers felt welcome, or encouraged, or emboldened enough to challenge what had for so long been seen as the only way to be a Catholic woman in a Catholic marriage.

What we have in *Marriage* is a gradual opening to new ways of thinking that manifested in a number of debates about key issues that played out over the course of years. While the editorial staff could weigh in on these issues in ways both heavy-handed and subtle, they were usually content to allow opposing voices to be heard. This approach gave laywomen the chance to speak frankly on the questions that concerned them about the most intimate aspects of their lives. The remainder of this chapter explores a handful of these debates from the second half of the 1960s through the mid-1970s, each of which demonstrates the boundaries imposed on laywomen's intimate lives through the restriction of gender identity, and the language some Catholics—women and men—were developing to lift them.

ESSENTIALISM

Let's begin with the question of what writers at the time termed "sex-role stereotyping." The affirmative case in the debate over this question, basically essentialism, has already been outlined, but what of the other side? By the midpoint of the 1960s, Catholic laywomen had had ample exposure in the national media to criticism of female essentialism, not only through the publication of Betty Friedan's *The Feminine Mystique* (which was widely reviewed, if skeptically, in Catholic periodicals, including *Marriage*) but also through other available feminist writings and coverage of the growing movement. What's more, educated and active Catholic laywomen would also likely have been aware of debates over women's equality that had begun to creep into Catholic circles through the Catholic feminist movement, then in its first phase. We know that any reader of *Marriage* who was also active in her NCCW affiliate would have been exposed to such ideas through the NCCW's national publications. The question was whether anyone would speak up in *this* forum, which was male-dominated and dedicated to strengthening Catholic couples. The answer is yes, and it is in this debate that laywomen's voices begin to emerge in revealing ways.

"I'm a housewife (or should I say homemaker) and mother of four, and I am tired of hearing of the glories of motherhood. 'Motherhood'—that golden word that is supposed to make us glow.... I'm one of those mothers that just doesn't 'glow.' Biologically, I'm a mother, but psychologically I might have been better fitted at anything else." Marge Morton did not glow, and she did not care who knew it. Similarly, Lucille Harper told a story of a friend whom she considered very "sacrificial," and it worried her. "She wants to excel as a woman, and to be considered feminine, which in her mind means to give beyond endurance.... Giving to the point of exhaustion isn't feminine, it's life-shortening." Here were two laywomen willing to state boldly, without qualifiers, what to this point was taboo: "natural" traits were anything but, and they could lead to psychological and physical harm for the Catholic women who attempted to conform to them.[26]

Perhaps for these reasons, and a host of others, it became increasingly normal to hear laywomen call for an end to sex-role stereotyping in the pages of *Marriage*. For instance, early Catholic feminist and philosopher Rosemary Lauer took aim at those who believed that a college education was wasted on Catholic wives because they would never use it in their role as mothers. "First of all," she began, "such a viewpoint presupposes that a woman can attain the complete development of her personality simply by being a wife and mother—a conviction that made sense only as long as theology professors could teach with a straight face the Aristotelian doctrine that 'men attain their perfection by developing their intellects; women attain theirs by bearing children.'" When she was finished with the theologians, she targeted another venerable institution a little closer to home for *Marriage*: "One hopes that it will filter through to the Cana conferences too and that all the unscientific nonsense about woman's 'intuitional' approach to reality as opposed to man's 'rational' approach will be consigned to the limbo it deserves."[27]

It is no coincidence, I think, that all three of these laywomen authors—Marge Morton, Lucille Harper, and Rosemary Lauer—appeared in the "Speak Up" section, a column reserved for extended reader commentary. Readers could submit an essay on any topic for potential publication in the magazine. Highly skilled laywomen writers were often featured in this section, and they tended to gravitate toward gender themes. I suspect this was one means by which the editors attempted to balance their tendency to select male authors in greater numbers as experts who earned full articles. Still, the essays they published are invaluable in a study attempting to reclaim the voices of laywomen, and one imagines the opportunity to have their say was more significant to them than the twenty-five dollars the women received in compensation.

Another Catholic feminist, Sidney Callahan, the author of the first Catholic feminist monograph, *The Illusion of Eve*, was invited to write for *Marriage* in 1965. She took the opportunity to weigh in on the debate over essentialism in what was for *Marriage* an extremely lengthy article as the Council was drawing to a close. "Those Council Fathers who wished more encouragement and recognition for women would do well to approve a strong declaration of married women's equality," she wrote. "But let the masculine half of the Church be wary of stating that women have 'special talents' (even as a tactic in their defense)." Offering *Marriage*'s female readers a new kind of vocabulary to critique what their church had taught them, Callahan pointed out "everyone should recall that part of the oppression borne by every minority group has been the dominant majority's insistence upon rigid definitions and distinctions."[28]

Sidney Callahan, perceived as a moderate insider in the intellectual lay Catholic community (her husband, Daniel Callahan, was the author of the widely read *The Mind of the Catholic Layman*) had the standing to get away with such a statement, but she was not the only one allowed to speak her mind in this forum. As we shall see, one of the places where laywomen spoke most freely about their own self-conceptions as Catholic women was in the "Reader Reaction" section, where people in this community could exchange ideas and debate questions of importance to them. The issue of essentialism was no exception. After a particularly conservative article on gender roles appeared, Kathleen Kinahan from Illinois wrote, "I think most women are sick and tired of being dissected in print, and are proceeding to 'do their own thing' as they see right. And certainly, many, if not most, women are going to turn off the opinions of a middle-aged marriage counselor (male) who wants women to stay in their place.... Women are human beings—they will no longer conform to one stereotyped image—please, accept us as ourselves, and drop the subject." In response to another such article, a pair of college seniors wanted it known that "not all females walking this earth feel a need to achieve self-identity through having children." Finally, Lucille Martin of New Jersey likely spoke for many when she requested "an editorial policy that refuses to

Complementarity and Intimate Life

accept for publication articles that encourage readers to be men and women first, and persons second." No such policy seems to have been adopted.[29]

HEADSHIP

Such questioning of complementarity and gender essentialism had real world implications for the laywomen who participated in it. Identity was more than how women viewed themselves; an ideological change in this area could potentially transform their marriages. To see how, let us return briefly to the Cana movement. Cana conferences and literature insisted "that fathers were the head and mothers the heart of each family, and remind[ed] participants that masculine aggressiveness and feminine docility formed the bedrock on which a successful marriage was constructed." In fact, the group that now influenced much of the premarital formation for Catholic couples in the United States went so far as to claim "that marriages often failed because men and women did not accept the innate qualities of their nature." The rightness of male headship was also reinforced in popular devotions of the day.[30]

The conversation that took place in *Marriage* over male headship in the Catholic family—really an extension of the discussions of essentialism—is one of the most surprising findings to emerge from this research. Unlike talk of women's place in the church, which frequently arose in the laywomen's organizations, the sensitive subject of power and submission in laywomen's domestic arrangements simply did not arise in their official outlets. However, the editors of *Marriage* wanted to open the floor for discussion of this aspect of Catholic marital relationships. The fact that such a conversation took place at all worked to undermine strict adherence to the principles of complementarity since it questioned beliefs at the foundations of the teaching.

The challenge to headship mounted in *Marriage* was not an inevitable response to feminist ideas entering the popular discourse in this period. Two other religious communities of the same era demonstrate that a reinforcement of headship was a popular response to feminism as well as an entry into conservative political activism. Many American evangelicals, for example, espoused male headship and female submission as markers of their Christian identity well after American Catholics ceased to proclaim them as central to their religious self-perception. R. Marie Griffith's study of evangelical women in the 1970s, particularly as revealed through their confessional stories in the magazine *Aglow*, shows that the women often promoted their own submission to male headship as a means of fixing troubled marriages and bringing the men in their lives to salvation. Furthermore, she finds the idea that only through submission will women find true freedom to be prominent. Neither idea emerges as significant in *Marriage*. The trends are markedly different as well; Griffith's findings show commitment to male headship on the increase through the 1970s, whereas it is clearly on the decline among the Catholics writing in *Marriage*. Julie Debra Neuffer also chronicles similar ideas that emerged in Mormonism in the early 1960s and spread to millions through the publication of Helen Andelin's *Fascinating Womanhood* (1963). Andelin argued that a potent combination of obedience and femininity would save American marriages. "Don't change your husband," she urged. "Change yourself."[31]

In the early 1960s, similar concerns about male headship began to appear in the magazine; as early as 1961, *Marriage* expressed its fears about men losing their authority in the family. Such worries, and accompanying defensiveness, often arose in the "Family Front" column, a regular feature written until 1965 by Richard and Margery Frisbie. Strongly antifeminist, the Frisbies were enthusiastic and frequent champions of complementarity in the first half of the 1960s. They assured readers in 1961, despite reports to the contrary, that "researchers found no evidence of the supposed decline in male status.... He still makes many of the final decisions and performs traditional male duties while his wife tends the house and children. The new element perhaps is how he achieves his position. 'He must prove his right to power, or win power by virtue of his own skills and accomplishments in competition with his wife.'"[32]

So committed were the Frisbies that, when in 1964 the Belgian cardinal Leo Jozef Suenens—well-known in that moment for advocating for women at the Council—spoke in Chicago, they asked him point-blank how he reconciled his views on women's rights with biblical calls for wives' submission. He answered that wives were like the Council fathers who submitted to papal authority, but "when you say 'let bishops be subject to the Pope' that doesn't mean there's no collegiality.'" The Frisbies reported he said this "with a twinkle in the archepiscopal eye," and they "were charmed by the image of the family as a miniature Council over which the Holy Spirit hovers while husband and wife pray and ponder over their decisions." His answer was perfect for the Frisbies because it suggested that traditional gender roles could fit into the plan of the dynamic, modern church.[33]

Female authors routinely supported male headship against a culture all too ready to let it go. Louise Shanahan pointed out that gender roles were in flux in 1962, and lamented that "in far too many homes there has been a shift from the emphasis on the husband as head to a two-headed idea of husband and wife sharing equal powers." She explained that the shift was "related

Complementarity and Intimate Life

to . . . the stress on personal fulfillment and happiness as a major goal in marriage," perhaps inadvertently implying that submitting to headship was not a pleasant experience for women. While Shanahan wanted women to understand that happiness should not even be their chief goal, other writers assured women that submission to male headship was the only means of achieving marital happiness. In "My Husband the Boss," Alice Waters advised women not to bolt if their husbands laid down the law: "No, girls . . . Remember, you'll have no neuroses, or psychoses—if you let husbands take charge, everything comes up roses!" A reader offered the ultimate reason for submission. "We obey our husbands," she wrote, "not because of what they ask but because we do love God above all."[34]

Perhaps in response to the growing backlash against male headship in the larger culture, other authors recommended that men demonstrate their authority through their role as fathers even more than as husbands. In the article "Why Is a Father," dads were advised to take control of potty-training "since the father represents authority to the child." The physician author argued, "It is important that the head of the family help his child make this first harsh adjustment to the demands of civilization for social conformity." Similarly, a 1964 article titled "Examination of Conscience for Family Men" recommended for the daily examen the questions "Do I recognize that I am each child's first vision of authority and consequently I am a symbol of God to my youngsters?" and "Do I act fully in accord with the precept that I am the *head* and my wife is the *heart* of our home?"[35]

The editorial staff of *Marriage* certainly seemed to believe in male headship in the early 1960s and frequently used their editorials to promote this view. A 1962 editorial complaining that not enough husbands read the magazine (a not infrequent lament by the editors) explicitly referred to men as head of the house; a 1964 editorial about wedding announcements noted that the groom did not appear: "Now, if the husband is really 'head of the wife,' as Scripture puts it, then why not show the head in the picture too?" These casual references, together with the proheadship "Family Front" column, and the frequency of other articles in support, suggest general agreement on the subject.[36]

However, something odd occurred in November 1964 when managing editor C. Q. Mattingly wrote the magazine's first pro–women's rights editorial. It contained an explicit statement against women's submission to male headship: "It is annoying for women to hear and read . . . that the family and community are in such a sad state because women will not *let* their husbands be head of the family." Citing the first creation story in Genesis, he coupled this statement with a salvo against complementarity, arguing that woman was "equal and of the same nature as man, not an inferior, and not set apart for 'separate' treatment."[37]

What are we to make of such a bold statement against headship, though, when a second editorial appeared in August of the following year that once again explicitly *affirmed* headship, this time from the associate editor Mary Alice Zarella? In an appropriate marriage, guided by the tenets of complementarity, "The woman is not a pale reflection of the male," she wrote. "As a wife she becomes more womanly. The husband becomes more manly. Deliberately they differentiate to achieve perfection." Furthermore, "the wife is not resentful of her husband's authority. Becoming complementary partners is a challenging and lifelong vocation." The about face may reflect a split on the editorial board, but the more likely immediate cause was fear over circulation. In the same issue as the editorial in November 1964, the editors placed a mildly feminist piece by Ann Ward titled "What Do Women Really Want?" The article provoked a flood of letters that the editors summarized for the February 1965 issue as overwhelmingly negative. The editors would not publish a pro–women's rights editorial again until 1975.[38]

Yet from 1966 on, the number of articles that called for an end to male headship outnumbered those in support. While the editors would not speak explicitly against headship again, and they continued to run pieces in support of complementarity, they provided myriad opportunities for those "annoyed" women, as well as sympathetic men, to speak for themselves. The magazine became a space where the Catholic community could think out the implications of male headship for Catholic couples, and contemplate alternatives. As a result, the magazine ceased to present a united front on the teachings of complementarity.

A good indicator that the editors had become more open-minded is the June 1969 issue, which contained opposing articles on headship, published on consecutive pages without editorial comment. The first appeared in the "Family Front" column from a female author, and asked (in honor of Father's Day) whether "young people today would find it easier to accept the authority of their parents and others placed over them if they had the example of wives accepting the authority of their husbands? Would men approach marriage differently if they realized that as the head of the family they were responsible to God for those under their care?" The article in response, from a male author, pointedly asked very different questions: "What is a man? What is a father? . . . Quick-and-easy traditional answers are as useless as physiological ones, e.g.: 'The father is the head and the mother is the heart of the good Christian family.' It means everything, means nothing, and is an insult to women. So we back up and observe again." Moreover, an article on sexual freedom in the following issue called "efforts to restore male dominance" both "reactionary" and "unrealistic." This male author claimed that "the insights provided by modern psychological knowledge support an equalitarian relationship between sexes rather than a dominant-subordinate one."[39]

Marriage's practice of featuring opposing opinions is best seen in the work of one contributor, the Catholic journalist and freelancer Louise Shanahan. Shanahan came out staunchly against egalitarian marriage in an article in 1962, but when her next articles on gender roles began to appear in the second half of the 1960s, she seemed willing to explore new ideas. It is worth looking in depth at her output because the editors returned to her again and again for her particular brand of article, an interview with experts in response to an important gender question of the day. At twelve articles, Shanahan is the largest single contributor in the sample.

It can be difficult to know what Shanahan herself believed because the majority of her articles quoted extensively from the chosen expert, and her framing of the articles always suggested that she concurred with whatever the expert said. As a result, her pieces could be wildly contradictory. In the eleven articles that Shanahan published in *Marriage* between 1966 and 1971, she managed to both affirm essentialism and proclaim it outdated, write with alarm about women's liberation and promote women's empowerment, warn of the impending disintegration of marriage as an institution and argue that marriage was actually in good shape after all.

The closest she came to endorsing egalitarian marriage outright is in the 1971 article "The Changing Husband Image," in which she interviewed five young couples about authority in marriage. Shanahan opened the article by asking, "Have the current trends articulated by women's lib groups caused unusual stress, fear, or anger on the part of the husband?" She concluded, however, that "all is not ominous and grim" and went on to quote a number of husbands who not only accepted shared authority with their wives, but embraced it. Said one young husband, "For all the nonsense of the extremists in women's lib, I think they are on the right track when they want to push women into other experiences out of the home. . . . I feel I am a much more flexible husband than my father was. Marriage a generation ago was considerably more rigid. The husband could be a tyrant and get away with it. Today that is out of the question." A young wife concurred: "The husband today is

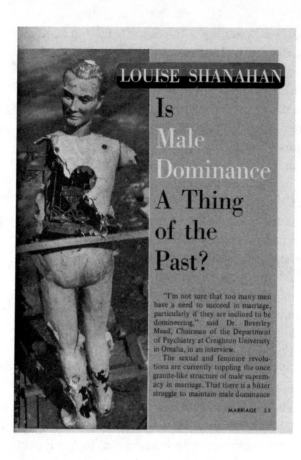

LOUISE SHANAHAN

Is Male Dominance A Thing of the Past?

"I'm not sure that too many men have a need to succeed in marriage, particularly if they are inclined to be domineering," said Dr. Beverley Mead, Chairman of the Department of Psychiatry at Creighton University in Omaha, in an interview.

The sexual and feminine revolutions are currently toppling the once granite-like structure of male supremacy in marriage. That there is a bitter struggle to maintain male dominance

MARRIAGE 23

The illustration for this Louise Shanahan article in *Marriage* (1970) conveys brokenness, male fragility, and profound confusion about changing gender roles. (Courtesy of St. Meinrad Archabbey)

no longer lord and master. It is much healthier for the marriage, and it doesn't take away a jot from his manhood."[40]

But Shanahan also gave equal time to the couples who preferred headship as a model, and noted men's increasing discomfort with egalitarian marriage and its effect on their gender identity. "My biggest complaint about women is that they have become obnoxiously aggressive," one husband remarked. "I think I'm like other men my age. I feel as if we are trapped in Unisexville." Shanahan also recognized that men might miss the right of command under the new model of marriage. "If there is an occasional ache in his heart when he remembers his father's thundering commands and a subsequent instant feminine response," she noted, "the neuter-generation husband may find compensations in the vast array of the means of self-expression available to him that were absent in his father's day." Yet she hardly saw this as a positive development. You could cut her sarcasm with a knife: "He may, if he feels like it, treat himself to one of those marvelous perfumed preparations that now take the place of less imaginative aftershave lotions. No longer is it a woman's prerogative to go out and splurge on a hat or cologne if she is feeling depressed."[41]

Despite these references to disgruntled husbands, frustration for *women* was a much more common theme in Shanahan's work. Not a feminist herself, Louise Shanahan rarely advocated directly for women's liberation (and in fact she took multiple swipes at the movement), but she often put forward the idea that women were limited and frustrated in marriages where they were controlled by their husbands. In "Money: His and Hers" (1966), for example, she interviewed several women who described how much they hated having no financial say in the household. Those who wrested back that power (and it was described as an abuse of power on the husbands' part) were clear about what it gave them. One noted that when she had some financial control she was "not merely someone's wife or mother or laundry service. I'm me. And it's a good feeling." Shanahan also wrote a very practical piece for wives in 1971 called "Marriage: Act of Negotiating." The tagline asked, "Why do women accept a second-rate marriage relationship?" Shanahan's chosen expert answered that women viewed themselves as subordinate because they had been conditioned by their husbands to see themselves that way. The rest of the article offered concrete techniques for women desiring to assert authority in their own marriages. "Practice with a friend," Shanahan recommended. Don't get emotional and "stay with the facts."[42]

Even Shanahan's most antifeminist and essentialist articles hinted at her awareness of women's struggles. An example is the astonishing "Are You Planning to Run Away?" (1971), in which she featured a female private detective who told wives enamored of feminism to rethink their plans of escape, to stay with their abusive or cheating husbands, and to consider if their own nagging didn't contribute to the problem. Yet in this same article she named women's deep well of frustration as the fuel that fed the women's movement in the United States. "Women's liberation is rocking the boat for women who have been smoldering for years," she admitted. In the previous year she wrote, "It is evident that those taking up the cudgels for the feminine revolution are expressing the frustrated feelings of women everywhere." Here was an author who, without embracing feminism, could give female readers permission to feel angry about their lot as wives under the burdens of headship.[43]

But, unlike Shanahan, many of the voices in *Marriage* on the question of headship were unequivocal. Once again, we can look to the letters to the editor for strong statements by women on practical questions of identity. "A single authority figure is outmoded," Mrs. Carroll A. Thomas wrote, and

"[I] hope our little girl and her brothers will grow to fully respect themselves and others as human beings, with responsibilities to themselves and to others." Suzanne L. Bacznak was in an egalitarian marriage and could confirm that it worked: "When my husband and I married we accepted the concept that two equal beings were joined together of their own free wills, each fully accepting the other." As so many letter writers did, Bacznak turned to the concrete rather than the theoretical: "On matters affecting the whole family we both talk over the decision to be made and discuss it fully until both agree. . . . In actual practice is this not what most happily married couples do? Work together. Why not realize this fact and accept it?"[44]

Other women commissioned to write for the magazine noted the ongoing shift toward equal partnership and wrote approvingly of it. In 1967, Iris Rabasca noted that the threadbare advice (head/heart) that mothers had long given to their engaged daughters would not do, as "many of today's young wives will no longer accept this 'sure cure' for a happy marriage, a bitter pill, too difficult to swallow." Such "compact clichés," as Rabasca labeled them, "seem to undermine [women's] individuality, their personalities, and their status within society, as well as within their marriage." Kathryn Clarenbach went even further that same year, claiming that abandoning headship would do more than just make women happier and more fulfilled: "I maintain that true partnership of husband and wife in the home will do more to strengthen family life in America than anything else."[45]

Equally common was the suggestion that men abused their power, or had the potential to do so; egalitarian marriage was promoted explicitly as a means of protecting women from abuse. Gloria Skurzynski laid the groundwork with "History's Woman Haters," a 1971 article detailing husbands' abysmal treatment of their wives in the medieval period. The editors tried to soft-pedal the article with its tagline ("If you think women are getting the medieval treatment, then you had better re-check your history"), and the author agreed that it was not accurate to call today's antifeminists "medieval" ("thank God!"). Yet Skurzynski wrote this piece for a reason, as a reminder perhaps of what wives could experience at men's hands when male authority went unchecked. In such circumstances, women were most valued for their youth and beauty, could not control access to their bodies, and were confined to the home, she reminded *Marriage* readers.[46]

Readers also heard in 1970 that "the male need to dominate is frequently at the root of much marital misery," and in 1971 that wives were "no longer merely chattels" of their "dominant and domineering" husbands. Women paid a mental price when men abused their authority, writers claimed.

One author noted "the dreadful damage done to women's psyches" by the tradition of headship. Another lamented the women who were at the mercy of their husbands' "moods and whims." A third described how women were encouraged to suppress their true personalities to be the wives that traditional husbands favored. "Brenda, don't be too aggressive," one woman reported being told by her parents, "because no man will love you." Finally, the 1969 Louise Shanahan article "The Tyranny of Love" took this to its ultimate end by describing an abusive marriage where the husband became "more and more domineering, ruthlessly disregarding her wishes with veiled threats about his masculine superiority." The wife could only ask herself, "Is it like this in other homes? Are wives who are doormats happy? Are women who attempt to live with their husbands as equals miserable?"[47]

Ultimately, as in "The Tyranny of Love," *Marriage* was much more inclined to pose questions than it was to provide definitive answers, but this is precisely what makes the magazine so remarkable in the context of the Catholic media in the 1960s: the answer to every question posed about intimate relationships was not complementarity. *Marriage* was willing to give women a voice in a wide-open debate over questions of authority, power, and submission in their own homes. While the editors rarely advocated for change in these matters themselves, they created a space where women could express a variety of opinions and advocate for themselves if they chose, or simply learn of alternatives to the way of life they had been conditioned to believe was natural and expected.

WORKING WIVES

An even greater preoccupation in the magazine was the debate over working wives, a consistent theme throughout the years of this study. Unlike the articles on essentialism and headship, the conversation over whether Catholic wives should work outside the home was almost exclusively conducted by women writers. Presumably women believed this topic fell squarely within their expertise and area of concern. Of the many objections raised against working wives in *Marriage*, most were representative of mainstream ideas, although writers could couch their arguments in Catholic terms. The precepts of complementarity were certainly raised, as were notions of prayerful housewifery meant to convey the deep spiritual importance of women's work in the home. The women who defended work outside the home mostly stuck with debunking myths and airing their frustrations over being judged neglectful and unwomanly. Their commentary on the debate as a whole hints at the editors' desire to move the conversation forward past the condemnation of women who dared take on paid employment. Toward the 1970s we begin to see a truly feminist perspective on the issue emerge in *Marriage*, largely couched in terms of the need for women's personal fulfillment.[48]

It's hardly surprising that the subject of working wives appeared with such frequency given the inordinate amount of attention paid to women's steady transition into the workforce after World War II. Commentators were responding to very real trends. Between 1940 and 1960, there was a 400 percent increase in the number of working mothers. In the 1960s alone, the number of women in the workforce increased from 23 million to over 31 million. The incessant attempt to normalize domesticity and the open hostility expressed toward women in the workplace in the same thirty-year period may be read as a defensive posture against demographic trends very much in evidence in writers' social networks and neighborhoods as well as in the statistics trotted out on every suitable occasion.[49]

Articles opposed to wives working seemed almost unavoidable in *Marriage* in the 1960s, their authors ready to throw every possible argument at a woman tempted to leave her kitchen. First, authors created the impression that the desire to work outside the home was abnormal. "Men love work but women love men," the Frisbies asserted, describing the correct order of things in 1961. Another writer claimed that "there is a tremendous emphasis on the importance of careers for woman, but I am afraid that our *mature* woman cannot get terribly excited about the subject." Housewives themselves supported these claims with articles like "I Enjoy Being a Housewife!" and "I Don't Want to Be Free."[50]

Advocates of housewifery argued that duty must be held above a woman's need for fulfillment outside the home. "This affluent American society has created many false images," Mary Ann Black said, "among them the damaging contention that women are entitled to freedom, freedom from the drudgeries of housework, freedom from the responsibilities of motherhood and freedom to be herself first and a wife second." Referring to "fulfillment propaganda," writers regularly blamed feminism for encouraging women to neglect their homes in search of self through paid employment, even though the increase in working wives predated second-wave feminism.[51] As one letter writer put it in 1971, "Let Betty Friedan play up my hidden potentialities that I'm supposed to be wasting on my spouse, three children and my home. As long as I have a chance left, and I still do, I'll remain a slave to a mannish man, three cherubs and a demanding home. Me, I am a slave; but I am free. I have love!"[52]

Complementarity and Intimate Life

In any case, women were unlikely to find outside work worthwhile, they were told. Most jobs available to women were boring and tedious (not unlike housework), far from the exciting careers for women spotlighted in the media. And if a woman made more money than her husband she would need to counteract it at home so she did not undercut her man. One such woman described the balancing act of maintaining her husband's authority when her salary was higher: "At home our children know who's boss, even in the little things. For instance, I always make sure my husband is served first at mealtime and has a chance at the biggest pork chop—or whatever." Was the "fulfillment" that came from working really worth it?[53]

Readers were also informed that working wives were both selfish and neglectful of their homes and families. "It is supremely undesirable that a married woman should take up gainful employment only for the sake of getting more out of life," one author said, "for then the family will suffer from her selfishness." A 1971 article purporting to help women decide whether or not to send their young children to day care in actuality heaped accusations of neglect upon working moms. For instance, the author claimed that children in day care "were unable to relate to overtures of love," and that full-time childcare "was often the pivotal factor in the case of a mentally disturbed child."[54]

Of course, authors also invested much energy in extolling the vital and intrinsic contributions of wives and mothers, relying heavily on the rhetoric of Catholic essentialism and complementarity. The editors could assist with this as well, as in 1961 when they prominently displayed a quote from Pope Pius XII in a section called "Think It Over": "Now the sphere of woman, her manner of life, her native bent, is motherhood. . . . For this purpose the Creator organized the whole characteristic make-up of woman, her organic construction, but even more her spirit, and above all her delicate sensitiveness. Thus it is that a woman who is a real woman can see all the problems of human life only in the perspective of the family." Catholic women had a sacred mission beyond the day-to-day work of the home that could not be disrupted by the siren song of the modern world. "The real job of a mother is to raise saints," as a reader reminded everyone in 1962.[55]

Authors did acknowledge with regularity that housewifery was difficult, as we have already seen, but unlike the "cries of the unhappy housewife" mentioned earlier, most articles kept an upbeat tone and sought solutions in keeping with the rightness of Catholic women's role as the heart of the home. For a period of time in the mid-1960s, writers in *Marriage* were particularly fascinated by the ideas of the Catholic writer Solange Hertz, the author of *Women, Words, and Wisdom* (1959).

Hertz's work appeared multiple times, excerpted at length as well as mentioned in other people's articles. Margery and Richard Frisbie described her philosophy for readers in "Family Front" in 1964. First, Hertz believed that housewifery was a vocation, and that it was "universal" for women. As such, she "consider[ed] all the current talk about women developing themselves outside the home 'tiresome.'" The heart of her writing, though, was the belief that a wife's work in the home should be treated as a call to the contemplative life.[56]

In 1965, the editors excerpted Hertz's book under the title "Meditations while Mopping the Floor." The chosen passages encouraged women to think of themselves as prayerful monastics as they went about their repetitive chores. Quite down to earth, Hertz did not pretend that housework was pleasant, but she did argue that it could be valuable if considered in the proper terms. Among other ideas, her theology promoted the idea that through the physical acts of housewifery—that is, through suffering—women helped redeem the sin of the world for which womankind was largely responsible: "Dirty dishes, dirty diapers, dusty floors, unwashed bodies . . . are quite simply effects of Eve's fall and must be accepted as such. In these physical aspects God keeps before our eyes the hideousness of sin. Leaving aside its obvious value as a penance, our battle against dirt, our repugnance for it, is a symbolic battle against sin. . . . It's the housewife's special little share in the Redemption to be able to atone for others' sins by washing others' clothes." Hertz and others like her used *Marriage* to encourage housewives and mothers to give their work meaning, and to prove—definitively, they thought—that Catholic wives did not belong in the workplace.[57]

But another set of articles existed alongside these works battling the trends of American culture. In 1962 *Marriage* published its first article in support of wives working, if only part-time. The author, Eleanor Culhane, made no radical arguments, but her piece is revealing for what it says about the debate itself. When the topic arose, she said, "the quiet game of bridge may erupt into a roaring volcano of emotion as partners divide and slams go unbid." Everyone had an opinion on what was incontrovertible: wives were going to work in ever-larger numbers, and not for the reasons everyone supposed, either. "For extra income, for an extra adult interest in life, for a welcome change from unrelieved domesticity which may actually enable her to be a better wife and a more patient mother," not to earn money for an extra television set. Nor, she added, were the children of these "frivolous" mothers out wandering the streets. Culhane neatly shows us what Catholic working women had to contend with in the 1960s.[58]

One woman who wrote of having to work by necessity spoke of being "condemned to death" for it, made to "bear the brunt of sarcasm and degrading remarks." Antoinette Bosco added that these women haven't "been proven guilty of anything, only accused," and that the debate over their choices had generated "more heat than light."[59]

A series of writers sought to shine that light by explaining what they believed to be misunderstandings about working wives. In the mid-1960s these most often included the idea that women worked to buy luxuries, a common theme in the history of opposition to working women and a preoccupation in a Catholic community concerned about materialism and secularization. More than one woman shared her personal experience to show that this was false, but it was left to the 1967 article "Women as Second Class Citizens" to state the obvious. Katheryn Clarenbach argued that the question "Should women work?" was "foolish" when you considered the number of women in poverty. "Women in the United States have always shared economic responsibility," she pointed out to this largely middle-class readership. Contributors also insisted that working women did not neglect their children; even the editors made the argument in 1964 that women were not "abandoning children and home just to make a fast buck 'out in the world.'" Besides, Bosco reminded readers, a Catholic wife who was unhappy at home was equally capable of messing up her kids: "Staying at home out of a sense of fortitude, martyrdom, or guilt does not communicate healthy emotional growth in her children."[60]

In the latter half of the 1960s and early 1970s writers in favor shifted away from a defensive posture to offer more expansive reasons for wives to work outside the home, reasons clearly influenced by the women's liberation movement. The most common theme offered was indeed personal fulfillment. One of the first articles to offer this view was "The New Woman," a piece written by a religious feminist in 1968. She noted that women do not make plans for themselves, in fact they balk at doing so. In consequence, "many women, even today find that they are not capable of thinking much beyond the age of forty or forty-five when all the children have left home. That this is so is an unparalleled waste and a great tragedy." She went on to warn that "intentionality alone can save us from drifting or floating to a premature form of living death where we find all our desires for personal satisfaction and fulfillment are empty and pointless." Another author argued that "because today's college-educated woman is trained for mobility and freedom, she cannot be eternally denied these things without dire consequences."[61]

Curiously, Marriage's editors reinforced the idea that women needed freedom to find fulfillment, but the editors did so in articles that supported the

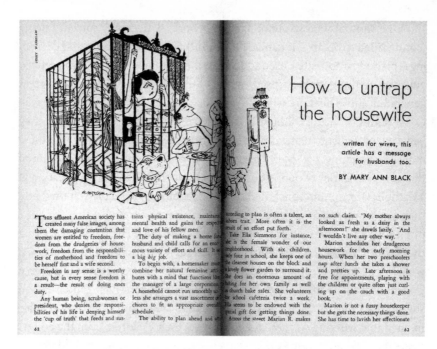

The editors' choice of illustration for this essentialist
article undercuts the author's message (1967).
(Courtesy of St. Meinrad Archabbey)

gender status quo. On three separate occasions they chose to accompany essentialist articles with illustrations depicting housewives bound, caged, or other-
wise trapped by housewifery. The traditional "How to Untrap the Housewife"
(1967) featured an aproned woman in a cage staring longingly at her family
(including the dog) watching television. In a similar vein, "What's a Nice Place
Like This Doing to a Girl Like Me?" (1973) showed a woman in an apron strung
up like a marionette with her own house maniacally pulling the strings. Most dis-
turbingly, Louise Shanahan's reactionary "Woman 1970: A Counsellor's View"
featured a drawing of a woman in kerchief and apron (naturally) bound by rope
to a broom at neck, torso, and ankles and suspended over her own mop bucket.
Marriage might continue to offer a voice to those who believed in complementarity, but the editors regularly found ways to raise the idea that women needed
more for their well-being than what the church had been willing to offer them.
The implicit became explicit in January 1973 when the priest John Catoir mused
on "The Future of Christian Marriage." Speaking specifically of women he urged,
"Marriage should not engulf people, should not trap them into a narrow space
in which they have no possibilities of growth." Catoir knew of what he spoke: he
was identified as chief judge of the marriage tribunal in Paterson, New Jersey.[62]

Complementarity and Intimate Life

The main thing to remember about being a housewife is that the average home is not exactly a rational, orderly place in which to live and work. It is usually composed of an assortment of individuals who vary in size, age, sex, appetite and interests. Frequently, this collection of people has nothing in common but the desire to get into the bathroom at the same time.

Any sort of "how-to" collection for housewives that ignores this basic fact is missing the point. Let us begin by recognizing the situation for what it is: impossible.

After you first ask yourself, "What is a nice girl like me doing in a place like this?" you will be in the proper frame of mind to take advantage of the suggestions offered here.

How to Get the Kids to Clean Their Room. It's no use to walk in and yell, "This place looks like a pig sty!" Your children don't know what a pig sty is. Threats are sometimes useful ("If you don't clean up this room by Friday, I'm giving your motorcycle to the Salvation Army!"), and bribery helps ("If you clean your room, I'll get you that portable color TV you've been wanting")—but it is unreliable, since you may be bankrupt if your children clean the room more than twice a year. Actually, twice a year may be enough.

Try praise, sincerely finding something about their room which

62 MARRIAGE

MARRIAGE 63

"What's a Nice Place Like This Doing to a Girl Like Me?," *Marriage* (1973). (Courtesy of St. Meinrad Archabbey)

Those who championed Catholic women's right to work recognized they needed to do more than convince wives to pursue their potential. Of more consequence, perhaps, were the practical obstacles, the "structures" that made women's work unfeasible, such as a lack of childcare and the objections of husbands. Virginia Heffernan, herself a sociologist and working mother of five, tackled these topics with gusto in 1971: "The larger society, as well as the small group of the family, has need of the qualities, talents and attributes women have to offer. With less hysteria, histrionics and name calling, we ought to be able to apply some rationality to the meeting of these various needs."[63]

Heffernan knew in particular that nothing would change for women until the men in their lives could be reconditioned to view their own role differently at home. She pointed out the young female professional whose "spouse has not the slightest intention of doing 'woman's work,' although he is more than willing to live on the double pay made possible by his wife's doing 'man's work.'" Giving up, perhaps, on the current generation, she recommended training boys to housework at a young age so they would not view it as merely "helping out." Some authors, like those who advocated for egalitarian marriage, tried to convince readers that husbands themselves would benefit from these changes. "Men were not necessarily happy in the old patriarchal society," Joan Schaupp claimed. "While women were restricted and confined,

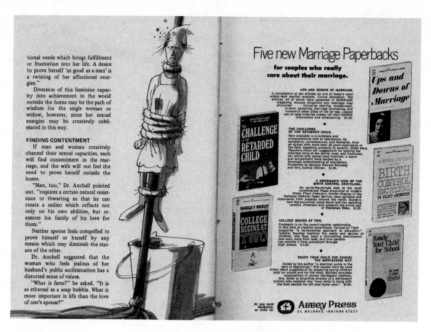

Illustration for "Woman 1970: A Counsellor's View," *Marriage* (1970).
(Courtesy of St. Meinrad Archabbey)

men often felt overburdened." She quoted one husband as saying, "It's an intolerable burden to have to be someone else's bridge to the world. It was a great relief when my wife got a job and became her own bridge."[64]

As usual, the most outspoken writers on this issue were the women featured in the "Reader Reaction" section. One of these was a woman writing in response to an article titled "Suicide and the Unhappy Housewife" (1970). Richard O'Donnell, addressing an increase in suicides among women, claimed that husbands were a much more effective cure for depressed wives than psychologists, if they would only pay their spouses some attention. According to O'Donnell, women "are begging for recognition within the framework of their own lives. It is possible that, for these women, the home—which should be the center of family life—has become a prison." He concluded, "The husband who does treat his wife with respect, and endeavors to allow her freedom beyond the four walls of their home, will soon discover that his wife is better equipped to bear those long days alone with the washing machine, TV and the children." Note the myriad ways O'Donnell stresses that men and women must remain within their traditional roles to prevent tragedy. She requires freedom, but only the freedom he allows her; she craves attention, but without challenging her life's basic "framework."[65]

Complementarity and Intimate Life

Letter writer Linda Hussmann was having none of it: "Could it be that the housewife—through a suicide attempt—is actually saying that her fullest human potential is not being reached," and, furthermore, that she will never reach her potential "no matter how many morning kisses she receives or how many doors her husband opens for her. *Every woman must open her own door.* She must begin *now* to seek the nature of her dissatisfaction *from other women.*" If you think this looks suspiciously like a laywoman championing consciousness-raising in the pages of a mainstream Catholic magazine, you are not wrong. "She can begin by reading what Betty Friedan has to say concerning the 'problem that has no name,'" Hussmann suggested. Then she addressed *Marriage*'s female readers directly: "Betty Friedan challenges all women *to begin to take their existence seriously.* Are you woman enough to take up this challenge?"[66]

Even in the mid-1970s *Marriage* was still providing a forum for those who opposed working wives, printing two articles in support of housewifery in the summer of 1973, for example. Yet I would argue that such articles were well outside the norm by this time.[67] One can see the movement on this issue in a rejoinder to those summer articles, "To Share Is to Live," written from the perspective of a young, modern working wife. Luise Cahill Dittrich, a newlywed teacher from Connecticut, wrote movingly of her fear of marriage. In itself this idea was completely foreign to *Marriage*, but the reason behind it was even more surprising. "What, I asked myself, is a smart, independent young woman like you doing in this stereotype of the American Way?" Dittrich wrote. "What of yourself are you hereby surrendering to the cheerful, chatty expectations of your mother and her neighbors? What possible quality of love can endure, let alone deepen, through bleary-eyed years of dishwashing and vacuuming and babies and mortgages?" Dittrich was careful to distance herself from the extremes of women's lib, but her beliefs are in line with liberal second-wave feminists, even if she did not choose to label herself as such. This teacher had no intention of giving up the full-time job she loved; she and her husband had found not just compromise but grace in their egalitarian relationship, where domestic duties were evenly split. No, her main challenge was being a wife in a house without becoming a housewife: "My deepest and subtlest apprehension was that the home itself, that bastion of security and comfort in an uncertain world, would somehow seduce me into a gradual acceptance of myself as housekeeper and mother—and no more." Dittrich found a solution, with her husband's help, and it echoed the conclusion of so many other women writers in *Marriage*: "the awareness to see each other as unique individuals rather than role-playing stereotypes."[68]

So far, we have covered significant aspects of the husband-wife relationship that can shed light on Catholic women's challenges to notions of womanhood in the 1960s and 1970s. Yet one aspect remains, and it was by far the most visible, most discussed topic in *Marriage*: marital sexuality. This is not at all surprising given the time period under study; in the 1950s and early 1960s, the community of educated lay Catholics that provided the readership for the magazine was in the throes of a momentous debate over artificial contraception that was in full evidence in the pages of *Marriage*.

That debate has been ably documented and analyzed in Leslie Woodcock Tentler's *Catholics and Contraception: An American History*, which proves beyond a doubt that laypeople fueled the conversation about—and the rejection of—the church's birth control ban.[69] Much of that debate focused on the practice of periodic continence, more commonly known as "the rhythm method," in wide use by Catholic couples as early as the 1940s and officially sanctioned for use by the Vatican in the early 1950s. When using rhythm, couples attempted to determine ovulation (eventually through the innovation of charting changes in a woman's temperature) and then timed intercourse to coincide with the "safe period" in her cycle. While many couples were relieved to have a means of family planning sanctioned by the church, and even found some spiritual good in the self-denial it required, rhythm occasioned much distress.

Articles about rhythm—how to practice it, how it failed, whether it failed, was it beneficial, should it be rejected—were ubiquitous. In fact, I would posit that if word clouds were available at the time, the center of *Marriage*'s cloud for the first half of the 1960s would be the word *rhythm*, hands-down. Notoriously unreliable, rhythm could not be trusted to prevent conception, and yet multitudes of dutiful Catholic couples doggedly gave it their best. Such couples wrote movingly of their struggles to raise families of eight, ten, or even twelve children, with barely a year in between births. They mourned their inability to express their love freely and railed against "love by calendar." Moreover, they moved adeptly among theological arguments of the day, advancing a view of moral theology rooted in lived experience rather than natural law. They also came to reject the idea, if gradually, that they should not use artificial contraception. After all, if the church allowed couples to choose to limit the size of their families through rhythm, what difference did it make if they used a barrier method or the much more reliable contraceptive pill to achieve the same end? As Tentler proves, such debates indicate that the laity was finding its voice and the confidence to reject the church's teaching authority on this matter.

Although the *Marriage* articles on rhythm are rich, abundant, and a boon for gender study, I will not analyze them here. Instead, I choose to investigate the writing that appeared *after* the debate about rhythm effectively ended. The debate had already faded from prominence in the Catholic press by the mid-1960s, as more and more couples chose to defy the Vatican on this issue. In fact, a survey showed that the percentage of American Catholic women between the ages of eighteen and thirty-nine who used a method of birth control other than rhythm was 51 percent by 1965, and 68 percent by 1970.[70] After filling their magazine with the debate, the editors themselves abruptly announced in November 1966 that rhythm was "a dead issue," that the people had moved on, and, furthermore, that the editors were "bored." The topic arose only occasionally from this point on. Artificial contraception itself appeared infrequently as a topic, even in the midst of the controversy surrounding the release of the birth control encyclical *Humanae Vitae* in 1968.[71]

In truth, while laypeople's responses to the ban on artificial contraception have been well documented, we know much less about the fascinating conversation that followed the debates over birth control.[72] As it turns out, Catholic laypeople did not stop talking about sex; they were just getting started. Those who had been practitioners of rhythm (or at least framed their understanding of sex in that context) needed to figure out what it would be like to experience marital sexuality without the huge burden of fear, anxiety, or guilt weighing on them.[73]

But they were also talking about sex to make sense of rapidly changing understandings of gender and the power dynamics within couples. As historian Beth Bailey reminds us, the sexual revolution encompassed more than an increase in sex outside of marriage, or even increased discussion or tolerance of such behavior. It "fundamentally challenged the dominant paradigm that located sex—and its control—in the difference between men and women. These revolutionaries claimed commonality; they sought freedom from strict male and female roles. They meant to remake sex by remaking gender." The conversations about sex in *Marriage* were nestled among discussions of headship, working wives, essentialism, and women's liberation, consistent with Bailey's claim. Laypeople, but primarily laywomen, were undermining complementarity as they discussed marital sexuality; they had more on their minds than birth control.[74]

It should be noted at the outset that, not surprisingly, these conversations had their limits. First, writers privileged heterosexual couples and were heteronormative in their approach. The magazine had no tolerance for homosexuality in this period, allowing a handful of negative statements to appear without a major counterargument in support. Gay men and women could not easily fit into a conversation that was dominated by the question of complementarity. Second, writers spoke almost exclusively about *marital* sexuality. Extramarital sex was not sanctioned and was spoken of in negative terms.

To begin, as might be expected at the dawning of the sexual revolution, numerous writers commented on the idea that they had received poor sex education that steeped them in an ethos of guilt and fear. As a result, we see a consistent effort to remain what we would currently term "sex positive," from the earliest days of the magazine. But as we know from the work of Catholic historians, a positive attitude about marital sexuality was nothing new in Catholic circles; it dates back to as early as the 1920s and was pervasive in the 1950s in the writings of laypeople and clergy, as well as in movements such as Cana and CFM. These writings often emerged from a set of people Leslie Woodcock Tentler so memorably named "The Holy Foolishness crowd," who promoted "a near-heroic vision of Christian family living" in their commitments to lay action and to their large families.[75]

The positive vision of marital sexuality that poured forth from these sources was frequently expressed in sacramental language. It was genuine, often profound, but it could also tend toward the rapturous and earnest. Authors often spoke of marital intimacy, and in fact orgasm, in spiritual terms. Philip Scharper described sex this way in 1966: "The marital act, which both symbolizes and brings about my complete surrender to and acceptance of the other also brings about an increase in charity, a dilation of my heart and mind, because it brings me, through the other, at least dimly into a contact with all mankind and with its head, the new Adam." Similarly, Reginald Trevett in 1961 argued for the centrality of God in the marriage bed saying, "Love then . . . utterly surrender[s] itself to the personal life of another, and by this surrender find[s] itself again in the fullness of trinitarian being." He continued, "The 'ecstasy' of orgasm symbolizes that fruitful death to self which is the heart of Love. To seek this ecstasy solely for its own sake leads to self-disintegration."[76]

One of the clearest trends in the *Marriage* articles immediately after the rhythm era is a backlash against such overly spiritual conceptualizations of sex. Writers, particularly women writers, seemed to be questioning whether this framing of marital sexuality best characterized the sexual lives to which

Complementarity and Intimate Life

Catholic couples should aspire. They also believed this framework made sex itself too weighty and abstract. One such writer was Angela Downs, who wrote an explosive "Speak Up" column in 1968 on the uselessness of so-called expert advice for Catholic couples in troubled marriages. Downs asked, "Must we speak of marriage as mystery? Of sex as mystery? Of human love as mystery? If I read one more 'mystery' in the religious press, I shall give one long blood-curdling banshee wail, and then retire quietly into a dream world where all marriages are made in heaven, become heaven on earth, then go back to heaven. . . . Seriously, must we retreat into mystery when it comes to sex, love and marriage, while at the same time we are trying to de-mystify . . . everything else?" Reader Diane McCurdy expanded on the idea: "[the church] obviously feels she must justify sex by sanctifying it, [but] sex is not *primarily* holy. . . . I reject . . . the notion that sex is the ultimate human experience. There are other things in life, really."

Why would these women wish to steer the conversation in this direc-tion? Neither Downs nor McCurdy were rejecting the holiness of sex so much as they were rejecting the unreality that such treatment of the subject perpetuated. Downs argued that such language attempted to mask the gen-uine problems of marriage; McCurdy pointed out that sacramental language tried to make sex into something it was not because deep down the church still believed sex was dirty and wrong.[77]

Articles of the rapturous type, which these authors opposed so strenu-ously, were nearly always gendered in ways that supported complementarity. Take for example Mary Maino's thoughts on women and sex in 1961: "By nature she is more passive, for she is the receiver in love-making: she is the vessel of life, nourishing, cherishing, and protecting it, not thrusting it upon others. . . . To her he may bring his less desirable self, and it is her work to serve the needs of his weakness when he does." Those who believed strongly in complementarity and were battling its erosion often used gendered per-ceptions of sexuality to argue for men's and women's fundamental difference. A common assertion was that women's role in the act of sex was evidence for a theology that insisted women were passive and receptive.[78]

By attempting to recast the language used to describe marital sexuality, these women writers were undercutting the teachings of complementar-ity yet again. Sex was not a device for the production of holiness in which women were innocent, passive recipients awaiting the rapture only God and their husbands could provide. In fact, if we read further in Angela Downs's commentary, she calls out husbands who would deny their wives birth con-trol, keeping women "barefoot and pregnant" in an effort to prove their own virility, hardly the selfless act of giving so many Catholic writers described sex to be in the early 1960s.[79]

Writers like McCurdy and Downs tried to bring sex down to earth where women were *real*, not essentialized creations of the Catholic imagination. Elizabeth Mulligan, a pre-Cana organizer, gave this advice in a 1970 article: "And above all, don't make sex so holy that it can't be discussed. It is God-given, yes, but very human in practice." Writers told young women that it was okay to experiment, make mistakes, and laugh at themselves. As Florence Weimrath memorably phrased it, "These bodies, like homemade bread, sometimes fail to rise to the occasion, but we accept the less-than-perfect loaf and hope for better luck next time."[80]

Most important, authors talked openly—as a corrective—of women's sex drive and capacity for pleasure. A mild example of this is a lengthy 1970 article titled "How to Enjoy Your Honeymoon." Written by a layman and a priest, primarily for the edification of young husbands, the two-part article explained in forthright step-by-step terms—basically—how to deflower your bride. This article was certainly gendered, but it also went out of its way to define pleasure in mutual terms: "[Sex] is so very great precisely because, in the consummation of love, each partner is doing to each other precisely what he *and* she most passionately desire to do, and in receiving from the other precisely what he *and* she most passionately desire to receive."[81] Readers also immediately countered any suggestion that women had a lower libido than men, or that they took less pleasure in sex. In this they were following the lead of sex researchers such as Alfred Kinsey, William Masters, and Virginia Johnson, whose findings had transformed common understandings of women's sexuality by this time.[82]

But women authors themselves wrote of sexual pleasure with much more gusto, further subverting expectations that a Catholic woman's climax should be linked to a spiritual orgasm. No article made this clearer than the delightful "Starting the Day with Love" (1971). The laywoman author laid out the simple pleasures of having sex in the morning. Citing research indicating that women were "more passionate before breakfast," she quoted woman after woman who attested to its joys. "'[It's] great!' a young grandmother declared, 'if time pressure, as to getting to work on time, doesn't force me to keep my eye on the clock, instead of on my husband.'" In the same issue, long-time letter writer and contributor Virginia Heffernan, well-known to the magazine community, had no problem declaring in a letter to the editor, "Seventeen years tomorrow and sex is still a joy." Laypeople, and particularly laywomen in *Marriage*, were ready to redefine laywomen's sexuality after rhythm, moving away from a ponderously sacramental formulation of marital intimacy toward a more realistic acknowledgement of a Catholic woman's role in sex that need not be linked to inherent traits.[83]

Laymen, however, were not always as willing as laywomen to separate marital sexuality from complementarity, even as they rejoiced in women's sexual pleasure. There were some outright statements against complementarity, to be sure. When a priest in 1965 described woman as "dependence-in-the-flesh" who submits to her husband's "amorous strengths," a male reader did not hold back, declaring this a combination of "ignorance with bad theology." All is mutual, he insisted. Each surrenders. In response to "How to Enjoy Your Honeymoon," another male reader took issue with the central concept: "The groom is assumed to be the leading force, directing the progress of events and able to easily overcome his own uncertainties and those of his bride. This picture seems to me to be almost insulting to many women who come to their marriage beds prepared to comfort and reassure as well as to be comforted and reassured."[84]

However, subtler articles that praised the delights of mutual pleasure while affirming traditional roles generally escaped notice, suggesting that on balance the readership would let references to complementarity slide if husbands were encouraged to see to their wives' pleasure. For example, articles liked to portray man as the knowing partner who could lead his more timid spouse to the wonders of a good orgasm. An example was an article titled "My Husband Is a Great Lover," a humorous 1963 piece written *by the husband in question* who interviewed his own wife (mother of nine) about his virility. She said, "I would say that God put in the male a superabundance of passion. . . . I would never have imagined I could come to have the same seeking and craving as my husband. It seemed unthinkable. In other words, this passion of the great lover is transmitted to the woman—and I'm blushing."[85]

Others highlighted the convenience of having a wife ready at home when she was wanted. In the article "What I Like about Making Love," Mario Panzen said, "I simply happen to enjoy making love to my wife. It's fun. And that she, in her body, is available and waiting for me at the end of a long and tiring day is a sustaining thought." Incidentally, this author also suggested that women should not be offended if their husbands sought out their wives for sex "to relieve feeling created by another woman." After all, he noted, "what domestic flower garden doesn't receive [more] attention after a visit to the local flower show?"[86]

Conversations around sex in this era also reveal tensions between husbands and wives over the wife's adoption (or potential adoption) of feminism. Pat Mainardi began her 1969 feminist manifesto "The Politics of Housework" with the line "Liberated women—very different from women's liberation!" How true it was. Many writers in *Marriage* celebrated the idea of Catholic women breaking out of their roles enough to embrace sexual pleasure openly, but feminism itself was a step too far for many. Fearing feminism, they warned readers to be on guard lest women's liberation inflict the ultimate damage: ruining their sex lives.[87]

As early as 1961 *Marriage* readers were confronted with the connection between acceptance of traditional gender roles and the quality of sexual experience when they were offered an excerpt of Marie Robinson's *The Power of Sexual Surrender* (1958). This popular book argued that a woman who accepted her traditional feminine role of surrender "almost always reaches a climax during the act of love. . . . But the number of times is unimportant. . . . What is important is the *kind* of orgasm she has." Consistent with the beliefs of many psychologists of the time, Robinson argued that the vaginal orgasm was a sign of true maturity and fulfillment and should be the goal for all married women.[88] Mario Panzen (of the flower show) addressed the same concept in speaking of his sexual relationship with his wife: "When a married woman accents her husband's maleness and the role of this maleness in her total life, she not only creates a positive tone for the myriad inter-relationships of the marriage, but sets an attitude which will carry over into the sexual side of the marriage." Ideally, she accented his maleness by adopting more strongly pronounced feminine behavior, heightening everyone's pleasure.[89]

This was the positive way of framing the question, but it was much more common to see the negative version: sex will be worse if the woman is liberated. One expert remarked, "It's becoming increasingly difficult . . . to be a male biologically and sociologically. . . . Now he's being threatened by Women's Lib, as if he didn't have enough problems about his sexuality already." Readers were told that sexually aggressive women were not only "incompetent bed partners" but should seek psychological treatment for emasculating their husbands. In the article "Danger—Working Wife!" a female writer asked, "Are you, as a working wife, endangering your marriage? . . . Does your sex life lack the zest it once had? Is your husband resentful?" Those who feared feminism claimed it was a threat to the mutual sexual pleasure (i.e., a product of complementarity done properly) championed so frequently in the magazine.[90]

Complementarity and Intimate Life

While *Marriage* did not commonly print the idea that feminism led to better sex, it did appear, and in surprising places. In 1968, it featured an article that was a particularly strong affirmation of traditional roles for women; however, tucked in as filler at the bottom of the last page was an excerpt from an article in *Psychology Today* arguing that "our culture is too hung-up about what is male and what is female, too quick to assert that there is a man's function and a woman's function and never the twain shall meet." This is surprising enough given its proximity to an article promoting complementarity, and there can be no doubt that the editors put it there on purpose. But the excerpt did not end there: "The major compensation for the man who is willing to make this kind of adjustment [to a more liberated wife is] the satisfaction of having at his side a great, vibrant, alive woman. This satisfaction spreads throughout the marriage, and one of its most potent effects is on the sexual relationship. From being 'masculinized,' the woman who has a sense of her identity as an independent person rather than as a mere appendage of her husband, is a more fulfilling sexual partner. At the same time she is a partner in every other aspect of marriage."

While champions of moderate feminism were not hard to find in the magazine, only a few authors went so far as to assert the sexual pleasures of women's liberation, probably because they feared such statements might be taken as approval of the sexual revolution. But for those who did, the joy that couples found in sex as a direct result of feminism was offered as further evidence for Catholic laywomen's emancipation. "Women are becoming able to express sexual aggressiveness without guilt and to pursue meaningful, fulfilling careers," Cliff Yudell wrote in 1971. "This is all to the good." Significantly, this quote appeared in an article titled "The Successful Marriage."[91]

. . . .

As we have already seen, in 1964 the editors went out on a limb and wrote an editorial against gender stereotypes for Catholic women, calling for equality and specifically decrying male headship and supporting working wives. They published their first feminist article in the same issue, but the backlash was extreme. As a result they backpedaled and quickly: three members of the editorial staff wrote in support of complementarity over the following twelve months, including C. Q. Mattingly, who wrote the original editorial. One of these pieces is worth discussing at length because it sheds light on how the staff seemed to have chosen to move forward on the issue of laywomen and changing gender roles.

Raban Hathorn, OSB, was charged with writing the opening editorial for the issue detailing the backlash in February 1965. To do so, he chose to recount his attendance at a recent conference panel titled "What Is a Woman?" (truly an artifact of the midcentury if ever there was one). Hathorn told how each panel member—"a single woman, a professional woman, a wife and mother, and a religious sister"—was asked to answer the question posed in the title, but instead "it was evident that each of the panelists approached the question by revealing her anxiety over the attitude of men toward women. Even the Sister, who related her experiences in a school of psychiatric nursing, began by telling how she was treated or 'mistreated' by the attitudes of the male personnel on the faculty and among the students. The upshot of the whole two days meeting was the resolution to discuss 'What is a man?' at the next session of the group." Hathorn seemed flummoxed by this: he thought he was attending a traditional panel on complementarity only to hear uncomfortable talk of "mistreatment" of women, and from a woman religious at that. If he sympathized with these women's experiences of sexism, he chose not to say so in the magazine that day. Instead, he followed the above quote with what at first seems an oddly misplaced statement about complementarity and *Marriage*'s editorial policy:

> [This] but strengthens the conviction on which our editorial staff
> has operated: it takes two to make a marriage, male and female, as
> God made them, to help, complement and fulfill one another. It is
> for that reason that we have consistently tried to get married men
> and married women to write for us. . . . And for the same reason
> we are grateful to our readers who write us so that their genuine
> reactions, published in our "Reader Reaction," can stimulate a lively
> give-and-take. . . . In this way we have been trying to fulfill our role as
> an open forum.

Hathorn seemed to be sending a message to those who wanted something more than *Marriage* could give in 1965: the best we can do for you, ladies, is to create a place where your voice can be heard.[92]

From here, the editors continued to pursue what could only have been a purposeful agenda, the deliberate exploration of changing perceptions of gender in the Catholic community. Why else would they run a seemingly endless number of articles on the subject? True to their word, they provided a forum where all sides could share their views, as we have seen on every issue outlined in this chapter. They also frequently juxtaposed wildly opposing positions, or slyly undercut their own authors (particularly conservative

Complementarity and Intimate Life

authors) with filler or illustrations that called those writers' ideas into question. Throughout, they gave laywomen the opportunity to speak, to question, and to redefine who they were for themselves and the Catholic men in their lives.

Did they bury complementarity and pronounce its last rites? No. Was every laywoman's voice raised in unison to decry her imprisonment at the hands of her culture? Not that either. *Marriage* archives a series of conversations and debates within a community that fostered diverse ideas about gender roles. What the evidence does support, though, is that by the 1970s laywomen had by and large rejected certain ideas about Catholics and gender. First and foremost, they no longer took for granted the idea that so-called God-given complementary gender roles should guide a couple's choices regarding the biggest decisions of their lives: the power dynamics of their marriages, their employment, their family size, their sex lives. They no longer assumed that gender was predetermined by God, was fixed and unchanging, and could not be challenged. They viewed feminist ideas as a legitimate part of the conversation, not as anathema to be rejected out of hand. Collectively, laywomen's writing dared to argue, as Antoinette Bosco suggested, that what had been on offer for Catholic women was "no longer enough for a fulfilling life."

Faithful Daughters

Vatican Council II in the decree on the Apostolate of the Laity
urges Christians to "become involved" in the work of the Church.
The Catholic Daughters of America have been "involved" through
the years and no doubt you remember the message of our
National Chaplain, Bishop Vincent S. Waters, given more than
ten years ago, when he said "That the holy Father, Pope Pius XII,
is now asking the Catholic women of the World to do what the
Catholic Daughters have been doing [for] close to fifty years."

Anna Ballard, Catholic Daughters of America National Regent (1967)

In 1966, the Catholic Daughters of America (CDA) invited a woman religious to speak at its national convention, an unusual occurrence. Mother
Mary Hennessey, RC (Sisters of the Senacle), a superior in her community
and the leader of a junior CDA group, stood before the assembled laywomen
and spoke in the voice of the new nun. As with the Theresians at the same
time, we see a sister playing the role of teacher, attempting to call laywomen
to renewal. "We have to decide whether we are going to seem to be something from another era that no one believes in any more, or someone who
finds in genuine Christianity what the world needs today," she explained.
Even more bluntly, she warned them that "you can find a bushel and hide
under it but it won't work." The changes of the Council were to be embraced,
according to this new nun. Any group that refused to do so would quickly
find itself irrelevant.[1]

The decision to invite Mary Hennessey came during a distinct moment
in the history of the CDA. In the several years following the Council, the
CDA (and its counterpart, the Daughters of Isabella) considered the emerging "spirit of Vatican II" and what effect it should have on their outlook,
program, and self-conception. In this brief window of time, we can see

middle-aged, fairly conservative, white laywomen in thought and action. They flirted with renewal, took the pulse of their own beliefs, read the documents, observed liturgical changes, and considered their own positions. After all, their bishops requested openness to change, and the women obeyed. As these more conservative organizational women weighed their options, they too participated in the greater laywoman project. But the Daughters are not the Theresians (or the NCCW, or WUCWO). Unlike the other communities of women in this study, their mid-1960s window closed without a major transformation in program or self-conception. They embraced what changes they found beneficial, but then said a firm "no, thank you" to renewal.

So do we conclude that their wariness of renewal amounts to sticking their heads under a collective bushel basket, as Mother Mary Hennessey claimed? It is far too simplistic, and dismissive, to write these women off as having rejected renewal in favor of an outdated version of Catholic womanhood. What's more, it allows the new nun to frame the question. To the Mother Superior the choice seemed clear: renewal or obsolescence. What you are is no longer necessary, she suggested, and you must seek a Christianity that is more "genuine" and better suited to the present. The Theresians and myriad other laywomen across the country in 1966 might have heard Mother Hennessey's words eagerly. Her enthusiasm, her authority, and her willingness to push—gently, respectfully—at the boundaries were exactly the formula to which many a laywoman might have responded in the heady days after the Council. But the Daughters, so attuned to their place in the spiritual and temporal hierarchy of the church, surprisingly did not allow women like Mary Hennessey to set the parameters of the debate for them. In contrast, their question seemed to be, "Does the older conception of Catholic womanhood still have value?"

They concluded that it did, which is why they did not allow the concurrent renewal and feminist movements to significantly transform them and their organizations. First, they believed that if they continued to fulfill their traditional roles as Catholic women they could help save the modern world from itself. Second, in rejecting the mid-1960s enthusiasm for change, they were fighting to retain their authority. To state it plainly, they saw feminism and Vatican II as threats to their own power, rightly viewing the transformations of the 1960s as eroding the sense of authority conferred on them by pre–Vatican II gender dynamics. The schema on offer from the new Catholic women did not expand the Daughters' reach so much as it questioned the authority they had enjoyed under a system that celebrated their loyalty and leadership. Finally, these women seemed to respond best to an atmosphere of threat, relishing the role of valiant and courageous loyalists. The enthusiastic optimism of the mid-1960s, which emphasized openness and possibility and deemphasized authority, left many of the Daughters at a loss.

To me, this narrative of consideration and refusal is just as compelling as the dramatic arc of the Theresians in the same period, because it reveals the complexity of the Daughters' position and of their carefully calculated responses. At the heart of this story is a group of women who prided themselves on their obedience and their leadership in the ongoing struggle to deflect the changes of the modern world. Then the man to whom they pledged full love and loyalty—the pope—asked that they find a new identity by now *embracing* the modern and transforming themselves in the process. And they tried. We can see a window of time when both groups of women attempted to reform themselves and their organizations in light of the "spirit of Vatican II," but the window did not stay open for long. The Daughters are an early indicator of resistance to Vatican II and fear of its results. Not wanting to disobey, as this would undermine their own identity, they nevertheless found ways not to conform to progressive expectations until the establishment, too, began to openly express its doubts. Ultimately, Vatican II was unable to convince them that the modern world was a positive good. Likewise, the women's movement offered little beyond a new focus for the Daughters' fear. Through their own version of the laywoman project, they came to believe that the old identity of the Catholic woman still had value, and they retained it. In doing so they enacted their own—loyal—rebellion.[2]

METHODOLOGY

This chapter will focus on two organizations: the Catholic Daughters of America (CDA) and the Daughters of Isabella (D of I). The CDA was the largest of the Catholic female "fraternal" orders in the United States, and the largest single affiliate of the NCCW. The Daughters of Isabella is also a fraternal organization, although at its peak it was only about half the CDA's size. As I will demonstrate in the next section, the groups were remarkably similar, only diverging in minor ways in the areas under scrutiny in this study. The CDA figures most prominently in the chapter due not only to its size but also to the fact that its archives are more thorough. Throughout the narrative I will use the term "Daughters" to refer to the members of both groups collectively since there is so little difference between them. When I am only speaking of the members of one of the groups I have indicated this in the text.

The two sets of Daughters shared more than an outlook and a penchant for ritual; they were also far more circumspect than the other communities of laywomen in this study. Committed to obedience and self-effacement both as organizational policy and as requisites for personal sanctity, the Daughters did not readily dissent or countenance dissent in others regarding matters of church teaching or the groups' governance. Moreover, they did not save much significant correspondence. They played their cards very close indeed, leaving a curious historian to wonder what went on beyond the official facade. You can be certain that some members held positions not in line with their leadership, but I make few claims to this effect because there is so little evidence of dissent in the official record. The Daughters proved the most vocal in their publications and at their conferences, and although these showcase "official" positions, they still allow us to discern change over time, rendering them invaluable. For a glance behind the scenes, both organizations also kept the minutes of their national board meetings. Reading the papers of the Daughters was a vastly different experience from reading those of the NCCW, or certainly WUCWO, the two organizations closest in size and membership. These women made neither demands nor sarcastic asides. Reading their documents was an exercise in listening for voices that, even at the time, often remained muted.

CATHOLIC "FATHERS" AND "DAUGHTERS"

Two organizations founded near the turn of the twentieth century chose to name themselves "Daughters" of the church. The Daughters of Isabella was founded in 1897 by mothers, wives, and daughters of various Knights of Columbus in New Haven, Connecticut. (The Knights of Columbus is a Catholic fraternal service organization founded in 1882.) Hoping to create a female counterpart to the Knights, and inspired by the renewed popularity of Queen Isabella of Spain after the 1893 Columbian Exposition in Chicago, these women named themselves after the woman who funded Columbus's expedition to the New World. Six years later, a second group of women tied to the Knights of Columbus, this time in Utica, New York, established an organization in Isabella's name. In 1921, following a protracted legal battle, this second group (now a national organization) was forced to surrender its name, calling itself instead the Catholic Daughters of America. Neither group was officially affiliated with the Knights of Columbus, although the Knights fostered the growth of both organizations.[3]

The two "Daughters" were remarkably similar. Both groups valued female leadership fostered within a strict hierarchical structure. Each established rituals, ceremonial dress, and elaborate passwords designed to highlight the groups' system of ranks and exclusivity. Until the 1960s, potential members for each "court" or "circle" were investigated to see that they were practicing Catholics and morally sound. Women in both groups pledged loyalty to the United States and the Catholic Church, from the beginning mingling devotional Catholicism (particularly Marian piety) and patriotic zeal. Historian David O'Connor notes the Catholic Daughters' eager involvement in anticommunism efforts through most of the first seventy years of the group's existence, a pattern that can also be seen in the D of I. Daughters of both groups championed Catholic teaching on gender roles, fully supporting female essentialism and the concept of complementarity.[4]

The similarities do not end there. These groups did the same types of charitable work, particularly parish-level service and fund-raising for missions and various war efforts. Each group also began a Juniors program to foster a commitment to the values of Catholic womanhood in each new generation. Both organizations' mottos contain the words *Unity* and *Charity* ("Unity and Charity" for the CDA and "Unity, Charity, Friendship" for the D of I), ironic given the groups' early acrimony and inability to consolidate. The two groups even share the same historian, who wrote the organizations' official histories just a few years apart.

The main differences between the groups have to do with membership. Both attracted a similar demographic; members were overwhelmingly white, middle-class, middle-aged, and conservative. The Catholic Daughters of America was the larger of the two, reaching a peak of 214,000 senior members in 1962; the Daughters of Isabella peaked in the early 1960s at 120,000 senior members. Beyond the numbers, the greatest difference between the two was the Daughters of Isabella's significant presence in Canada (especially Québec), making the group more international in scope and bilingual.[5]

The most important thing the groups share, of course, is their choice to name themselves "Daughters" and to retain that name throughout the twentieth century. To begin with the obvious, the term first suggests relationship. These women claimed a relationship with the church, a connection in which they took pride. In sharing the title *daughter*, members could also view themselves as sisters, with the positive feelings of mutual support and affection that term connotes. (The term *sister* was unavailable to them because they likely associated it with women religious, and later, with the feminist movement.)

Faithful Daughters

The term *daughter* also carries a connotation of dependence, but the matter is more complex than it first appears. In selecting the term, the founders chose to highlight different characteristics than the Knights of Columbus, whose name was deliberately chosen to suggest manly defense of the faith. Daughters (ideally) were to be obedient, malleable, and supportive, acquiescing to the beliefs and objectives of their guardians. Yet both women's groups began as daughters of Isabella, an independent and, many would add, ruthless queen, although the more unsavory facts of her reign were downplayed by both groups.[6] To be Isabella's daughter suggests an assertion of power and the right to lead, coupled with demure obedience.

The name *Daughter* also vividly reflects the relationship of the CDA and D of I to male Catholics, once again suggesting the tug-of-war between asserting power and offering obedience. The majority of senior Daughters in both groups appear to have been married, but they did not call themselves the "Catholic Mothers" or "Wives" or even simply "Women." While there is little reason to doubt their commitment to home, marriage, and motherhood, in their courts and circles these women functioned as individuals apart from their husbands. In the material left behind by these groups, laymen rarely appear. When they do, it is usually costumed as Knights for ceremonial purposes. The Daughters may have believed in the ideals of the eternal woman (receptivity, dependence, self-sacrifice), but in their organizations these women functioned as if laymen did not exist.

Husbands may have been deliberately excluded, but "fathers" they had in spades. Here, then, is the most obvious relationship evoked by the term *daughter*: parent and child. When perusing CDA or D of I publications or conference proceedings, priests are ever-present: delivering speeches, clarifying doctrine, offering benedictions, smiling patiently as yet another middle-aged woman in white gloves handed over a check. Daughters in both groups deferred to their chaplains and pastors on matters ranging from national policy on the Equal Rights Amendment down to whom could be admitted into a local chapter. The Daughters' chaplains served as advisors and, increasingly as the 1960s advanced, as interpreters of the church's place in the modern world. In marked contrast to the NCCW leadership in the same period, I could not find any statements or comments criticizing Catholic clergy, even obliquely. These women took pride in being faithful daughters, and that included honoring their priestly fathers.

Images from the late 1950s and early 1960s demonstrate both the pride of place priests were offered, and their authority. For example, a photo of the CDA Supreme Directorate at a 1958 ceremonial dinner shows the group's

Daughters of Isabella, 1962 National Convention.
The group's chaplains are prominently placed.
(Courtesy of the Daughters of Isabella)

chaplain, Bishop Vincent Waters, ensconced paternally at the head of the table, with daughters arranged down both sides. Likewise, in a sea of Daughters of Isabella in a photograph from the 1962 national convention, the two supreme chaplains are most prominently placed (even though they obviously blocked the shorter women behind them). As might be imagined, the gender dynamics of the Daughters' world—revolving nearly exclusively around the interactions of laywomen and celibate priests—was not without awkwardness. Take, for example, an image from the Junior Daughters of Isabella. The priest charged with presenting a medal to the "Outstanding Junior Daughter of Isabella of 1961" reveals through his face and body language his discomfort with his proximity to these women, particularly the teenager, as does the girl's mother, who oddly clutches her daughter's arm as the priest approaches. Only a priest could properly convey such an honor, and he fulfills his role. However, no one in this tableau seems quite comfortable.[7]

Mostly, though, the Daughters and their clergy served as a mutual admiration society, in which laymen need have no presence. A preconference issue of the CDA's newsletter spoke excitedly of those who would attend the 1958 convention, particularly "our Hierarchy and our priests." "Our Hierarchy," referring to the group's own officers, shows their commitment to women's leadership, but there is no missing the fondness and pride expressed in "our priests." The Daughters of both organizations showed their respect for their priests constantly, frequently pledging their loyalty explicitly. Nearly every CDA conference in the 1960s featured a resolution in support of the clergy, from the pope to local pastors. A typical resolution read, "Allegiance, loyalty, devotion and love to our Holy Father Pope Paul VI." They further resolved "that in filial obedience to the Holy See we respectfully pledge full cooperation with our ordinaries and pastors; we pledge them our assistance in

Miss JoAnn Valerio receives the Outstanding Junior Daughter Award of 1961.
(Courtesy of the Daughters of Isabella)

their endeavors and in all of their works for the Church in our country, our diocese and especially in our own parishes." Similarly, the D of I pledged their "wholehearted support of all Bishops and Pastors in all their undertakings" and resolved to "be ever responsive to their requests for our assistance." The CDA national regent claimed in 1969 that "it is inherent in our organization to be loyal and to love the Church and its leadership."[8]

In return, the groups' chaplains spoke admiringly of the Daughters, complementing them on their dedication and support. In particular, priests buttered them up by claiming that the Daughters were both the church's bedrock and its salvation in tumultuous times. "The Catholic Daughter and her Little Sister hold the key to the future," Chaplain Vincent Waters claimed, "because in Woman's hands is the culture of the Nation and the World." Two years earlier in 1962, Waters said of the CDA (quoting Paul's letter to the Philippians), "You live in an age that is twisted out of its true pattern and among such people you shine out as beacons to the world." Another chaplain, fretting about a lack of respect for the pope, said, "Thank God, you Catholic Daughters of America are giving a magnificent example." Such praise of Daughters' solidity amid chaos increased as the 1960s advanced.[9]

Yet mutual admiration did not signal an equal relationship. While the Daughters did not stray from pledges of absolute loyalty (at least in public), priests felt free to openly criticize the Daughters. "You know, my dear good women," a chaplain began in a conference address, "if you have any fault in the past, and you haven't had too many, the one great fault that you had was that you depended entirely upon your priests to do so much for you." This must have seemed doubly harsh, seeing that Daughters were taught to rely on their "fathers" for guidance. A few years later, after a meeting of court chaplains, the national chaplain chose to present a list of nine criticisms to the national board, including that priests didn't like to attend court meetings because they were "too long, too boring, and do not start promptly." The priests also felt it appropriate to tell the board that the CDA's magazine had "too many pictures of too many bishops receiving too many checks." As if this wasn't blunt enough, they added, "It is not good for the image of the organization to have so many pictures of older people." No record remains to tell how the Daughters received such comments, or how they handled being criticized for the very behavior that the Father/Daughter relationship encouraged.[10]

ON THE BRINK OF THE COUNCIL

Bishop Vincent Waters, supreme chaplain of the Catholic Daughters of America, took a dim view of the future. In a homily to thousands of gathered Catholic Daughters in 1962, he warned that "[the World] is on the point of moral and spiritual death, you cannot be indifferent." Then he brought out the big guns. Recommit to your role as Catholic women, he said, and "you will help the Church save the world from Paganism and Atheism and restore Christian Civilization to the world, to your children and to your children's children. Now is the time! This is a Catholic Woman's Crusade for God— God wills it—you cannot fail."

While other organizations in this study were at their sunniest in the early 1960s, anticipating a future church enlivened by the Council, both groups of Daughters embarked into the conciliar era in an atmosphere of apprehension. This despite the fact that both organizations reached peak membership, and their greatest influence in the American church, in the early years of the 1960s. They approached these years with trepidation in part because of the changes already well under way (especially the decline of devotional piety), but also because the Daughters tended to cultivate an atmosphere of fear long before the 1960s brought the largest changes that would so unnerve them.[11]

The list of threats that the Daughters cataloged was long and frightening. In her letter to the membership in 1958, Supreme Regent Frances Maher outlined the need for the CDA's service, citing "the evil influences around us." These included the "distressing deterioration of public morals," "young people bolting from the laws of morality," and "the blows struck at the sanctity of Marriage." Evil only spurred them on, however: "We would be ungrateful not to be a leader of Catholic Action in these perilous times." Fear of immorality included distress over the spread of pornography. "More and More Good Reading Is a Fallout Shelter against Smut," read a headline in the Catholic Daughters' newsletter, News and Views, in 1962. The author made the hyperbolic claim that "more destructive than the atomic or hydrogen bombs is the Bad Reading Explosion that is taking place in our country."[12]

The decline of public decency threatened the well-being of Catholic girls in particular. Reportedly, Supreme Regent Anna Ballard once said to Vincent Waters that "the time approaches when a Catholic girl can't walk down the street without carrying a gun to protect her honor, life and purse." After relating this anecdote to the membership, Waters argued that "the Catholic Girl is probably in the greatest need that the world and the Church has experienced because of the crumbling of Christian culture and the take-over of the animal that is the evident method in the world, the flesh, and the Devil."[13]

Warnings against the infiltration of immorality into the home were mixed with fears of slipping morals within. Both groups of Daughters tilted at the windmill of immodesty in the 1950s and 1960s, calling attention to the scandal of strapless wedding gowns in partnership with the Marylike Crusade, a national movement to confront immodest dress.[14] The CDA decried Catholic women's groups who organized fashion shows where strapless gowns were featured. "What kind of style it is—Christian or pagan—doesn't matter much to the unthinking," a priest wrote in News and Views. "And, mind you, not a few of the organizations that sponsor these 'Catholic' style shows are dedicated to the Blessed Mother. . . . If they do not have enough respect for the Mother, they surely will not have respect for the Son." Once again, the chronicling of threats was a call to female leadership. "What we need and need badly from our Catholic women is leadership—leadership in the right direction," the priest concluded.[15]

The vocation crisis was high on the list of threats at the turn of the 1960s, the same fear that brought the Theresians into existence. Both the CDA and the D of I made vocation promotion a high priority. In an article titled "Storming Heaven for Vocations," Lucy Callahan reiterated the popular theme that mothers were to blame for the crisis. "God does his part," she offered, "so the reason for the dearth of vocations must lie in us." While both groups regularly prayed for vocations, passed conference resolutions on their promotion, and included inspirational articles on vocation in their magazines, Callahan had a more radical solution: all-night prayer vigils. Taking the example of a CDA court in Northern Virginia, Callahan advocated having every court pray in church from 10:00 PM to 6:00 AM without anyone leaving. According to Callahan, "The church selected will not be large enough to hold the crowd who will consider this a most unusual privilege." Even this, the gravest of threats to the church community, could be countered with female action.[16]

Add to the list of threats communism, the threat of creeping materialism, and the most basic fear of change itself. By nature, however, the Catholic Daughters were disinclined to cower; they were ready to meet the frightening times head-on. "You might ask, 'What can I do alone?'" Vice Supreme Regent Margaret Buckley wrote in 1958. "It is not the number, but the willingness" that would win the day. "It is the keen vision, the intense conviction, the blood of the martyr, the prayer of the saint, it is the heroic deed, it is the concentrated energy of a look or a word which is an instrument of Heaven."[17]

No one could summon heroic deeds like the CDA's Vincent Waters. His rhetoric reached its peak intensity in 1962 as the CDA reached peak membership. Writing for the national convention, Waters took as his theme "The Challenge of the Sixties." He opened by laying out the state of the world in stark terms, describing it as an ongoing battle for souls between "the World, the Flesh, and the Devil," on one side, and "God, His Grace, the Sacraments, His Holy Mother, and the Saints," on the other. Waters outlined the siren song of the World, with its "materialistic charm" and its ally the Flesh "with all its human, unruly passions." He assured the Daughters that God gave them free will, hoping they would join the battle by practicing virtue and eradicating vice.

But in this fight the Daughters were not called to lead so much as to follow. Waters's language here is worth extended quotation because it illustrates his expectations of near-militant obedience on the part of these women in the pew. According to Waters, the "CHALLENGE OF THE SIXTIES is a challenge of the good by the evil one in the universe." He was certain that the Blessed Mother would respond and lead. "She defends her children and does for them what only the Mother of God can do for them—thinks for them, prays for them, obtains the help they need, and fights if necessary like a tigress against all the hordes of the evil one, to save the souls of her children. . . . [She] goes ahead of her Legion of devout followers to push back the hordes of the enemy. . . . May you Catholic Daughters be in the forefront of the battle alongside your Mother and her Legions, ready to meet the CHALLENGE OF THE SIXTIES!!" The Daughters are offered the vision of the woman warrior or crusader, in the unlikely figure of the Virgin Mary as tigress. The invocation of Mary aside, such imagery is strikingly reminiscent of the temperance movement at the turn of the century, whose members also referred to themselves as armed crusaders fighting against the hordes of a modern enemy. The imagery is certainly not without precedent, but it reads as out of place, offered as it was within days of the opening of the Second Vatican Council. In particular, the claim that Mary *thinks*, as well as prays, for her daughters shows how far the CDA was from the emerging picture of an empowered and increasingly independent lay apostolate.[18]

Initially, neither group of Daughters met the Council itself with fear; they viewed the 1960s with palpable anxiety but responded to the Council with mild interest and promises of support. Simply put, they responded as one might expect from two groups that regularly pledged absolute loyalty to their pope. They were not quite sure what such an enterprise entailed (few Catholics were), but they would go ahead and pray for it, and with gusto. At the 1962 convention the Catholic Daughters' supreme regent recommended "that the CDA sponsor a crusade of prayer for the success of the Ecumenical Council, and that every member be asked to say three Hail Marys daily for the intention of our Holy Father, Pope John XXIII until the end of the Council." Her announcement was completely in keeping with the group's self-conception. She likened their prayer to a "crusade" and then meted out a quota of Hail Marys to the membership.

Her crusade was no idle promise. The CDA published annual statistics on prayers and devotions offered by the courts. One such list in 1960 noted that 905 courts said the rosary together, while 650 distributed prayer cards; 737 courts prayed for conversions, although only 142 participated in "the Apostolate of the Prayer Card for Dying Non-Catholics." Similarly, the Daughters of Isabella also viewed their duty to the Council in devotional terms. Members were told that "each of us must respond [to the Council] readily by prayer and by living a life in which the lovely vision of Christian virtues shine and permeate [sic] the life of the family and society with this ideal in imitation of Our Blessed mother, Spouse of St. Joseph."[19]

What they knew of the Council before it began seemed to conform to their own hopes for the future of the church and did not suggest that their role as Catholic women would change. They knew they were being asked to step forward and serve to support the pope's agenda, but as proponents of Catholic Action this was entirely in keeping with their worldview. Both groups assumed the Council was primarily about evangelization, again, a primary goal of each organization. Beyond that, they sensed a call to ecumenism, which they were also prepared to support. (The Vatican called it an "Ecumenical" Council after all.) Looking at these initial expectations of the Council with the benefit of hindsight reminds us how unprepared these women were for what was barreling toward them. Their belief that the upcoming event was primarily a means of strengthening and propagating the faith seems far off the mark, but at the time they were responding to John XXIII's own statements, noted in both groups' literature.

At the close of 1961, the pope issued the document *Humanae Salutis*, which formally convened the Council, although the first session did not begin until the fall of 1962. Bishop Waters excerpted the following passage for the CDA membership: "The upcoming ecumenical council will be held at a moment when the Church is caught up by an ever more consuming desire to restore and fortify its faith, to draw renewal of spirit from contemplating the image of its own remarkable unity. It likewise experiences a quickening sense of its duty, not only to increase the efficiency of its life giving efforts and advance the sanctification of its members, but also to further the diffusion of revealed truth and update all its other activities." Here was language that the Daughters understood: "Restore and fortify," "remarkable unity," "sense of duty," "sanctification," and "diffusion of revealed truth." How familiar it must have sounded, and how easy it was to pledge support for a program so in keeping with their own values. The last phrase, "update all its other activities," contained the bombshell, of course, but how were they to know what was coming?[20]

As we have seen with the Theresians, the rank-and-file membership relied upon educated mediators to translate and explain this momentous event. This was especially true of the CDA and D of I, since their memberships were well trained to receptivity and obedience. Not surprisingly, the chaplains took the lead, although laywomen also wrote about the Council for both organizations. But the Daughters' introduction to the Council did not unfold like that of the other organizations in this study. The Theresians grew increasingly animated by the Council's promise of renewal and their role in it; the NCCW's and WUCWO's leadership backed the Council wholeheartedly, but less from a sense of loyalty than from a genuine excitement about change. Moreover, the early days of the Council also caused these laywomen to begin to question sexism within the church. But discussions of the Council among the Daughters in the early 1960s emphasized continuity rather than renewal, and traditional service rather than new roles. Those who would teach the Daughters about this looming event often linked information about the Council with traditional rhetoric about female essentialism and complementarity, as if to temper the hopeful (or reassure the fearful) in the days of uncertainty.

Let's start, again, with Bishop Waters. Right after relaying the Holy Father's words quoted above, the supreme chaplain outlined the laywoman's role: "Catholic Daughters you have to back up the words and works of our Holy Father. You have to be the support of your Bishops and priests in this age of the Council." So in the future, as in the past, the Daughters were to stand as silent support for the work of others. Waters reminded them that such support required courage and resolution. "You should resolve," he said, "to avoid sin and bad example to others." Moreover, he counseled them "to be active in promotion of the womanly virtues of Christian modesty in dress and behavior." Finally, he urged them to "convince others of the true nature of the Church, as the one, Mystical Body of Christ." To prepare for their work of supporting the Council, then, their chaplain called them to personal sanctity, modest womanly behavior, and evangelization. By evoking familiar gender norms, Waters signaled continuity with the past, not a rupture.[21]

Shortly after the close of the first session, the *Isabellan* also offered a reflection on the Council. Unlike Bishop Waters, who styled the Council as the work of the hierarchy to which the women owed allegiance, Claretian father Basil Frison asked the D of I rank and file to take ownership of the event. "You belong to it," he declared, "and the Council belongs to you." His article "God's Candles" took a warmer view of the times, referring to the present as an "age of chances and challenges." He saw the Council as a call to "restore Christ's Church to her pristine beauty"; for Frison, Vatican II would make the modern holy, and women would be actively involved in meeting that challenge.[22]

But this glowing vision of the Council—which might inspire the D of I to move beyond knee-jerk loyalty—was inextricably entwined with two pages of full-blown gender essentialism, some of the most blatant rhetoric found in either collection. "God's Candles" spun an elaborately drawn-out metaphor likening Catholic women to the flowers of the yucca plant. Just as the yucca was often referred to as "God's candle," so Catholic women should be "like 'God's Candles' on the altar of creation and in the midst of society." Frison claimed that woman was endowed with "natural attributes, tendencies, instincts which are strictly hers, or which she possesses to a degree different from man."

Moreover, "woman was also assigned specific tasks." Chief among them was "the mission to spend herself in sacrifice" as the candle burns itself away on the altar. The metaphorical call for female self-immolation was a familiar, if relatively rare, theme of essentialist rhetoric in this period. Readers were also likely not surprised either by Frison's take on woman's purpose, that "the end for which the Creator fashioned woman's entire being is motherhood." As if to prove himself a modern man, Frison then quoted a late 1961 statement by John XXIII on women: "One result of . . . social progress in the last fifty years has been to take women outside the four walls of their homes and place them in direct contact with public life." To Frison, as to the pope, this was a welcome development, because it meant that Catholic women would bring their unique characteristics and innate holiness to bear upon the world. "The beauty of the home," he wrote, "where the queenly love of mother and wife reigned, is now being made manifest to the open world, in the whiteness and in the fragrance of the bell-shaped yucca flowers of noble womanliness."

His last section was on the Council specifically, and while written in positive, welcoming tones, it may have proved ultimately confusing to his laywomen readers. On the one hand, he first urged them to see the Council as their own, to pray for its success, and to take up the challenges of bringing the church into the modern world. But at the conclusion he named Catholic woman's true role in renewal. Frison believed the best thing Catholic lay-women could do was to be the best possible examples of Catholic life that they could be. "The Catholic woman . . . must consecrate the world with the beauty and fragrance of her genuine Catholic life," he said. "The Ecumenical Council will ask Catholic women to renew their Catholicity, and thus become a greater inspiration for the world and a benediction which consecrates creation about them." Such a directive hardly invited the Daughters to move more than a few inches beyond a traditional outlook. Anyone who has tried to dig up a yucca from their yard might suggest another meaning for Basil Frison's metaphor: the Daughters, like the yucca, were deeply rooted and would not be easily shifted.[23]

Anna Ballard, vice supreme regent for the CDA during the run-up to the Council, also framed the Council in gendered terms that limited its potential. Just after the close of the first session, she wrote with the most enthusiasm she would demonstrate in print about the Council. She described the CDA as "an organization which is now and ever has been doing something real and concrete in the work of the Church—an organization which is planning and preparing to cooperate with its spiritual leaders and to be actively identified with the program that will be released by the Second Vatican Council." She then remarked on what she really enjoyed most about the spirit of the times: "What could be more stimulating than to be closely associated with women, upholding traditions, and working unselfishly for the same high purposes?"

Both ideas—tradition and unselfish service—signaled continuity with past ideas of female essentialism, as did comments Ballard made in 1962 before the NCCW national convention. Here she told the assembled laywomen, "As Catholic women proud of our Church and our Country, we have a real challenge in these trying times, a challenge to be *the silent but active* force in Church affairs, and an active and articulate force in everything affecting our Country." Laywomen must divide their action into two categories based on their surroundings: silent in church affairs, but vocal in public life. This leader of women did not view the Council as an opportunity for significant change. She hoped for an expanded reach under the new system but not for an altered worldview.[24]

The Daughters may not have been prepared for change, or have found it particularly welcome, but innovation was not their strength; they represented a constituency of laywomen who prized what they had. In fact, a large portion of their identity was rooted in their ability to *defend* what they had. It is striking how frequently the Daughters described themselves (or were described) as valiant, heroic, and courageous, particularly in the period just before and during the Council. When the CDA's supreme regent was named a "Lady of the Equestrian Order of the Holy Sepulchre" (a prestigious external award) in 1964, the organization celebrated the honor with a full-page photograph of their leader in floor-length cape and gloves, holding a cross reminiscent of a military medallion. The award was meant "to revive in modern form the spirit and ideal of the Crusades with the weapons of faith, the apostolate and Christian charity." Only an organization that built its identity around the concept of defense would style its apostolate as a weapon.[25]

The Daughters of Isabella also adopted a martial spirit. Their official song, "We're the Daughters of Isabella," opened with the lines "History is filled with deeds of daring / with women sharing, side by side / changing destinies/bringing liberties, and now, with courage / one and all we sing with pride." At the 1966 convention, participants were warned to take off their badges when they went into cocktail lounges and to refrain from singing the D of I song. Where there's a prohibition, there must have been an offense, so we might imagine groups of tipsy Daughter conventioneers belting out verses about their own courage at the top of their lungs. Unlady-like, to be sure (hence the warning), but how they must have enjoyed it.[26]

Commentators, usually priests, in both groups described what might be seen as dull work—upholding traditional values in the church and the home—as adventurous. Military metaphors abounded, glorifying aggressive defense of the faith. "Wherever the faith of Christ has triumphed, it was the woman who helped attain the victory," the D of I was told in 1963. "Has not the lot of the 'valiant woman' been an exciting and demanding one, resulting frequently in suffering and often in martyrdom?" another priest asked the CDA. In case martyrdom proved too exciting, even for the Daughters, the priest also advocated a return to Marian devotion. "To follow the example of the Blessed Mother in the space age may sound old-fashioned and dull. On the contrary, it would offer excitement [and] bring great heroism."

The Daughters believed in the church, reveled in it, enjoyed it, and defended it from perceived attack. They supported Vatican II at the outset because it fit their self-perception as loyal foot soldiers ready to extend and strengthen the faith. In time, though, they began to realize that they might have misunderstood. Catholics need not fear the modern world, the Council seemed to say, or the Protestant or Jew. Catholics could openly disagree, question tradition, be open to what was new in the world. These changes signaled that the Daughters, as conceived, might be out of a job. New threats emerged on the horizon toward the end of the decade (con-traception, abortion, feminism, loss of faith) that revived the need for the valiant Catholic woman, but before these crystalized, the Daughters were challenged to see if they could fit themselves into a new mold. Before they could judge the fit, the laywomen needed to figure out the nature of these new expectations.

SORTING THE MESSAGES

As we have seen in all of the groups under study, both sets of Daughters worked through a welter of ideas about women's changing roles and renewal simultaneously, because the changing times forced them to confront both at the same time. But more than serendipity led them to explore the two together. Vatican II asked laywomen—as laity—to change their identities significantly. The Daughters knew to ask what the hierarchy left largely unasked and unanswered: Does the Council call us to change *as women* as well? This question lay at the heart of the Daughters' laywoman project, which preoccupied them for a limited period in the mid- to late 1960s.

The NCCW took the question one step further, leading them to a basic feminist critique: If the church is not willing for women's role to change within the church, doesn't that limit the promise of renewal? The Daughters' papers, however, do not show a preoccupation with feminism such as the NCCW demonstrated in the same period. Their records only rarely reveal even mild feminist criticism of the hierarchy, tradition, or theology; the Daughters never lost their obedience and shied from voicing criticism. Nor did they engage in debates over the appropriate limits of Catholic feminist activity, since they only occasionally entertained ideas that could be construed as feminist.

The Daughters did not take a feminist turn, but that does not mean that they ignored the furor on their doorstep. They discussed the changing roles of women as did all the communities of women, but instead of focusing on women's *rights* they sustained a lengthy conversation about women's *duties* in the age of renewal. Had expectations of women changed in the church as well as in the world? Did the church support such changes? How could a Catholic laywoman best serve God in these circumstances? To what positive ends could women's new freedom be applied? And perhaps most important of all, do we, the bedrock of the church, really need to change at all? This was not a given; by decade's end both groups of Daughters were inclined to deny the need for fundamental transformation of women's identity, purpose, and duty. In the following section, we will see which ideas they entertained, and which they ultimately rejected.

To get a handle on how the Daughters' understanding of their duty as Catholic women was challenged by the Council, we might return to the immediate preconciliar period, and the Junior Daughters of Isabella. For a girl to receive the "Eagle of the Cross" award, given to the outstanding Junior Daughter of the Year, she had to demonstrate her superior characteristics in the following areas (presumably in this order): practical Catholicity, dependability and cooperation, personality, leadership, scholastic achievement, and commitment to the Junior D of I. "Practical Catholicity" came up quite a bit in the records of both groups of Daughters prior to the Council, and it undergirded their understanding of the Catholic woman's duty. To be "practical" in your Catholicism was to create and uphold the scaffolding that kept a family rooted in the faith. A woman attuned to her duty would fill her home with Catholic devotional objects, insist on family prayer over and above blessings at meals. She would make sure her family went to church and received the sacraments, and most important that her children were educated in the faith. Presumably a Junior Daughter demonstrated her "practical" sense of the faith by her avid participation in religious education and her mastery of devotional practices. Next on the list we find "dependability and cooperation," further demonstrating the need for Catholic women to provide the firm, if passive, foundation of the faith. We might also hazard a guess that a group prizing "personality" over academic honors did not hope to promote critical, questioning leaders. The D of I was not alone in their use of the Juniors to inculcate in their young women the sense of duty they themselves valued. The CDA's Juniors took the prosaic "Be Useful" for their motto.[27]

Anna Ballard reiterated several of these themes in "The Laity—A Reservoir of Catholic Strength," an essay for the CDA newsletter in 1963. The title suggests the laity's pre–Vatican II importance: solidity. She opened with a quote from John Tracy Ellis that hinted at the laity's changing role, but Ballard's response was merely to say that the CDA was well aware of how significant laypeople were. We have "cooperated with spiritual leaders and will continue to cooperate in every way possible in the work of the church," she said. But "cooperation" signaled Catholic Action, not an independent laity. Ballard went on to say that CDA was "an organization which is now and ever has been doing something real and concrete in the work of the Church." Again, her essay highlights the dependable, reliable, and passive, a reservoir upon which clerics might draw for help. But the *Decree on the Apostolate of the Laity* would demand much more: an educated and independent laity empowered to do the work of the church in the world. And this included women.[28]

By 1965, this message began to seep into the Daughters' consciousness, inviting them to begin a process of transformation. "The time has passed when we can be satisfied to have women just as pew sitters," a bishop was quoted as saying in the CDA newsletter. "We must take their womanly existence seriously." This entailed encouraging women to "develop initiatives of their own. . . . The Church has barely started to tap these wonderful resources dormant in women." Later that year, the same newsletter featured an excerpt from a speech by Pope Paul VI on the new liturgy. Whoever chose this excerpt knew her audience well. It begins with an acknowledgment from the Holy Father: "It is in the nature of a practical as well as of a spiritual reform of set religious habits, piously observed, to cause some agitation, not always pleasant to everyone." A Daughter might think, "Yes, he understands how hard this is for me." But Paul VI intended to coax such Catholics away from what was safe. He told them not to expect "that after a while we shall again become quiet and devoted or lazy as of old." "No," he said, "the new order will have to be different and will have to prevent and shake the passivity of the faithful." What a shock to see these two words—"quiet" and "devoted"—linked to the word "lazy." Suddenly practical Catholicity came to signal complacency and stagnation.[29]

The Daughters had always viewed themselves as strong, but the Council required a new kind of strength, the courage to risk becoming something new, to be shaken up. This was not in their wheelhouse, and if renewal was going to be effective, they needed to be taught that they were both ready for change, and that they could be excited about it. As a Catholic Daughter said to the membership in 1966, "THE FACT IS THAT TO DO ANYTHING IN THE WORLD WORTH DOING WE MUST NOT STAND BACK SHIVER-ING AND THINKING OF THE COLD AND DANGER BUT JUMP IN AND SCRAMBLE THROUGH AS WELL AS WE CAN."[30]

The CDA's response to the introduction of women into the Council is also instructive on this point. At the opening of the Council's third session in 1964, a handful of Catholic women auditors were allowed to attend the pro-ceedings for the first time. The fifteen women were not allowed to speak in the assembly and were confined to their own section and even their own cof-fee bar, although some were invited to contribute to several of the documents in process, and some of these contributions were significant. An account by Sister Mary Luke Tobin, SL, an American auditor, conceded that "although we did not create a countervailing current turning around the attitude toward women, our presence was noticed immediately by the press, and at least a few bishops began to see the problems more clearly."[31]

The arrival of women at the Council provoked a range of reactions in American laywomen, from the Catholic feminists who used it as an opportu-nity to call the hierarchy on its blatant sexism, to the more moderate NCCW which qualified its obvious pleasure with a brief "It's about time." As we saw in chapter 3, the occasion even prompted the editors of *Marriage* magazine to publish their first pro–women's rights editorial. The CDA, in contrast, seemed not in the least disgruntled, only awestruck. Newsletter editor Phi-lomena Kerwin remarked, "This is the beginning of something that was unheard of years ago. . . . In order to begin to comprehend the wonders of the age in which we are living we need to remind ourselves that nothing like this has happened since the days of the Apostles. . . . Since the coming to the papal throne of that astonishing personage known as John XXIII we have been accustomed to marvels. Women being seated in the Council Hall with the Council Fathers is a measure of the tremendous changes which are tak-ing place in the Church." More than anything, Kerwin seemed gobsmacked as she tried to express her reaction to the "marvels" she was witnessing.

Far from being bitter at the delay, Kerwin responds like a loyal daughter, profoundly grateful to the fathers for their willingness to bring women to the table at all. One senses, too, her excitement at the "tremendous changes" on the horizon.[32]

Some members were happy to acknowledge women's abilities beyond traditional gender roles. As early as 1961, a letter to the editor commenting on the Daughters of Isabella's new magazine declared that Catholic women were evolving, and the organization could reflect those changes. "We need a magazine for the modern Catholic woman with an international scope," Miss Maria Fairfax argued. "Today's Catholic women are active, intelligent people living within the sphere of this twentieth century. They realize the needs of the time and devote themselves to fulfilling them." These sentiments became more frequent by the mid-1960s as the effects of the Council began to be felt. In 1966, D of I member Patricia Adams remarked, "Obviously, the barnacles of past tradition that impede progress must be scraped from our structure; apathy among our members must be replaced with a burning desire for each to do her part in making the Church what Christ intended it to be—an organization attuned to the needs of today's people and problems."[33]

Both of these passages link inspiration to duty, anchoring a transformed female identity in new works of charity. But unlike the past, the Daughters were now told that before they could engage in charitable work they must educate themselves so they might rely more on their own intelligence and judgment. What a change from Bishop Waters's insistence in 1962 that the Daughters let the Blessed Mother think for them. Father William Connare brought to the 1964 CDA conference the gentle message that the Daughters needed to train themselves for a new kind of charity. "This is the age of the laity," he said. "This is the age when you must have an intelligent, a trained and a devoted laity if your apostolate is to continue. . . . You know the grand work that you've been doing these years will have to continue . . . but unless we have women in the years to come who understand the social doctrine of the Church and teach it, we're lost." To ask the Daughters to serve as intelligent experts, particularly on Catholic social teaching, was novel to say the least.[34] Daughters of both groups were frequently exhorted to engage in serious study. Primarily, this involved reading the Council documents, but both groups' publications featured suggested reading lists and occasional reviews of prominent theological works of the day.

Others suggested that the Daughters' new duty was to transform themselves as individuals, through not just education but also personal spiritual renewal. The members were told on numerous occasions that this personal renewal should originate in a commitment to love more deeply. "Our organization must be renewed through a renewal of ourselves that springs from a single source, *love*, which finds expression in a renewed turning to man. This is our great vocation," explained the D of I's supreme regent in 1967. Mother Mary Hennessey went so far as to suggest that Vatican II as a whole was best understood as a call to love more deeply, telling the CDA in 1968 that "the Church in its renewal is essentially trying to carry on a revolution of love and service."[35]

The chaplain head of the CDA's "Share the Faith" (Evangelization) department also took love as his theme, noting how it could lead laywomen outward into the world. "We have to learn how to love right here, and our love must be a large love, a great love, an all-embracing love." Once again, we hear the CDA in the mid-1960s called to expansiveness. If love was practiced on this scale it would first transform the organization: "There won't be any cliques; there won't be any exclusive small groups; there won't be any talk which can belittle or hurt others." But the ultimate goal was Christian witness to the world, he said. "From the Court, we will spread [love] into our parishes, into our diocese, into the whole country and the world."[36]

There is a fine line between charity and love, of course, and many Daughters would certainly argue that their familiar acts of charity *were* expressions of love. In 1964, Supreme Regent Anna K. Buckley urged members to increase the numbers of women who supported the missions, an extremely popular activity in CDA courts. "Such publicity is best obtained through vestment making and mission exhibits," she noted, "for the tangible evidence of the work of loving hearts and hands always inspires love for the missions." To express your love of God, church, and neighbor in the past you performed a concrete service in your home or court. You can almost hear a Daughter asking, "Why isn't the work of my hands enough anymore?" But such work was now suspected of causing insularity and complacency. A laywoman speaker at the 1968 convention concluded that service in isolation was insufficient. A modern woman does not stay in her home to bake bread for the hungry, she insisted, but leaves "the protective middle class security of her own world" to go into the streets to meet the hungry person firsthand.[37]

So the first messages the Daughters received about women's changing duties in the age of renewal were (a) that a Daughter should shift from a posture of defense against the modern world to a posture of openness and enthusiasm, (b) that being a pew sitter was no longer sufficient, (c) that "practical Catholicism" no longer strengthened the faith as much as it upheld values now viewed as suspect, (d) that Daughters should be not passive and obedient but educated and intelligent, (e) that good Catholic women did not love deeply enough, and (f) that familiar acts of charity fostered a ghetto mentality in Catholic women and did not go to the heart of the world's needs.

When historians write of the laity in the Vatican II transition, much of the focus is on changes to liturgy and prayer. *Sacrosanctum Concilium*, the document that transformed the liturgy, demands historical attention because its effects were so dramatic, changing as it did the central act of worship for all Catholics and demanding their deliberate participation. But the Daughters, surprisingly, do not talk about the liturgical changes very much; such changes were noted with interest and readily accepted. True to form, the hierarchy gave the Daughters a directive and they conformed to it. But the changes noted in the preceding paragraph were so much harder to grasp, process, and accept, first and foremost because no single document spelled out such expectations. There was no *Decree on Woman in the Modern World*. Who and what were they to believe?

The Daughters made a good faith effort, engaging in the laywoman project perhaps more reluctantly than other Catholic organizational women. In the thick of the messages flying about their ears, most of which were a challenge to their well-established and beloved worldview, both organizations made a conscious effort to listen and weigh what was being asked of them. Not only did they encourage their conference speakers to help explain the Council to them, but they also used their publications as means of educating their constituencies. Keep in mind that they need not have done this; they could easily have continued with pictures of church suppers and diatribes against communism and smut (which still appeared, but with less prominence and frequency). Even on the issue of feminism, which the organizations found deeply troubling (although we do not know if this was true of all members), the Daughters made an attempt to engage some of the ideas gaining traction in the larger culture.

Response to feminism varied among the various stakeholders in the organizations. The chaplains seemed most eager to deaden the appeal of feminism by arguing that in the Catholic Church it was unnecessary. But a few other female speakers and authors tried to formulate a vision of change for Catholic women that would challenge them, improve their lives, and empower them, without asking them to relinquish complementarity or to criticize the church as unjust. It's not feminism, but it does help explain the gradual changes that traditional-minded Catholic laywomen made through the 1960s.

As might be expected, the chaplains were keen to contribute to this conversation. Chaplains frequently took as their theme "the Nature of Woman" in a variety of guises. Generally, the priest would reiterate woman's call to receptivity, her aptitude for small-picture detail work, the importance of motherhood, the example of the Blessed Mother, and woman's role in fostering the faith of others. Again, such outlandishly essentialist articles were not uncommon in the Daughters' literature, and we need not go into them in detail.

Of more interest are the articles and speeches that changed subtly in the face of feminism, tweaking their messages to address women who might be inclined to sympathize with what they were hearing outside of their courts and circles. These pieces often conceded that women should be highly valued and afforded dignity, but they asserted that the church already did that, and better than anyone else. "Ahistorical" and "revisionist" do not begin to cover the egregious falsehoods several of the chaplains were trying to pass off as historical fact to the Daughters in an effort to counteract feminism. At least four different chaplains claimed that the Catholic Church was responsible for bringing about women's equality. The argument claimed that conditions for women were brutal under paganism. "Taking the world at large," State Chaplain Joseph Beatty explained, "before Christ, woman was in a condition of unspeakable degradation—unspeakable, indeed, for I have not dared tell half of it." Not only was she used as chattel, but she "was deemed unworthy of moral consideration." The woman of ancient Israel had it no better, according to Vincent Waters: "Her role was to work, to obey her husband, to bear children, and to please."[38]

But "into such a world entered Christ the God-Man, the Redeemer, His Person, His teaching, His truth, His church, His example changed the whole status of women. *No greater change is found in the Social History of the World than that brought about by Christ and His Church in the status of women.*" Waters then observed that "women are seen as man's equal" in the New Testament. Waters took care to demonstrate that while Christ may have liberated all women, he was no scary feminist: "Christ did not, indeed like a wild revolutionary, attempt to change immediately all the customs of the ancient world." Instead he established the principles that would "gradually" lead to her emancipation, and "the popes . . . have continued the teaching of the Church on the Status of Women." In following this line of argument, Waters was taking his cue from the Council fathers themselves. In their 1965 message to the women of the world on the Feast of the Immaculate Conception, the Council said, "the Church is proud to have glorified and liberated women and, in the course of the centuries, in diversity of characters, to have brought into relief her basic equality with man."[39]

Let's begin with what might be lost in the reaction to such hyperbole: Waters is affirming women's equality. He says so quite plainly. But his understanding of "equality" or "liberation" was quite different from that of a feminist in 1966. He meant that Christ affirmed women's essential dignity, and that he made them equal partners in the work of salvation. As for the church, Waters and the other chaplains cited how it elevated the Blessed Mother to exalted status as evidence for how it liberated women.

The idea that the Catholic Church has promoted women's equality throughout its history is patently absurd, but to the chaplains, the church seemed a force for women's ultimate freedom. Vincent Waters honestly believed that he was promoting equality for women. He cited Galatians 3:28 ("In Christ there is neither male nor female"); he noted the Council's call for women to be more active in the church's apostolate. But "equal" to Waters meant "special and different." Glorification of woman's role was meant to substitute for self-determination, which was not possible for women under this interpretation of Catholic cosmology. Anyone who can say "a woman's function, a woman's way, a woman's natural bent is Motherhood," has not the vaguest understanding of why a woman might need or want to be liberated. We might also question Waters's commitment to equality when he spoke approvingly of the gradual, that is, millennia-long, approach to implementing women's rights.[40]

The chaplains did provide evidence for the church's version of women's liberation. Vincent Waters cited complementarity, the concept most deplored by Catholic feminists, as an equalizing force. In recognizing women's essential (and eternal) difference, the church gave women special, very weighty, responsibilities. These included motherhood, the salvation of the family, and the work of peace. Joseph Beatty did his best to make women's work in the church seem more important. They didn't just teach Confraternity of Christian Doctrine (CCD), they were "the collaborators of Providence in the education of peoples." The everyday laywoman didn't just raise her children in the faith, she was "the genetrix of saints." Not only that, but Beatty tried to elevate women's work to the level of ministry. "She is truly the priestess of the home," he claimed. She does "a veritable priestly work."[41]

But these articles, however affirming of women and their worth, if not their rights, carried warnings as well. Hubert Newell told the CDA that the affirmation of women's rights "challenges our interest and merits our support" as long as everyone interprets equality in such a way that "will enable woman and not serve as a pretext to lower her to a position that might be degrading. . . . To speak of equality in such matters is a hoax that can ruin woman, and spiritually impoverish the world." If women were fooled into leaving their work to chase equality, the consequences would be dire. They must accept their role, Vincent Waters claimed, so "that the important human values may not be lost."[42]

Vincent Waters ended his 1966 sermon on women's equality with the idea that women owed the church their gratitude for the gifts of equality they had been given. "Christ saved you from slavery," he said. "The Popes of our time challenge you. The Vatican Council challenges you to be real Daughters of the Church, to be real Children of Mary, to be real Catholic Daughters of America." In other words, the challenge issued by the Council fathers to women was to remain as they were in changing times for the good of the world; being a "real" Catholic Daughter should be freedom enough.[43]

Of the commentaries on women's rights by women, I found only three documents that forwarded anything approaching a feminist argument. One appeared in the D of I newsletter, and two were delivered at CDA conferences (one was a keynote address, albeit by a non-Daughter). Needless to say, this sample is not sufficiently representative to prove anything about the Daughters' views of feminism. The lack of documents, and the nature of the feminism they express, suggests to me that feminism was a minority opinion within the organizations, although we cannot know how many individual members espoused feminist ideas. Nevertheless, this smattering of essays does suggest which questions Daughters seemed to be asking about their changing roles as women.

In her 1962 essay "This Is a Woman's World," Lillian Kennedy asked explicitly, "Has her role changed? Or has the concept of 'dependence' merely been broadened to meet with the demands of this twentieth century?" This set up her main point, that modern Catholic women were not interested in returning to a traditional state of dependence. She acknowledged that the Daughters viewed feminism as suspect: "There has been much senseless jargon and fussiness about . . . the feminist movements, about suffrage or woman's rights and equality with men, call it what you will." But she pointed out the positive results saying, "Yet when the chaff has been sifted away woman has emerged as an independent being."[44]

It would be quite easy to lose her larger point in the essentialist themes that follow. Kennedy asserts a familiar notion of woman's difference, claiming that woman is the great moral force in the world. "[Man's] part is to fashion the world," she says, "hers, to maintain the moral standards thereof."

Kennedy's rhetoric does not sanction female passivity, but it does suggest that men come first: "Her function is to beckon man ever forward to great moral achievement, nor should she allow him to rest in aught other than the highest he is capable of."[45]

Kennedy does not question woman's role so much as she challenges how women should go about claiming it: "For centuries, nothing perhaps so hampered the proper development of woman as the exaggerated notion of her dependence on the man." Instead, she is "qualified to be man's independent ally and co-worker." Difference, then, is used as an argument to defend women's autonomy. A similar theme can be found in the NCCW's modest feminism in the same era. What woman needed, Kennedy wrote, was, first, self-reliance and strong character to assert herself enough to get her work done in the world without interference. Second, she needed to unite with other women for solidarity and support. Thus, essentialism is tempered by the slightest hint of feminism, as in Kennedy's closing paragraph: "The Catholic woman of today attains her queenly sovereignty by uniting . . . all the prerogatives of woman. It is for us to pursue and encourage whatever tends to compass the realization of a strong, self-dependent, intellectual, and loyal womanhood."[46]

Mother Mary Hennessey also delivered an essentialist message, this time to the CDA, but of a more modern stripe, and accompanied by an actual feminist critique. "Clearly the Church does not use the full potential of the Catholic woman, lay or religious," she remarked, citing a recent article from the progressive magazine the *Critic*. Moreover, Catholic women were restricted "by the canon law with its concept of women at least two centuries behind the times. . . . These iniquities must change." This type of language, quite rare for the Daughters, must have provoked some conversation at the 1966 convention. However, Hennessey's feminism—explicitly linked to her identity as a new nun—was tempered considerably by what is an essentialist, but not particularly traditionalist, argument.

Hennessey believed that the ultimate takeaway from Vatican II was that the people of God needed a more feminine orientation. She remarked early in the talk that women religious had lost their bearings long ago by practicing "traditionalism—rigidity—formalism—authoritarianism—and suspicious separatism," all of which she considered to be masculine characteristics. We "lost what was truly feminine and took on what was the legalistic, almost militaristic ways of men." She said her fellow sisters had discovered the call back to personal contact and service through the teachings of the Council, and urged the Daughters to do the same. She believed that "the more fully a woman is a woman the more whole she will make the Church and the world." Is this essentialist? Certainly. But it is also an admission that the church needs to be reformed and at women's instigation, an alien thought for many of the loyal Daughters.[47]

The third document was delivered as the 1968 convention banquet keynote by a laywoman who was not a Daughter. As any outside speaker would, Mrs. Arthur L. Zepf opened by heaping praise upon the CDA for the charitable work it sponsored abroad. Zepf herself served extensively abroad as an international aid worker. She used her talk, though, to help the CDA membership define the changed nature of the modern Catholic woman. Before she even began to describe this figure, Zepf noted how out of touch the hierarchy was. "Is the Church talking to [the modern woman]? or perhaps better yet, does the Church know her well enough to know how to talk to her? . . . The Church is talking to our great-grandmothers." Zepf structured her address around ten words that defined the modern Catholic woman. Among them was "knowledgeable," under which heading she asserted that women were well-educated and capable and should not be bound "with ironing boards, playpens and clotheslines." She said that the song "Don't Fence Me In" was the new woman's theme. "For I know more—and I care about more."[48]

Zepf also noted that women were now mature enough to take responsibility for their own actions. As a case in point, she noted the co-eds now in jail for protest actions. "Appalled though some of us might be," she noted, "we need not agree with [a female student's] protest . . . to recognize a 'new Woman' no longer concerned about sanctuary in the sorority of the 'fair sex.'" Most of all, she said, the new Catholic woman was "free." Here she openly criticized the hierarchy that favored "legalism" and passing "directives in favor of the institutional Church" instead of the people of God. She also offered a very mild criticism of pastors, those most beloved figures for the Catholic Daughters: "No more is she the woman who will limit her parish concern to areas her pastor will approve for feminine consideration." Instead, she wants to meet the needs of the world with openness and courage, and without limitation. And, Zepf adds, she meets them as a woman, which includes a natural inclination to seek peace and guard human life.[49]

Although there is some additional evidence of feminism among individual members, particularly in the D of I, its presence was not broadly felt. What we can say of the few articles and speeches discussed above is that they show the Daughters displaying a willingness to hear ideas that might have been uncomfortable for many. They also demonstrate on what terms the

Daughters were willing to engage with feminist ideas. Unlike the chaplains, women who discussed feminism were much more sympathetic to the need for change, and were freer in naming contemporary problems for women. None of these women speakers claimed the church was the source of women's equality. Another stipulation seemed to be that essentialism be reaffirmed despite the need for change. The Daughters heard a feminist message, set against the backdrop of the Council, that called for greater autonomy for women without fundamentally changing their roles.

TRYING ON THE SPIRIT OF VATICAN II

In 1966, Patricia Adams gave a talk to the Annual Congress of Religious Education that revealed the questions worrying the Daughters of Isabella at the beginning of the Vatican II transition. In the notes of her talk, the following sentence is isolated and all in caps: "CAN THE DAUGHTERS OF ISABELLA AND OTHER CATHOLIC ORGANIZATIONS FACE THE PROBLEMS OF CHRISTIAN MATURITY?" She says this central question resulted from a time of soul-searching in the organization. In 1965, "we were in the throes of evaluating the past, revamping our structure while looking to the future." Adams insisted that they were ready to grow up, that "our objective is *not* to be an end unto ourselves" but a force for good in an increasingly troubled world. According to Adams, the second question driving the Daughters in the age of renewal was continued relevance. Were the large Catholic laywomen's organizations needed anymore? Could they do the work that needed doing? She concluded that yes, they were needed more than ever. "Do we have the right to consider ourselves obsolete during this painful time of rejuvenation in our Catholic Church; dare we ignore our commission of being Prophetic People?"[50]

How aptly she phrased it: the "painful time of rejuvenation." What was meant to be a moment of energy and unity could at the same time cause great discomfort. In the words of a chaplain, developing a new program wouldn't be easy: "It is the way of the crucified." This section explores the concrete actions both organizations took to respond to Vatican II. These steps move beyond rhetoric and indicate what each group was able to accomplish in the implementation phase after the Council. But while the groups did make an effort to change themselves, by the turn of the 1970s the Daughters entered a period of retrenchment. Suspicions that renewal had gone too far, coupled with alarming developments in the larger culture, led the Daughters to the conclusion that a defensive posture did, in fact, suit their nature and their work best. Despite steeply declining numbers (or perhaps because of them), the Daughters began to back away from the spirit of Vatican II.[51]

But first, let's see what changes they chose to implement. Both organizations opted to simplify their rituals and the trappings of office in a direct response to Vatican II. This was the "scraping away [of] the barnacles of tradition" that Patricia Adams referred to in her CCD address. Both groups dropped the title *Supreme* for officers and chaplains in the 1960s, replacing it with *National*. Members proposed the change in the CDA as early as 1964, in order "to be in line with the updating that the Second Vatican Council is calling for in the Church." At that early date the supreme regent shrewdly responded, "As far as the updating of it in order to be in line with what the Second Vatican Council is calling for, I can't see that it has any relation there because there's been no change in the titles of the clergy." Not having seen any evidence of the promised collegiality among the hierarchy, she asked that the motion be voted down (although it passed a few years later). The Keokuk, Iowa, Circle of the D of I also cited Vatican II as a reason for simplifying its organization. A resolution to the 1966 convention read, "Be it resolved: that we . . . feel that since our Holy Mother the Church is dispensing with many 'outdated' and 'outmoded' ceremonies and bringing our Faith 'closer' to us all as individuals, that 'NOW' is also the time for the D of I to 'DELETE' the word 'SECRET' from our Constitution. Let us instead, open our meetings to *ALL* good Catholic women members of the Holy Mother Church. Thus, we would be 'OBEYING' the order of His Holiness Pope Paul by 'NOT' discriminating against others." The Isabellans had no trouble believing that the pope had their back on this issue. Such changes, though minor, illustrate that the membership was trying to adapt in the wake of the Council.[52]

Of more substance were changes in how the courts and circles functioned on the local level. Both groups attempted to minimize language and rituals that served to target particular members for undue scrutiny or humiliation. The D of I eliminated a ritual that a member had to perform if she arrived late or left a meeting early (which was noted to be highly embarrassing and time-consuming).[53] Moreover, the CDA voted in 1967 to change the term *expelled members* to *dismissed members*, perhaps softening the harshness of such an action. In 1964 the CDA eliminated its "investigating committees," which had previously determined a candidate's suitability for membership. We might not call this a huge step forward, as the organization decided that it was sufficient to have a priest's signature attesting to the candidate's character.

When it came to accepting the Council, the Daughters seemed most eager to accept liturgical change. Both organizations followed liturgical developments carefully. Even before the Council, both regularly sent delegates to the annual "North American Liturgical Week" meetings sponsored by the Liturgical Conference, and had the women report back to the membership. At these events, the Daughters heard cutting-edge theology, rubbed elbows with scholars and liturgists, and most important, participated in the experimental liturgies celebrated by those who wished to enliven and deepen Catholics' experience of worship well before the Council was even contemplated. *America* magazine called the 1962 Liturgical Week "one of the most important events in the life of the Church in North America." The CDA's delegates that year did not report back much of import, noting only that members served as "hostesses" for the event, staffing the information desk and performing "behind the scenes" work. But as the 1960s advanced, delegates' reports increased their detail and enthusiasm.[54]

CDA supreme secretary Mary Kanane attended the 1964 conference and noted that each day's highlight was the community Mass. Such masses demonstrated active participation, the priest facing the congregation, and the distribution of communion at stations throughout the hall. Kanane also participated in a "Mass of Tomorrow" spoken in the vernacular. Kanane took the time to note that studying the liturgy was not about rules and rubrics, "such accidentals as the cut of a sacred vestment" for example. Instead, Catholics should study liturgy "in its theological, historical, spiritual, pastoral and juridical aspects." Kanane may have thought this message particularly suited to the Daughters, who naturally inclined toward formalism and rule enforcement. Daughter of Isabella Helen Bennett attended the 1967 Liturgical Week, which she described as "a happening." She too reported positively on a "Mass of the Future," telling the D of I membership that participating in liturgy opened people to the Holy Spirit. Only then could the message of the Council be carried out "to create a new image. It is only by experimenting that this goal can be achieved."[55]

True to form, when leaders urged their memberships to participate more fully in the mass, these calls were usually prefaced with a comment that a member of the hierarchy approved of it. In 1971 Kanane urged the membership to pass a motion calling for women to offer their services as lectors (this was the first year women were allowed to serve as lectors, but only when a qualified layman was unavailable, and only if she stood outside the sanctuary gates). Kanane assured the women that "Bishop Bernard Flanagan was in favor," so there could be no objection.[56]

Faithful Daughters

Intriguingly, the CDA attempted to place at least one of its own rituals within a liturgical context. In 1973, the organization decided to create a new ritual for the installation of court-level officers that would take place within a parish's Sunday Mass. They did so at the prompting of the state court in Kentucky that first created the ritual. Two reasons were given for such an innovation. The first mention of this ritual explained that "as there are few times a woman has the privilege to approach a priest for his special blessing for herself, this enhances the office as well as the image of the office." This statement, hidden in the minutes of an annual board meeting, is touching in its simple request. The Daughters prided themselves on selflessness throughout their history, selflessness and often self-effacement. When was a laywoman invited before the congregation for a special blessing? At her wedding perhaps, or the christenings of her children. But even here, she was recognized as wife or mother, not for her own leadership and achievement. And what of single laywomen, who were likely never to receive such a recognition at all? Inserting the installation of officers into a liturgical setting shows that these women viewed their work and themselves as worthy of recognition by the church in the heart of its worship, not simply as an extracurricular activity of the parish hall.

Later in the discussion, someone from the ritual committee explained that "the object here is to emphasize the priesthood of the laity by doing the installation by a priest." Members of the board warned that some priests would object. In that case, could an officer perform the ceremony in the Mass? They decided that in such a case, it was better left out of the Mass as "the whole concept of the priesthood of the laity and the consecration and dedication of these individuals to the good of the Church is lost if the priest does not give the charges." Even though the national chaplain offered an imprimatur, that is, his official permission to perform such a ritual in the Mass, the board suspected that priests might still refuse these laywomen their recognition as leaders of the church and the blessing of their work by their communities.[57]

Other changes were prompted by both Vatican II and the cultural shifts that were becoming impossible to ignore. Both sets of Daughters expressed increasing fear for their Juniors in the 1960s, not only because membership was dropping but also because they recognized that their approaches were simply not connecting with the youth of the era. The Daughters seemed to make a concerted effort to change how they viewed their young women, deemphasizing "practical" Catholicity and highlighting individuality. In fact, this development may have been the Daughters' only concession to the growing feminist movement, even though it was not mentioned as such explicitly.

In 1964, a Miss Roberts spoke at a rather optimistically titled conference session on the Junior CDA, "Our Potentials—Limitless," but her optimism was predicated on transforming the organization. "We must aim not to keep up with the modern times but [stay] ahead of them," she said. "It is not by rules and regulations that girls become fine leaders, but by being loved and treated justly, and even being given a sense of their own individual worth." Bishop William Connare took this a step further, advising would-be counselors of the Juniors to let the young women speak their minds, even if it meant criticizing the church. As we know, this went completely against the grain for long-time Daughters. But, Connare insisted, "the worst thing in the world is to sit upon the critics of the Church. Let our young people criticize ourselves, even the Senior program. Listen, just listen, that's all, and encourage them to develop their own ideas."[58]

Finally, in 1971 the D of I sent a representative to a meeting about the Marian Medal, an award presented to qualified members of the Junior CDA and Junior D of I, as well as to Catholic Girl Scouts and Campfire Girls. All present recognized that the award was terribly outdated, with some going so far as to suggest that they should "soft-pedal" Mary so they might attract more girls. The D of I representative could not go this far, but she did agree that the focus of the award should recognize a modern Catholic girl's knowledge of the faith. Far from the "practical" model, this committee recommended a program that emphasized theological training, ecumenism, "in-depth study of liturgy," and the discussion of ethical matters such as "drugs, women's liberation, population explosion, etc." The main goal, she suggested, "would be to inspire and motivate girls to go beyond the ordinary." Perhaps looking at their young women inspired the Daughters to embrace some measure of change, if not for themselves, then for the women they feared would soon be walking away.[59]

THE WINDOW CLOSES

The largest attempt to change the organizations in light of Vatican II was the CDA's "Sevenfold Program." As early as 1966, CDA leaders and members began urging the group to make major changes to its "program," which represented not only what ideas and works the group wished to promote but also how its officers and staff would be organized to reach the CDA's goals. This was no small undertaking. Ultimately the Sevenfold Program was unsuccessful, revealing—from its inception to its final analysis—how uneasy the CDA became with renewal by the turn of the 1970s.

The 1966 convention focused very heavily on the implementation of the Council, featuring sessions such as "The Renewed Church," "The Study of Vatican II Decrees," and even "New Opportunities for Catholic Women." At this first conference after the close of the Council, the CDA passed a new "Statement of Principles" at the behest of Supreme Regent Margaret Buckley. This list balanced the desire to address renewal with the need to honor the Daughters' traditional commitments. The Daughters set forth eight principles, beginning with a commitment to study the Council documents and Catholic social teaching, and a pledge to participate in the new liturgy. The CDA then upheld its commitments to ecumenism, community service, and civil rights, as well as reaffirming decency in dress, and support of the president's agenda in Vietnam. Finally, the Daughters voted unanimously that "our program be UPDATED in accordance with the directives handed down by Vatican II especially as they apply to the laity." As if to emphasize the group's openness, the conference edition of *News and Notes* featured a quotation from the progressive archbishop Paul Hallinan: "There is no earthly way we can live in the past except in a museum. The Catholic Church is not a museum—it is a living community." But in keeping with its split sensibility, Chaplain Connare called for a change of program that same year that could indeed have come out of a museum. "You must help form a program which can make you the effective and imaginative wives and mothers of the next decade," he wrote. But still, the call for change was in the air.[60]

Despite the building momentum, the new, now "national" regent Anna Ballard seemed reluctant to pursue a new program. In her first report to the national board in early 1967, Ballard suggested that the CDA did not require fundamental change. "Many suggestions have been received recommending and I quote 'that the program by updated.' Members . . . know full well that in accordance with requests such recommendations were filed, but no actions were taken." She went on to say that everyone knew that change could be a good thing, but that the CDA from its inception had embodied the spirit of unity and charity and had cooperated with its spiritual leaders.[61] Finally, she made a remarkably candid statement, revealing her position on renewal. She remarked, "Vatican Council II in the decree on the Apostolate of the Laity urges Christians to 'become involved' in the work of the Church. The Catholic Daughters of America have been 'involved' through the years and no doubt you remember the message of our National Chaplain, Bishop Vincent S. Waters, given more than ten years ago, when he said 'That the holy Father,

Pope Pius XII, is now asking the Catholic women of the World to do what the Catholic Daughters have been doing [for] close to fifty years." She boiled Vatican II down to two words—"become involved"—and then insisted that the CDA had always been involved. Moreover, she cited two male authorities in one sentence to affirm her belief that the Daughters need not change anything. If Pius XII and Bishop Waters thought we do good work, why should we change? At the end of her report she conceded that the organization might need to change but only "to meet the demands of the present period, for we know these are challenging times."[62]

That spring, Ballard wrote a piece for the new CDA *News* titled "National Regent Stresses Role of Women in the Apostolate of the Laity Movement." But the gist of the piece was to say that the program was fine as it was. She argued that "the Catholic Daughters are fortunate in having a well-rounded program with various facets to meet the challenges of the ecumenical age." She added a shot of Marian piety to emphasize her turn to the past: "The role of women is great, but to fill it, we have the Model of all Women, the Queen of Heaven as an example." Ballard attended her first convention in 1929 as Massachusetts state treasurer, and her membership predated that. Reportedly, she was "an expert on ritual," entrenched in the day-to-day workings of the organization and its hierarchy. Her reluctance to make a dramatic break with the past is understandable.[63]

But Ballard must not have been convincing, because the national board did move forward with a new program, which it revealed to the membership at the national conference in late 1968. By this time, Ballard had been replaced as national regent by Anna Baxter. Baxter was at that time the longest-serving officer in the CDA, having begun her tenure in 1925. At least outwardly, she supported renewal, saying in 1970 that "as members of a pilgrim Church, we are charged for a brief moment in history with a precious trust—the renewal of our organization and the building of the new program." But like Ballard before her, Baxter was more cautious behind closed doors.[64]

In early 1969, soon after her election, she wrote a report for the national board in which she too spoke frankly about the changes the church required of them. In that report she used the telling phrase "the ordeal of change, of renewal," hinting at what such shifts cost an organization so deeply rooted as the CDA. She referred in this report to a crisis, but not one of faith. Rather, she warned that the "crisis of loyalty" had "reached a new peak." Her hope was that in the midst of this crisis the CDA would "be found true and trusted." She went on to say that the organization must use all of its resources to promote loyalty and expand membership: "In this age when traditions are being challenged, we are faced with the greatest test of our leadership throughout all jurisdictions in the history of the Order." (The context of the larger document suggests that the crisis she refers to is the backlash against *Humanae Vitae*, Pope Paul VI's birth-control encyclical, promulgated six months earlier.) Her language in this report does not suggest a woman eager to transform her organization to conform to a nebulous progressive spirit of renewal. This is a woman diving back behind the bunker wall.[65]

Yet the Sevenfold Program was rolled out in 1969. Various officers introduced each section of it to the membership in the newsletter. You can already sense the limited scope of the program change when you read that the key word the designers chose for the program was *involvement*. This term seems rather passive, even for the Daughters. We should not jump to the conclusion that merely showing up was sufficient for the CDA. The program outlined a vast array of opportunities for service, and the Daughters expected everyone to do their part. But what we do not see is a significant change in the nature of that service, or its conception. Did the new program really reflect the spirit of the Council?

Each of the program's seven aspects featured involvement of some kind, from "Personal Involvement" to "Ecumenical Involvement" to "Involvement of Youth." Many of the women chosen to introduce these initiatives leaned traditionalist. Under "Personal Involvement," members were told that the CDA offered many opportunities to uphold "His Divine Truth, Justice, and Order in human affairs." The person who explained "Civic Involvement" described the United States as "the dwelling place of ideals and principles" and urged members to promote the "soul of America." The only section that seemed substantially affected by the Council was "Social Involvement," whose author stressed the creation of personal relationships with the poor (not just the writing of checks), and direct knowledge of social issues.

In the end, the Sevenfold Program was ineffectual. Even the CDA's official history, a glowing account of the group's past, had trouble making the case that it succeeded. After noting that the program was "imbued with the Spirit of Vatican II," the author concedes that "in the end [Baxter's] program was more a refocusing of the many works and services rather than something entirely new." By 1973, National Chaplain Bernard Flanagan expressed his opinion that "up to this point we are not really implementing the Sevenfold Program. It has been set down on paper, but not carried out as effectively as it might be." Moreover, he stated bluntly, the various aspects of the program required "expertise that you don't have." (Again—only the fathers were permitted to be so honest about the Daughters' failings). At the following year's board meeting, the national regent conceded that not only was the program not widely implemented, but that not enough courts were truly familiar with it.[66]

At this point, the CDA and the D of I diverge for a time. In the late 1960s and early 1970s, the D of I found in its regents a series of women deeply committed to renewal. This did not make them less conservative in outlook, but they did demonstrate more genuine openness to change in the church, and at times had to placate a more traditional membership. Historian Carol Dorr Clement notes that the changes the D of I promoted in the area of women's roles may have been small, but they were meaningful. For example, Dorr argues that "Isabellans often found it difficult to speak in public. For years they believed that they were to be anonymous and humble in their charitable actions." Yet living through the 1960s and 1970s taught them to be "a clear sign of the charity of Christ in the world." Isabellans became more courageous, more autonomous, and more willing to speak about their works of charity to the people around them. In 1974, National Regent Marie Heyer wrote eloquently about how the D of I should view change: "All life, we know, is always in a state of flux. We realize that to enjoy dignity and the rich essence of human living, we must ourselves participate intellectually in the changing life of today. We must avoid negative attitudes. We must orient ourselves toward positive and fundamental principles."[67]

Yet the times seemed to conspire against the Daughters of both groups. Membership began to recede in both organizations as members aged and the new women of the post–Vatican II era declined to replace them. The popularity of highly structured all female societies was fading; white gloves and parliamentary procedure now had to compete with new, more loosely constructed groups. If a young Catholic woman wanted a single-sex group, she might instead choose a neighborhood consciousness-raising meeting. If she was drawn to male-female groups, she might join a social justice organization, or a prayer group in the charismatic renewal. Such groups felt more in tune with the times, more responsive to renewal, and required less of a time commitment, a key point for young Catholic women who increasingly worked full-time even after they married and had children.

Such groups may also have been more responsive to young laywomen's desire to process the pressing issues of the day, including women's liberation, changing ideas about women's roles in the home, the sexual revolution, and laywomen's growing dissent on the issue of artificial contraception. Catholic women wanted and needed to discuss these very personal matters in the context of their faith; the Daughters were not prepared at that time to allow conversation on such topics, unless it was to reaffirm the church's official positions. In 1974, a chaplain cautioned the CDA that the Juniors were displaying an undercurrent of rebellion. Like other young people they seemed to be "trying to rid themselves of all authority. . . . It would be detrimental if the Senior CDA were to let this happen. Control has to be maintained." [68]

The Daughters began to return to the worldview of "fear and threat," not dominant since the pre–Vatican II period, which the decline in membership no doubt exacerbated.[69] Rhetoric from chaplains and the leadership hinted at the dark days facing loyal Catholic women. In the middle of rolling out the Sevenfold Program in 1969, which should have been a hopeful event, the leaders could not hide their fear. One officer called the present "this most tragic moment in the history of our Church and our country." That same year the CDA national regent also returned to the military metaphors. "With a sort of spiritual black death creeping into even the smallest of our communities," she warned, "it seems fitting that this meeting re-emphasize our Crusade of Prayer for the strengthening of our Faith for unity within the Church and for the salvation of our country." Here Anna Baxter puts the Daughters in the context of not one but two medieval references: the plague and the crusades.[70]

And yet the Daughters were not paranoid. After year upon year of upset in the 1960s, 1969 seemed the worst of the lot. Nationally, the Vietnam War was raging and antiwar protest was turning violent with the emergence of the Weathermen. Radical feminism, having emerged in late 1968 on the national scene, was in its ascendency and was splashed across the evening news. Deadly urban uprisings and assassinations still lingered in recent memory. The Daughters had good reasons to believe the world as they knew it was falling apart.

Developments in the church were shocking as well, particularly the backlash against *Humanae Vitae*, which was at its height at the end of the decade. Unfortunately for the Daughters, the crisis over birth control was not the only threat to their beloved church. As early as the 1968 conference, the CDA started to hear speeches from their clerics arguing that Vatican II had gone too far. The main purveyor of this view was Father John Walde, moderator of the Share the Faith department. "We were all thrilled when the word went out that there was going to be a General Council of the Church," he said. "We all shared the idea that this was going to be a tremendous impulse to making our faith known." Instead, renewal was hijacked by those who wanted to question doctrine instead of spread it around the world, and the result was chaos. Too many people were questioning authority, he said, too many "taking liberties" with the Mass, too many abandoning devotion to Mary. "The great majority of ills of today stem from the fact that Our Blessed lady has been demoted," he lamented. By 1970 Walde took this rhetoric even further, warning of "the destruction of all supernatural beliefs" due to the questioning brought on by the Council. Around the same time, the CDA national board debated changing the name of the evangelization department from "Share the Faith" to "Preserve and Share the Faith," revealing their return to a defensive position.[71]

Even before the worst of the crisis started, the Daughters were reminded by those who cherished them that it was women such as themselves that could save the church and the world, if they would only stick to the values that had served them so well in the past. You will "help keep a balance in the bark of Peter," one cleric assured them. Patricia Adams told the Isabellans that "God expects each of us to do our part to help this teetering world get back on course."[72]

We see the Daughters return to older forms at the turn of the decade, as if to hunker down and stabilize the ship. Both groups put renewed emphasis on the rosary and Marian devotion, speaking often about Mary's "demotion." Spiritual bouquets also reappeared. The CDA began to put more energy into its "Women for Decency" campaigns to combat cultural decay. In 1969 the D of I passed a resolution to promote "home visitations to indifferent and careless parents" in their parishes. More emphasis was placed back on the conversion of others, rather than on the personal conversion of the self. The Share the Faith section of the Sevenfold Program exuded certainty in the midst of crisis: "The Church does not ask us to compromise with error."[73]

While the leadership of the CDA seemed onboard with retrenchment, the D of I leadership was more supportive of renewal; the worrying rhetoric about Vatican II excesses does not appear in the D of I at the same time. But the same feelings of fear do appear in the membership, and what we see is the leadership trying to convince a lot of nervous Isabellans that all will be well. A similar dynamic shows up in the NCCW in the same period, when a more liberal leadership became out of step with its membership.

At the 1968 D of I convention, the leadership passed a resolution suggesting the reluctance of some members to enter into the spirit of the Council. The resolution began, "Pertaining to the renewal in the Church: Whereas, In the present era of the Second Vatican Council many well-meaning Catholics have engaged in fruitless and unavailing pining for past usages to the detriment of their own spiritual orientation and advancement in the way of Christ. . . ." So some of the Isabellans were "pining" for the past even amidst the organization's overhaul at middecade. A note in the minutes of the 1970 convention hints at how tumultuous this period was. In 1966 "many changes were made to the Ceremonial. In 1968 some of these changes were rescinded and the original practice resumed. In these two conventions, more changes were voted in the Ceremonial than had been made in the five previous biennial Conventions. Confusion was the result."

Despite the changes made to restore the old way at the 1968 convention, some in the membership were still dissatisfied. At issue was a loss of formality. In 1972 someone from the floor proposed the "reinstatement of formality in business meetings, including return of the 'SALUTE.'" The reason? "It is felt that a great amount of dignity has been set aside along with respect for our regents." The copy of the minutes deposited in the archives features the penciled annotations of someone, presumably one of the leadership, who wrote "NO, NO" across the page. The resolution was reintroduced, and again rejected, two years later.[74]

The leadership of the D of I may have been more inclined than that of the CDA to continue the work of renewal into the 1970s, but on what would become the most dominant issue for the Daughters going forward, they were in strict agreement. The Daughters of both organizations were women moving back into crusader mode, for all of the reasons listed above. What they lacked was a cause beyond a general sense that the world was going to hell in a handbasket. They found their cause at the turn of the 1970s: abortion.

In the early 1970s, the Daughters became more vocal in their opposition to the women's liberation movement. What they had basically ignored in the 1960s could no longer be tolerated after the rise of the radical feminists and the growing focus on abortion rights. In 1967, the CDA voted unanimously to drop the organization's membership in the World Union of Catholic Women's Organizations (WUCWO). This is surprising in that just nine years earlier the CDA sent 112 delegates to the WUCWO world convention. As we have seen in chapter 2, however, WUCWO had emerged as an unapologetically Catholic feminist organization by this time, which likely explains the CDA action. The CDA leadership also made an explicit statement on rights in 1972 saying that the CDA "affirms the support of equal rights for women, recognizing always however, the complimentary role that the Creator himself has given men and women."[75]

In honor of International Women's Year (IWY) in 1975, the D of I passed a resolution on the role of women. Nearly every Catholic women's organization I have studied issued some kind of statement concerning IWY; it was an enormous event, and a group's response to it was much less about women than it was about feminism. The D of I's statement makes their opposition to feminism so obvious that no one could miss the message: "Be it resolved: That we the Daughters of Isabella renew our devotion to Mary, the Mother of God. Let us study her great qualities of mercy, compassion and concern for her fellow man and seek to follow her example. Let us be proud to fulfill our role as women and to serve diligently to accept our duties such as womanhood imposes." True to form, the Daughters turned the conversation back from rights to duties.[76]

What caused them to emerge as such strong opponents of women's rights were the twin issues of the Equal Rights Amendment and the threat to legalize abortion, although primarily the latter. By 1972, opposition to abortion moved to the top of both organizations' conference resolution lists, a spot once occupied by the implementation of Vatican II. CDA chaplain John Walde stoked the fires with his antifeminist, antiabortion rhetoric. "Today it seems that, some women at least . . . have come to the conclusion that their body is their own to do with as they wish," he said. They seek only pleasure, and then dare to prevent human life. "A sin like [abortion] cries to heaven for vengeance," he claimed, and ultimately it "could destroy our whole civilization." Such end-of-the-world rhetoric seemed to suit the Daughters who remained in the organization. Both groups began active campaigns to end abortion and prevent the passage of the ERA. Expressing her admiration for the leader of the opposition to the ERA, one CDA leader remarked "how strange that I should come to know, love and admire Phyllis Schlafly over these past eight years." Both official histories of the Daughters note that from the early 1970s onward, antiabortion protest became central to the identities of both groups.[77]

The Daughters differ from the other communities of women in this study in their motivations. The women of the Theresians, the NCCW, and *Marriage* seemed intrinsically motivated to engage in the laywoman project. The work they left behind suggests exploration, an eagerness to ask questions, a deep desire to confront the growing discrepancies between their own self-conceptions and the church's teaching in a moment of fluidity. In contrast, the Daughters' laywoman project emerged more as an outgrowth of their reluctant organizational reassessments in the immediate postconciliar period. As can be seen in all of the groups, when they began to educate themselves about Vatican II they could not help but talk about themselves as women and ask if their role might need to change. When they were challenged to adapt, they did so in good faith; they read, they wrote, they prayed, and they reconsidered. Some seemed genuinely inspired, but for the majority little in the new order of things seemed to fit, particularly the new ideas about Catholic women.

The other groups were rebelling against the hierarchy by challenging the teaching that gender is fixed and unchanging, yet were complying with the directives to support renewal. The Daughters were the opposite. They understood better than anyone that Vatican II did not change church teaching on gender roles, no matter how people chose to interpret its "spirit." They were, however, empowered enough in this moment to rebel openly against other conciliar reforms. In this they were declaring their power as Catholic laywomen to direct change in the church, and they did not apologize for it.

To them, the new Catholic orientation toward openness, as well as the women's movement's insistence on rights over duty, did not seem appropriate responses to either the evils of the world or their own fear. Not too long after, the Holy See would come around to their view and spend much of the 1980s and 1990s trying to roll back the changes Vatican II inspired, placing the Daughters firmly back in the position of obedience where they liked to reside. But the Daughters' empowered choice to reject a modern outlook, in part as a means of preserving their preferred gender identity, came at a cost. As Mother Mary Hennessey warned, refusing to change brought increasing irrelevance in the eyes of younger Catholic women. Membership steadily fell, median age increased, and the Daughters of the present lost their chance to shape the Catholic daughters of the future.

Epilogue

Legacies

Francis, to his credit, says again and again that a "deeper
theology of women" is needed. I take this to mean that
at some level he knows that he doesn't know what this
"feminine genius" is—and nor does anybody else.

Rita Ferrone, "Francis's Words about Women" (2017)

It is safe to say, at least in the view of the Vatican, that Catholic laywomen are having a moment. Numerous Catholic media sources for the past few years have cautiously noted Vatican efforts to place more laywomen in leadership positions and involve them in decision-making. News stories point to the appointment of *two* laywomen as undersecretaries in the new Dicastery for Laity, Family, and Life, for example. Likewise an article reports (in a tone that may or may not be deliberately sarcastic) that "the Commission for Latin America held a plenary assembly on the issue of women, and, in an exceptional move, invited some 15 women to participate." What's more, the often progressive Voices of Faith conference, a gathering of women designed to amplify Catholic laywomen's voices from around the world, has been held within the Vatican walls for the last four years. Pope Francis himself has repeatedly called on the church both to give women more power and to listen for their voices, most notably appointing three female consultors to the Congregation for the Doctrine of the Faith, a historic first, and instituting a commission to study the viability of a female diaconate.[1]

These attempts to include laywomen should be applauded, but let's look a little closer. Not long after the appointment of the two undersecretaries, the cardinal who heads the Dicastery for Laity, Family, and Life rejected three of eleven female speakers for the Voices of Faith conference, without any explanation. As it turns out, the cardinal determined each was too outspoken on issues of LGBTQ and women's rights to be approved, even though

Voices of Faith had always been careful to avoid the question of women's ordination, at the Vatican's insistence. The conference's organizers chose to move the gathering outside of the Vatican rather than change their program. Digging through the new Dicastery's fine print also helps us see the limits of the sudden opening to laywomen's leadership. In a recent revision of the Dicastery's statutes, the new Article 9 states: "The Dicastery works to deepen the reflection on the relationship between men and women in their respective specificity, reciprocity, complementarity and equal dignity. Valuing the feminine 'genius,' it offers a contribution to ecclesial reflection on the identity and mission of women in the Church and in society, promoting their participation."[2] Written into the governing language of the body that oversees the laity worldwide is a definition of men and women as distinct and complementary. Not surprisingly, "the feminine 'genius,'" so flattering a phrase, remains undefined. To do so would require a listing of essentialist traits guaranteed to produce some unpleasant headlines for a church already struggling to retain young women.

Pope Francis's statements on women during his pontificate have been, at times, encouraging, but they are of a piece with the statutes of the Dicastery. He speaks firmly against wage discrimination and calls for more women theologians, for example. He knows that Catholics should have women in the room when vital conversations take place and decisions are made. But Francis has an understanding of gender that is still rooted in the postwar world. In a 2015 general audience he said, "We still have not grasped fully the things that the feminine genius can give us, what society and we can be given by women who know how to see things with another pair of eyes that complement men's ideas."[3] In other words, laywomen's importance lies in their essential difference. To question this conception of womanhood is to bring chaos. "Gender theory is an error of the human mind that leads to so much confusion," Pope Francis has said.[4]

Despite my deep respect for Pope Francis, I will say frankly as a Catholic and a scholar that I do not believe that gender theory is an error of the human mind. Nor, as is already apparent, do I believe in female essentialism. It has been proved beyond a doubt by historians that the way gender is constructed and performed changes over time and in different contexts; neither "gender" nor "female" is fixed. So where does this leave me, reflecting on my research in sight of the Pope Francis hand puppet my daughter made in her kindergarten class on the first day of his pontificate? ("His name is Francis, Mommy, and he only has one lung!!!") Here I am, a Catholic laywoman myself, raising a daughter and son in the faith, watching history repeat itself as laywomen are once again flattered and invited to the table, but only if our genius is proved sufficiently feminine. What can we take away from the laywoman project that might help us navigate the gender politics of this moment?

The liturgist Rita Ferrone, in reflecting on Pope Francis and women, has written, that he "evidently feels deeply that women are important and he knows they are undervalued in the church. But when it comes to the point of saying why women are important and what is valuable about women, there is less clarity. The second underlying problem implicit here is that women are not easily 'defined' and perhaps should not be."[5] Pope Francis, so forthright on a host of issues, is in a pickle. He likely knows that much of what was written on gender in the church prior to the 1960s is not helpful, steeped as it is in the language of submission and obedience (a language he does not choose to use as it endangers the equality he seems to desire for women). Yet what has been written since the 1960s is heavily influenced by women's liberation, and therefore jettisons the idea of essentialism. He wants new women theologians who will espouse essentialism, and strong laywomen who will presumably make their voices heard while enforcing their own restriction under complementarity.

The Catholic laywomen in this study would likely find this situation all too familiar. They were also living through a moment when their participation and leadership seemed suddenly welcome. They too heard the flattery, even as the barriers around their participation were erected and enforced. They fielded and even more frequently posed the questions of what a Catholic woman is and what gifts she has to offer this community. But when they responded to those questions—over a decade's worth of thoughtful reflection—the official church seemed not to hear their answers, or willfully ignored them.

Rather than be disheartened at the continued exclusion of laywomen from positions of authority and the well-worn justifications for that exclusion, as it would be quite easy to be, I prefer to take what lessons we can from the women who have been here before. The first lesson, I think, is that laywomen need to speak fearlessly and relentlessly on questions of their own identity. They must also confront how rigid constructions of gender and the clericalism they support weaken, and in fact threaten, the church entire. Although not all of the laywomen featured here were in agreement, the very fact that they spoke publicly and for so long in an attempt to redefine who they were for a new age challenged the notion that gender was unchanging and only the ordained had a right to define it. Their work was not solely about themselves; they were trying to fix a contradiction at the very heart of the modern church.

The second lesson is that the women who wrote and organized and taught these ideas altered the church, even though it is tempting to believe at times that nothing has changed. I'm not saying that the American Catholic Church is no longer gendered or that it does not discriminate against women. However, the needle has moved in significant ways, and we must acknowledge that. If we don't, we slight what these women accomplished. My daughter serves at the altar; my son crowned Mary in second grade. Their catechesis is free of the gender essentialism that would have my daughter believe her primary vocation is self-abnegation and my son's is headship. That outlook did not simply disappear on its own: laywomen and their allies needed to confront it and dismantle it inch by inch.

Third, let us say a word in praise of Catholic women's organizations, which trained women for leadership and found a home for their talents. More important, however, these organizations served as educational enterprises, and were the means by which curious, committed laywomen disseminated ideas they hoped would transform Catholic culture. All of the communities in this book carried on their projects of transformation within established Catholic structures, often in cooperation with clergy, women religious, and occasionally laymen. With energy and imagination, established organizations as well as new networks of laywomen could serve a similar purpose in the twentieth-first century.

The final lesson, though, is that the laywoman project could only accomplish so much if it could not gain women real power in the church hierarchy. Laywomen spent years attempting to answer the questions now being posed about gender, and as far as the hierarchy is concerned, it's as if it never happened. At the very least, the official church needs to do more than offer them a chance at the microphone, or a seat on a committee. If laywomen are to be offered a voice, they must also be given the authority to make decisions that have weight, and the power to exercise that authority, even over a man in a roman collar. At a bare minimum, they need the power to speak on their own self-conception, vocation, and identity—in a diversity of voices—and have it be reflected in church teaching. The lived experience of the church changed as a direct result of the work of the laywoman project. This is their legacy. The laywomen of this moment have the power to create a legacy of their own.

Notes

INTRODUCTION

1. *Lumen Gentium*, chap. 4, sec. 33. The Dogmatic Constitution on the Church was one of the key documents of the Second Vatican Council and focused on the church's authority and mission. It was promulgated in late 1964.

2. Father James Murtaugh, "Address," Chicago Archdiocesan Council of Catholic Women Fall Assembly, October 1963, Proceedings, box 25-P7220, ADMN/ACA, 14. A version of this research on Catholic laywomen and their clergy advisors in the Vatican II era was published previously in *U.S. Catholic Historian*. See Henold, "Woman—Go Forth!"

3. It is worth noting that the laywoman project was taking place at the same time as a conversation about the "emerging layman," which has a literature of its own. Titles include Callahan, *The Mind of the Catholic Layman*; Thorman, *The Emerging Layman*; O'Gara, *The Layman and the Church*; Schillebeeckx, *The Layman in the Church*; and Roche and De Roo, *Man to Man: A Frank Talk between Layman and Bishop*. Books in this genre tend to discuss laymen as laity, indicating that the authors were far more interested in defining lay status, power, and ministry than in discussing questions of gender. In fact, "layman" was assumed to include women, although men were treated as normative and women were rarely mentioned. In contrast, authors engaged in the laywoman project tended to discuss laywomen as women, engaging gender in ways ignored by the male authors in this field. The only authors in the laywoman project who produced book-length studies in this era tended to be the emerging Catholic feminists. See, for example, Cunneen, *Sex: Female; Religion: Catholic*; and Callahan, *The Illusion of Eve*.

4. Sugrue, "The Catholic Encounter with the 1960s," 62.

5. I planned to include a chapter in this book analyzing the laywoman project of the Ladies of Peter Claver (the women's auxiliary to the Knights of Peter Claver), the largest

organization for African American laywomen. Unfortunately, the organization's archives are not open to professional researchers at this time.

6. Books on the history of Vatican II abound. For a useful overview of debates in the field over how to interpret the impact of Vatican II, see Cummings, Matovina, and Orsi, *Catholics in the Vatican II Era*. For a broader understanding of the reception of Vatican II over time, see Faggioli, *A Council for the Global Church*; and Faggioli, *Vatican II*. For reception in the American context, see, for example, Kelly, *The Transformation of American Catholicism*; and McDannell, *The Spirit of Vatican II*. For a discussion of "rupture" versus "continuity," see O'Malley, *Vatican II*.

7. For discussions of Catholics and suburbanization, see McDannell, *The Spirit of Vatican II*; Massa, *Catholics and American Culture*; Dolan, *The American Catholic Experience*; Kelly, "Suburbanization and the Decline of Catholic Public Ritual in Pittsburgh"; and McGreevy, *Parish Boundaries*. For laypeople and Catholic Action, see Bonner, Denny, and Connolly, *Empowering the People of God*.

8. See Tentler, *Catholics and Contraception*.

9. Johnson, *One in Christ*, 3. For more on Catholics in the U.S. civil rights movement, see Davis, *The History of Black Catholics in the United States*; Southern, *John LaFarge and the Limits of Catholic Interracialism*; McGreevy, *Parish Boundaries*; Koehlinger, *The New Nuns*; Cressler, "Black Power, Vatican II, and the Emergence of Black Catholic Liturgies"; and Copeland, *Uncommon Faithfulness*.

10. Bonner, "Who Will Guard," 225; Johnson, "Taking Marriage 'One Day at a Time,'" 3.

11. See Kelly, *The Transformation of American Catholicism*, 227; and Kane, "Marian Devotion," 116.

12. See O'Toole, "In the Court of Conscience," 172; Morrow, "Change in the Conception of Sin"; and O'Toole, *Habits of Devotion*, 5.

13. Westoff and Bumpass, "The Revolution in Birth Control Practices," 41; Johnson, "The Home Is a Little Church," chap. 6.

14. Kelly and Kelly, "Our Lady of Perpetual Help," 6; Kane, "Marian Devotion," 116.

15. McDannell, "Catholic Domesticity," 49; see also Johnson, "The Home Is a Little Church."

16. Johnson, "The Home Is a Little Church," 114–15; Harmon, *There Were Also Many Women There*, 244.

17. For a discussion of recent historiography of feminism, see Gilmore, *Groundswell*; and Laughlin and Castledine, *Breaking the Wave*. For a study of 1950s organizational women pursuing what we would now consider to be feminist goals before the resurgence of feminism in the mid-1960s, see Johnson and Johnston, "Unfamiliar Feminisms." On the issue of conservative women and how they fit into a historiography shaped by feminism, see Nickerson, *Mothers of Conservatism*, conclusion.

18. Blair, *Revolutionizing Expectations*; Rogow, *Gone to Another Meeting*; Cobble, "More than Sex Equality"; Weaver, "Barrio Women"; Mathews-Garner, "From Ladies' Aid to NGO," 100. The Women's Division of Christian Service was the precursor of the United Methodist Women.

19. Second Vatican Council's "Message to the Women of the World," December 8, 1965, quoted in Bishop Stephen A. Leven, "Votive Mass for Peace," Conference Proceedings 1968, folder 1968, box 24, NCCW/CUA, 140.

20. For an insightful look at the "lived history" of Vatican II in localities around the world, and a discussion of the importance of the lived history approach, see Cummings, Matovina, and Orsi, *Catholics in the Vatican II Era*.

21. Betty Jarmusch, "Power Struggle in the Supermarket," *Marriage*, January 1972, 62.

22. Mrs. Lucille W. Martin, letter to the editor, *Marriage*, March 1972, 69.

PROLOGUE

1. Sister Mary Yolanda, BVM, "Vocation: From Doubt to Decision," *Today*, March 1959, 18–21.

2. K. A. L., "Vocations Begin (and End) at Home," editorial, *Information*, March 1960, 60.

3. Among the forty-one articles, four authors could not be determined; K. A. L., "Vocations Begin," 61.

4. Rev. Henry E. Strassner, "Four Sermons to Parents on Vocations," *Emmanuel*, March 1959, 122–23; Douglas Roche, "Vocations in the Family," *Marriage*, March 1962, 47; James F. Kane, "Parents Key to Vocations," *Ave Maria*, June 1963, 13; James D. Moriarity, "Vocation Losses by Default," *Homiletic and Pastoral Review*, March 1959, 535. Serra International was founded in the late 1930s as an exclusive organization for laymen who wished to promote vocations to the priesthood. Its counterpart for laywomen, the Theresians, was not founded until 1961.

5. For more on the materialist crisis, see Kelly, *The Transformation of American Catholicism*, 8–9. For more on materialism and gender, see Johnson, "The Home Is a Little Church," 79; Berthold T. Fahey, O.Carm, "Parental Objections," *Mary*, April 1962, 13.

6. Donald F. Miller, C.SS.R., "How Parents Block Vocations," *Liguorian*, September 1960, 3.

7. Kelly, *The Transformation of American Catholicism*, part 1. For a discussion of the complexities of the shift away from Cold War–era devotionalism, see Chinnici, "The Catholic Community at Prayer," 83.

8. Although this was not mentioned in any of the articles studied, this theme also dovetails with heightened fears, in the larger culture, of "Momism," the much condemned practice of stifling mother love supposedly responsible for encroaching homosexuality.

9. Fahey, "Parental Objections," 15; Fr. Gerard McCrane, "Mothers Today Do Not Want Their Children to Be Heroic," *Maryknoll*, March 1964, 30 (emphasis added).

10. McCrane, "Mothers Today," 30; del Rey, *Bernie Becomes a Nun*, 15.

11. Irene Boyd, "Patty Enters the Convent," *Family Digest*, March 1959, 10; Godfrey Poage and John Treacy, "What Parents Ask about Vocations," *Ave Maria*, March 1959, 12–14.

12. Rev. Robert A. Burns, OP, "Creating a Vocation Atmosphere in the Home," *Proceedings*, National Sisters Vocation Conference, 1964, folder 15/box 88/TUSR/WLA, 19.

13. "Vocation Crisis Must Be Solved," *Homiletic and Pastoral Review*, February 1959, 464.

14. "God to Souls—Souls to God," *Isabellan*, December 1962, box 12/DI/CUA, 10 (emphasis in original).

15. Moriarity, "Vocation Losses," 536.

16. Poage and Treacy, "What Parents Ask," 14; Miller, "How Parents Block Vocations," 2; Strassner, "Four Sermons," 124.

17. "Vocation Crisis Must Be Solved," 464. For a concise explanation of the decline of parochial schools, see Dolan, *The American Catholic Experience*, 441–42.

18. Bishop Stephen Woznicki, letter to Mrs. Scott D. Hurlbert, February 6, 1961, folder Statements–Board of Directors/box 26/NCCW/CUA.

19. Sister Jean Marie, O.S.B., "I Decide My Destiny," *Catholic School Journal*, March 1961, 52–53; Sister M. Dominic, R.G.S., "For Teenagers Only," *Family Digest*, March 1962, 41.

CHAPTER 1

1. Douglas Roche, "Vocations in the Family," *Marriage*, March 1962, 47–48.
2. Elwood Voss, "The Theresian Purpose," c. 1970, folder 13/box 90/TUSR/WLA, 1.
3. Voss and Mullen, *The Theresian Story*, 2, 53.
4. McCartin, "The Sacred Heart of Jesus, Thérèse of Lisieux," 63.
5. Voss and Mullen, *The Theresian Story*, 2 (emphasis in original).
6. Bishop Charles A. Buswell, letter to Elwood Voss titled "The Theresian's Prayer," c. March 1963, folder 8/box 21/TUSR/WLA.
7. Sister M. Simone, O.S.B., "Theresian Meetings," Proceedings, National Sisters Vocation Conference, 1965, folder 10/box 87/TUSR/WLA, 26; "The Theresians of America," pamphlet, c. 1968, folder 8/box 4/TUSR/WLA, 9.
8. "Quotations from Monsignor Voss on the Theresian World Apostolate," Presidents' Handbook, 1972, folder 9/box 2/TUSR/WLA.
9. Italian American Catholicism is one exception to this. Robert Orsi found Italian Catholics to hold especially priests, but also women religious, in lesser esteem. See Orsi, *The Madonna of 115th Street*.
10. McCartin, *Prayers of the Faithful*, 12–13.
11. Mrs. John Downs, "A Laywoman Looks to the Sisterhood," Proceedings, National Sisters Vocation Conference, 1964, folder 15/box 88/TUSR/WLA, 47; Rev. F. A. Marrocco, "Vocations to the Sisterhood—Responsibility of All," Proceedings, National Sisters Vocation Conference, 1964, folder 15/box 88/TUSR/WLA, 4; Virginia Siegle, "The Theresian Apostolate," New Mexico State Conference, 1966, folder 7/box 92/TUSR/WLA, 2.
12. Marrocco, "Vocations," 4; Cynthia Bordelon, "Theresian Programs and Activities," Proceedings, National Sisters Vocation Conference, 1964, folder 15/box 88/TUSR/WLA, 26 (emphasis in original).
13. Bordelon, "Theresian Programs," 27; Siegle, "The Theresian Apostolate," 2; Marge Herrig, "What Adult Women Think of the Changing Sister," Proceedings, National Conference, 1967, folder 14/box 89/TUSR/WLA, 5.
14. Mrs. Raber Taylor, "The Theresian Influence," Proceedings, National Sisterhood Vocation Conference, folder 10/box 87/TUSR/WLA, 30.
15. Mrs. Carl Miller, "Establishing a Theresian Unit," Proceedings, National Sisterhood Vocation Conference, 1965, folder 10/box 87/TUSR/WLA, 17–21.
16. Taylor, "The Theresian Influence," 28 (emphasis in original).
17. Kane, "'She Offered Herself Up,'" 88. Vestiges of this type of prayer persist in American Catholicism. Surely I was not the only Catholic teenager who was told to "offer it up" when she complained to her mother of some hardship. I also vividly recall sitting in my hospital bed with my newborn daughter, tears running down my face at the pain of nursing. My mother, a progressive Catholic woman, must have been channeling her own midcentury childhood when she said solemnly, "Offer it up—this is how you earn the jewels in your crown."
18. Kane, "She Offered Herself Up," 100.

19. Fr. Howe, letter to Elwood Voss, March 12, 1963, folder 8/box 21/TUSR/WLA; Bordelon, "Theresian Programs," 25; Marrocco, "Vocations," 6; Elwood Voss, as quoted in Bordelon, "Theresian Programs," 25.

20. "The Theresians of Shrine High Newsletter," April 1967, folder 22/box 36/TUSR/WLA; "The Theresian," Santa Monica High School Theresians, November 1967, folder 22/box 36/TUSR/WLA. Shrine High School was the school connected to the national Shrine of the Little Flower in Royal Oak, Michigan, founded by the controversial Father Charles Coughlin. Incidentally, it is also my alma mater.

21. Mrs. Charles Lovette, "The Purpose of the Theresians," Proceedings, National Sisters Vocation Conference, 1964, folder 15/box 88/TUSR/WLA, 8, 11 (emphasis added).

22. Downs, "A Laywoman Looks to the Sisterhood," 48.

23. Downs, "A Laywoman Looks to the Sisterhood," 46; Sister Kathleen Mary, SL, "The Modern Girl," Proceedings, National Sisters Vocation Conference, 1966, folder 3/box 95/TUSR/WLA, 6.

24. Siegle, "The Theresian Apostolate," 2.

25. Sister Elena, CSC, "Vocation Principles," Proceedings, National Sisters Vocation Conference, 1966, folder 3/box 95/TUSR/WLA, 4–5 (emphasis in original); Sister Thomas Aquinas, OP, "Religious and Lay Cooperation in the Light of Vatican II," folder 7/box 92/TUSR/WLA, 5; Father William Steele, "Personalism, Liturgy and Vocations," folder 7/box 92/TUSR/WLA, 5.

26. Lovette, "The Purpose," 9; Kathryn Cribari, "Something Else Again," The Theresian, Summer 1971, folder 4/box 104/TUSR/WLA, 9; Sister Annina Morgan, SC, "The Importance of Communication between Sisters and Young Women," Theresian National Conference, 1968, folder 17/box 91/TUSR/WLA 3 (emphasis in original).

27. Taylor, "The Theresian Influence," 29–30; Dan Maio, "A United Effort for Sisterhood Vocations," conference booklet, 1965, folder 9/box 94/TUSR/WLA, 11.

28. Steele, "Personalism, Liturgy and Vocations," 5.

29. American Lay Women, conference booklet, National Sisters Vocation Conference, 1964, folder 15/box 88/TUSR/WLA, 12.

30. Sister Margaret Mary, "A Need for Youth in the Vocation Apostolate," New Mexico State Conference, 1966, folder 7/box 97/TUSR/WLA, 1.

31. Mrs. Charles Strubbe, "A Time for Giving," Theresian National Conference, 1971, folder 6/box 92/TUSR/WLA, 2–3.

32. Minutes, Theresian Board of Consultants Meeting, Spring 1970, folder 3/box 23/TUSR/WLA, 4; Voss and Mullen, The Theresian Story, front material.

33. See Koehlinger, The New Nuns. See also Borromeo, The New Nuns.

34. Theresians of Long Beach newsletter, January 1970, folder 23/box 36/TUSR/WLA, 2;"Theresian Questionnaire," Theresian, Summer 1969, folder 4/box 104/TUSR/WLA, 9.

35. Saint Mary's College in Indiana was the first institution to offer a PhD in theology for women in the 1960s.

36. Sister Elena, "Vocation Principles," 1–3.

37. Sister Thomas Aquinas, "Religious and Lay Cooperation," 2.

38. Sister Elena, "Vocation Principles," 4; Sister Thomas Aquinas, "Religious and Lay Cooperation," 2.

39. Sister Margaret Mary, "A Need for Youth," 3–4. The author's order is unknown.

40. Father William Steele, letter to Elwood Voss, September 2, 1969, folder 9/box 4/ TUSR/WLA, 1; Minutes, Theresian Board of Consultants Meeting, Spring 1970, folder 3/ box 23/TUSR/WLA, 5.

41. Sister Elise Marie, "Theresians of America Student Activities," report to National Consultants Meeting, 1969, folder 2/box 23/TUSR/WLA; Minutes, National Consultants Meeting, 1970, 2.

42. Minutes, National Consultants Meeting, 1967, folder 1/box 23/TUSR/WLA, 11; program, Theresian National Conference, 1970, folder 9/box 94/TUSR/WLA; Minutes, National Consultants Meeting, 1970, 5. It is worth noting that such fears emerged in the nascent Catholic feminist movement in the same period. Lay feminists were concerned, rightly as it turned out, that women religious would come to dominate the leadership in Catholic feminist organizations.

43. Ebaugh, Lorence, and Chafetz, "The Growth and Decline," 175; "Report to Consultants' Conference—Adult Membership," c. 1968–1969, folder 2/box 23/TUSR/ WLA; Sara McCarthy, letter to Elwood Voss, August 29, 1969, folder 9/box 4/ TUSR/WLA.

44. McCarthy to Voss, August 29, 1969; "Report—Adult Membership" (emphasis in original).

45. Elwood Voss, memo to Executive Board, September 4, 1969, folder 9/box 4/TUSR/ WLA, 1.

46. Steele to Voss, September 2, 1969, 1.

47. Voss, "The Theresian Purpose," 1.

48. Voss, "The Theresian Purpose," 1.

49. Minutes, Consultants, 1970, 2; Elwood Voss, letter to Executive Board, September 1, 1970, folder 3/box 23/TUSR/WLA, 1; Voss and Mullen, *The Theresian Story*, 14.

50. Voss, letter to Executive Board, September 1, 1970, 1; "President's Message," *Theresian*, Summer 1971, folder 4/box 104/TUSR/WLA, 3; Sister Kathleen McNamara, *Women of Vision*, 1972, folder 10/box 104/TUSR/WLA, 6.

51. Cribari, "Something Else," 6–7.

52. Betty Barrett, "Unique We Are," *Theresian*, Autumn 1970, folder 4/box 104/TUSR/ WLA, 15; "Clothing Workshop Report," 1970 conference, folder 13/box 90/TUSR/WLA, 1.

53. Mrs. Joseph Zavadil, "Emerging Role of Laywomen in the Church," New Mexico State Conference, 1966, folder 7/box 92/TUSR/WLA. Friedan says explicitly that "women of orthodox Catholic or Jewish origin do not easily break through the housewife image; it is enshrined in the canons of their religion, in the assumptions of their own and their husbands' childhoods, and in their church's dogmatic definitions of marriage and motherhood." She also calls out prominent Catholic laywomen writers by name, specifically Jean Kerr and Phyllis McGinley, in her assessment of freelance nonfiction writing in the 1950s. Of these writers she remarked, "They are good craftsmen, the best of these Housewife Writers. And some of their work is funny. . . . But there is something about Housewife Writers that isn't funny—like Uncle Tom, or Amos and Andy. 'Laugh,' the Housewife Writers tell the real housewife, 'if you are feeling desperate, empty, bored, trapped in the bedmaking, chauffeuring and dishwashing details. Isn't it funny?'" Many Catholic feminists in the mid-1960s gave only conditional support to the book, not because it called out the church (which they did as well) but because it located women's fulfillment almost entirely in the world of work and

neglected both the question of vocation and the idea of spiritual fulfillment. See Friedan, *The Feminine Mystique*, 351, 57.

54. Friedan, *The Feminine Mystique*, 5.

55. Sister Margaret Ellen Traxler, excerpts from National Conference address, 1969, folder 19/box 87, 1–2.

56. Minutes, Theresian Board of Consultants Meeting, 1970, folder 3/box 23/TUSR/WLA, 2; "Miss Kathy" [Kathy Cribari], "New (Not So New) Woman," *Theresian*, Autumn 1970, folder 4/box 104/TUSR/WLA, 5.

57. McNamara, *Women of Vision*, 180.

58. Father Robert Wilson, "Woman—Go Forth," *Theresian*, Summer 1971, folder 4/box 104/TUSR/WLA, 4; Sister Grace Jose, OSF, "Feminine Fulfillment," *Theresian*, Autumn 1970, folder 4/box 104/TUSR/WLA, 6.

59. For a primary source detailing the eternal feminine construct, see von le Fort, *The Eternal Woman*. See also Henold, *Catholic and Feminist*, chap. 1.

60. Sister Grace Jose, "Feminine Fulfillment," 6; Wilson, "Woman—Go Forth," 4; E. Dawne Jubb, MD, "Woman in the Age of Aquarius," National Conference, 1971, folder 6/box 92/TUSR/WLA, 3;

61. Father Bernard Mullaney, "A Time for Giving Birth," 1971 National Conference, folder 6/box 92/TUSR/WLA, 4; Father Bernard Mullaney, "Spirituality in the Theresian Community," National Conference, 1973, folder 14/box 93/TUSR/WLA, 2.

62. Liturgy booklet, Board of Consultants Meeting, April 1971, folder 4/box 23/TUSR/WLA, 4–5, 15.

63. Liturgy booklet, 3–4, 16.

64. Mrs. Frank (Rita) J. Metyko, "A Time for Community," 1971 National Conference, folder 6/box 92/TUSR/WLA, 14–16 (emphasis added).

65. Jubb, "Woman in the Age of Aquarius," 2–5 (emphasis in original).

66. "Sisters Are Needed," excerpted from the *Brooklyn Tablet*, *Theresian*, Summer 1971, folder 4/box 104/TUSR/WLA, 10. One such example can be found in the prescriptive "Separate Spheres" ideology promoted in the antebellum period in the United States, when in a time of great economic and social upheaval moral authorities encouraged women to emulate a particular set of female traits.

67. "Mary," letter to Elwood Voss, c. 1971, folder 4/box 23/TUSR/WLA, 1; Kathy S., letter to Elwood Voss, January 3, 1973, folder 5/box 23/TUSR/WLA, 1; *Theresian News*, December 1972, folder 2/box 104/TUSR/WLA, 1 (emphasis in original).

68. Cribari, "Something Else," 6.

69. Sister Patricia Mullen, memo to Board of Consultants, July 9, 1975, folder 6/box 23/TUSR/WLA, 1. The date on the document reads "July 1975" but I believe this was a typo. Each year's conference was planned starting in the spring of the same year.

70. Mrs. Maelsel Yelenick, Theresian Position Paper, c. 1976, folder 6/box 23/TUSR/WLA, 1.

71. Patricia Mullen, "Theresian National Conference" planning memo, Summer 1976, 1; Elwood Voss, "Opening Address," National Conference, 1976, folder 6/box 23/TUSR/WLA, 1.

72. Voss, "Opening Address," 3; Mullaney, "A Time for Giving Birth," 1.

73. For more on the underground church, see Henold, "Breaking the Boundaries of Renewal."

74. Steele, letter to Voss, September 2, 1969; Voss, "The Theresian Purpose," 2.

75. Advertising flier, 1970 National Conference, folder 13/box 90/TUSR/WLA; Steele, letter to Voss, September 2, 1969. For a discussion of these developments, see Schulman, *The Seventies*, chap. 3.

76. By the early 1970s feminists were increasingly shifting to the word *ministry*, a term rarely applied to laywomen in the past, to describe their work, leading to the call for women's ordination to the priesthood by the mid-1970s.

77. Long Beach Newsletter, January 1970, 2; Jo Taylor, "Newsletter—Community Dimension," c. 1976, folder 6/box 23/TUSR/WLA, 1; Sister Patricia Mullen, "Theresians of the Future," National Conference, 1976, folder 5/box 93/TUSR/WLA, 2.

78. Sister Jane Abell, OP, "Women in Support of Women," National Conference, 1978, folder 3/box 89/TUSR/WLA, 7–8.

79. Barrett, "Unique We Are," 14; introduction, *Theresian*, Summer 1971, folder 4/box 104/TUSR/WLA, 3.

80. "A Sense of Mission," *Theresian News*, July/August 1979, folder 2/box 104/TUSR/WLA/1.

CHAPTER 2

1. "The Buried Talents Symposium," *Sign*, October 15–19, 1966, 17. An earlier version of the research in this chapter appeared in Bonner, Denny, and Connolly, *Empowering the People of God*, 197–221.

2. Margaret Ellen Traxler, statement before the Illinois House, March 22, 1973, National Coalition of American Nuns Records, 2/2, Marquette University Archives. See also sociologist Ruth Wallace's denunciation of the NCCW for its stance on the ERA in 1975; Wallace, "Bringing Women In," 301.

3. Wallace, "Joseph H. Fichter's Contributions," 361; Weaver, *New Catholic Women*, quoted in Kelly, *The Transformation of American Catholicism*, 35. For another case of moderate organizational women being criticized for their lack of feminism, see Johnson and Johnston, "Unfamiliar Feminisms." The authors argue that organizational women in the National Council of Women Psychologists in the "interwave" period did demonstrate a form of feminism that historians later judged insufficient to meet "feminist" standards.

4. The National Council of Jewish Women (NCJW) showed a similar commitment to feminist goals but also chose not to self-identify as feminist. See Rogow, *Gone to Another Meeting*, 113.

5. The NCCW does not fit comfortably into existing narratives of women's right-wing activism, despite its opposition to abortion and the ERA. While certainly sympathetic to the antiabortion movement that predated *Roe v. Wade*, abortion was not a central focus of NCCW activity at the leadership level in the 1960s. For more on the Catholic antiabortion movement, see Williams, *Defenders of the Unborn*; and Taranto, *Kitchen Table Politics*.

6. For a discussion of traditional women's organizations that pursued modest feminist goals without self-identifying as feminist, see Blair, *Revolutionizing Expectations*. See also Mathews-Gardner, "From Ladies' Aid to NGO."

7. National Council of Catholic Women, home page, http://home.catholicweb.com /NCCW/index.cfm.

8. Margaret Mealey, Report to the Board of Directors, December 1959, box 10/NCCW/CUA, 1; Margaret Mealey, Report to the Board of Directors, January 1964, box 10/NCCW/CUA, 5.

9. "Family and Parent Education," 1960 Conference Proceedings, box 23/NCCW/CUA, 52–53; Margaret Mealey, letter to Catherine Schaefer, August 2, 1967, folder NCCW-Mealey, Exec Dir Corr/box 161/NCWC/USCC) OGS/CUA.

10. Alexander Sigur, "Women in the Apostolate of the Church," 1960 Conference Proceedings, box 23/NCCW/CUA, 73; John S. Spence, "Woman's Particular Role," 1964 Conference Proceedings, box 23/NCCW/CUA, 50.

11. Sigur, "Women in the Apostolate of the Church," 73; Rev. Leo W. Duprey, O.P., "Challenge to the Nature of Woman," May 1963, box 34/NCCW/CUA, 1; Spence, "Woman's Particular Role," 53; "Nature of Woman," fact sheet, 1963 NCCW Institute, box 34/NCCW/CUA, 3.

12. Margaret O'Connell, editorial, "Women at Vatican II," *Word* 2, no. 2 (November 1965): 3 (emphasis in original).

13. Mary Perkins Ryan, "The Liturgy," 1964 Conference Proceedings, box 23/NCCW/CUA, 86. For an analysis of Ryan's preconciliar writings on families and liturgy, see Harmon, *There Were Also Many Women There*, chap. 5. In the postwar period, Ryan was a great supporter of laywomen applying liturgical concepts in their role as homemakers.

14. Massa, *The American Catholic Revolution*, 158.

15. Arlene Swidler, "Church Communities Commission: Overview," 1968 Conference Proceedings, folder 1968/box 24/NCCW/CUA, 88.

16. Margaret Mealey, Report to the Board of Directors, January 1966, box 10/NCCW/CUA.

17. Margaret Mary Kelly, "Cooperation with Vatican II," *Word* 2, no. 1 (October 1964), folder 1964/box 66/NCCW, 11 (emphasis in original).

18. Margaret O'Connell, editorial, *Word* 4, no. 8 (May 1967), folder 1967(1)/box 66/NCCW, 3.

19. Mrs. Louis H. Sweterlitsch, "NCCW: People and Structures," 1968 Conference Proceedings, folder 1968/box 24/NCCW, 77; John Tracy Ellis, "The Catholic Laywoman and the Apostolate of Our Time," NCCW National Conference, November 6, 1962, box 34/NCCW/CUA, 3.

20. Mary Perkins Ryan, Report of the Spiritual Development Committee, 1964 Conference Proceedings, box 23/NCCW/CUA, 190; "Organization and Development," *Word* 3, no. 5 (February 1966), folder 1966(1)/box 66/NCCW/CUA, 7.

21. "Committee on Libraries and Literature," Proceedings, 1960 Convention, box 23/NCCW, 68; Margaret Mealey, "50th Executive Director's Report," *Word*, c. 1970; Kelly, "Cooperation with Vatican II," 11.

22. Workshop session notes, NCCW National Conference Proceedings, 1966, box 24/NCCW/CUA, 82; Mrs. John A. Paddenburg, "Opportunities in the Church Communities, Myth or Reality?," NCCW National Conference Proceedings, 1966, box 24/NCCW/CUA, 56.

23. Arlene Swidler, "Church Communities Commission: Overview," National Conference Proceedings, 1968, box 24/NCCW/CUA, 88–89; "Signs and Wonders," *Word* 5, no. 4 (January 1968), folder 1968/box 66/NCCW/CUA, 3; box 186/NCCW/CUA. Timothy Kelly's research on the Archdiocese of Pittsburgh shows that when the NCCW affiliate there flirted with feminism in 1966 it was rebuked by priests, supporting the claim

that the NCCW leadership was more willing to provoke the clergy in this period. See Kelly, *The Transformation of American Catholicism*, 237.

24. The only long-form scholarly work on the NCCW in this period can be found in Ruth O'Halloran's dissertation on the NCCW's history. In it O'Halloran argues that the NCCW was not antifeminist in the 1960s and 1970s, and that it did express feminist ideas. Her dissertation does not pursue the nature of that feminism or its relationship to Vatican II, however. See O'Halloran, "Organized Catholic Laywomen," 221.

25. Mark Massa makes a similar argument about the difficulties in employing political labels in the postconciliar period. See Massa, *The American Catholic Revolution*, 160–62.

26. See Henold, *Catholic and Feminist*.

27. On the history of radical feminism, see Echols, *Daring to Be Bad*; and Buchanan, *Radical Feminists*. For the history of Catholic feminism's radical wing, see Henold, *Catholic and Feminist*.

28. A helpful comparison is Appalachian women who worked in the antipoverty movements of the 1960s and 1970s. They too responded to and incorporated feminist ideas in this period without making feminism central to their activism. At times they also clashed with more orthodox coastal feminists. See Wilkerson, *To Live Here, You Have to Fight*. Historian Erin Kempker also describes the "low-key feminism" of women's rights advocates in Indiana. While they, unlike the NCCW, supported the ERA, they demonstrate the variety of approaches to feminist activism by moderates. See Kempker, *Big Sister*.

29. Mig Boyle, Report to the Board of Directors, January 1968, box 11/NCCW/CUA.

30. "Of Human Life: A Conversation," *Word* 6, no. 2 (November 1968), folder 1968(2)/box 66/NCCW/CUA, 5–11.

31. Arlene Swidler, "Make Theology Your Business," *Word* 7, no. 3, folder December 1969/box 66/NCCW/CUA, 4–11; Arlene Swidler, "Feminist Liturgies," *Catholic Woman* 1, no. 1 (January 1975), folder 1975/box 66/NCCW/CUA, 3–5. In the previous year, Swidler published a book on feminist liturgy titled *Sistercelebrations: Nine Worship Experiences*. Historian Timothy Kelly also reports that in 1966 Swidler gave a talk to the Diocesan Council of Catholic Women of Pittsburgh on "Modern Women in the Church." See Kelly, *The Transformation of American Catholicism*, 237.

32. Theodora Briggs Sweeney, "Children, Church,—and Lib," *Word* 8, no. 1 (January 1971), folder 1971/box 66/NCCW/CUA, 18–19.

33. Paddenburg, "Opportunities," 57.

34. Mrs. Louis H. Sweterlitsch, "NCCW: People and Structures," 1968 Conference Proceedings, folder 1968/box 24/NCCW/CUA, 74.

35. Lillian O'Connor, "Women: Their Own Worst Enemies," *Word* 5, no. 3 (December 1967), folder 1967(2)/box 66/NCCW/CUA, 6; Sweterlitsch, "NCCW: People," 8; Joanne M. Moran, editorial, *Word* 7, no. 1 (October 1969), folder 1969(2)/box 66/NCCW/CUA, 2.

36. Joanne M. Moran, editorial, *Word* 7, no. 9 (June/July 1970), folder 1970(2)/box 66/NCCW/CUA, 2.

37. Mary Perkins Ryan, quoted in Swidler, "Make Theology Your Business," 9. Dan W. Dodson, "Why Women's Organizations?," 1968 Conference Proceedings, folder 1968/box 24/NCCW/CUA, 41, 46.

38. "Statements Adopted by Board of Directors at Annual Meeting," January 22–25, 1968, folder Statements of Board of Directors/box 26/NCCW/CUA, 2; Kelly, "Cooperation with Vatican II," 4.

39. Mary Perkins Ryan, "The Liturgy," 1964 Convention Proceedings, box 23/NCCW/CUA, 84.

40. Kelly, "Cooperation with Vatican II," 11; Margaret Mealey, Report to the Board, January 1964, box 10/NCCW/CUA.

41. Proposed resolution at 1966 Convention by Church Communities Committee, box 24/NCCW/CUA; Rosemary Kilch, editorial, Word 3, no. 9 (June/July 1966), folder 1966(1)/box 66/NCCW/CUA, 3.

42. Swidler, "Make Theology Your Business."

43. Helena Malinowski, "Beyond Stereotypes: Contributions of Women Theologians," Word 6, no. 2 (November 1968), box 66/NCCW/CUA, 12–13.

44. The NCCW was not alone in linking Vatican II and feminism; self-identified Catholic feminists made the same connection. See Henold, Catholic and Feminist.

45. Historian Dorothy Sue Cobble outlines a trend at midcentury she calls "Social Justice Feminism," in which advocates of equality for women worked within existing organizations and movements oriented toward other causes, such as the labor movement and the civil rights movement. The NCCW can be interpreted to fit within this framework, pursuing rights within its larger focus on church renewal. See Cobble, "More than Sex Equality."

46. Margaret Mealey, "Executive Director's Report to the Board," February 1970, box 12/NCCW/CUA, 1. For the details on the brief merger of the NCCW and the NCCM, see O'Halloran, "Organized Catholic Laywomen," chap. 5.

47. This theme was likely drawn from Deuteronomy 30:19, "I call heaven and earth to witness against you today that I have set before you life and death, blessings and curses. Choose life so that you and your descendants may live." New Revised Standard Version.

48. Mealey, "50th Executive Director's Report," 5–6.

49. Such a position is not unprecedented. For instance, it was not uncommon for American suffragists to argue using both the rhetoric of female essentialism and the rhetoric of equality and rights in the last twenty years of the suffrage movement in the United States. See Cott, The Grounding of Modern Feminism, 19.

50. Desmazières, "Negotiating Religious and Women's Identities," 76.

51. Rossi, "The Status of Women," 300–324.

52. Rossi, "The Status of Women," 316.

53. Proceedings, International Study Days, November 6–9, 1966, folder 13/box 3/COCN/UNDA, 3.

54. "From Study Days to the Congress in Rome," Proceedings, 1967 WUCWO congress, Rome, folder 23/box 2/COCN/UNDA, 67; WUCWO congress working paper and program notes, October 4–7, 1967, folder 26/box 2/COCN/UNDA.

55. Lillian O'Connor, "For a Better World Tomorrow," Proceedings, 1967 WUCWO congress, Rome, folder 23/box 2/COCN/UNDA, 105.

56. María del Pilar Bellosillo, "WUCWO after Vatican Council II," Proceedings, 1967 WUCWO world congress, Rome, folder 23/box 2/COCN/UNDA, 74–78.

57. María del Pilar Bellosillo, "Opening Speech," WUCWO Assembly of Delegates Report, October 1970, folder 30/box 2/COCN/UNDA, 3–7.

58. María del Pilar Bellosillo, "Aims and Programme," WUCWO Assembly of Delegates Report, October 1970, folder 30/box 2/COCN/UNDA, 25–29.

59. Marge Brooks, poem, Roster Team Training Institute, Marymount College, n.d. folder 1/box 1/COCN/UNDA; liturgy handout, "Sharing of a Shalom Meal," February 4, 1972, folder 24/box 3/COCN.

60. Lillian O'Connor, "Prayer for WUCWO Day of Prayer," 1973, folder 24/box 3/ COCN/UNDA; Lillian O'Connor, memo, c. March 1973, folder 25/box 3/COCN/ UNDA.

61. Margaret Mealey, note to Lillian O'Connor, March 18, 1973, folder 25/box 3/ COCN/UNDA.

62. Desmazières, "Negotiating Religious and Women's Identities," 80–84. The Holy See increasingly came to view WUCWO as a representative of "radical feminism" in the church, particularly under the pontificate of John Paul II in the 1980s, and worked to promote its own "new feminist" ideology within the organization by the end of the Decade of the Woman. New feminism emerged from Pope John Paul II's theology of the body and reaffirmed traditional gender roles for Catholic women.

63. Cummings, Matovina, and Orsi, *Catholics in the Vatican II Era*, xvi.

64. Margaret O'Connell, editorial, *Word* 2, no. 11 (October 1965), folder 1965/box 66/ NCCW, 3.

65. Letters to the editor, *Word* 7, no. 8 (May 1970), 1970(1)/66/NCCW/CUA, 21; Rita M. Burke, letter to Catherine Schaefer, March 18, 1969, folder NCCW General Correspondence 64–70/box 161/NCWC-USCC/CUA.

66. Mrs. Ralph LeBlanc, letter to the editor, *Word* 6, no. 5 (August/September 1969), folder 1969(1)/box 66/NCCW/CUA, 16; Mrs. Richard Spiering, letter to the editor, *Word* 7, no. 3 (December 1969), folder 1969(1)/box 66/NCCW/CUA, 15; Catherine M. Cullimore, letter to the editor, *Word* 6, no. 4 (June/July 1969), folder 1969(1)/box 66/ NCCW/CUA, 17.

67. 1968 National Convention Program Evaluation, NCCW/CUA.

68. Report from the 1972 General Assembly, box 26/NCCW/CUA, 27.

69. NCCW National Board Meeting Minutes, January 1969, box 12/NCCW/CUA.

70. General Assembly Minutes, September 5–7, 1974, NCCW Minutes, 1 (58–79)/box 10/NCCW/CUA, 14.

71. C. M. T., "Notes on Church-State Affairs," 196–97. Other scholars who classify the NCCW as part of the "New Right Coalition" include Conover, "The Mobilization of the New Right," 636; and Siegel, "Text in Contest," 310.

72. For two sources that discuss the rise of women's organizations on the religious Right, see Critchlow, *Phyllis Schlafly and Grassroots Conservatism*; and Schreiber, *Righting Feminism*. Notably, there are no references to the NCCW in Critchlow.

CHAPTER 3

1. Antoinette Bosco, "What's Really Happened to Women?," *Marriage*, March 1971, 60.

2. Bosco, "What's Really Happened?," 60.

3. Bosco, "What's Really Happened?," 61–63.

4. Bosco, "What's Really Happened?," 59.

5. Editorial, *Marriage*, October 1963, 1; editorial, *Marriage*, May 1968, 5. These are the only years for which circulation statistics are available. Unfortunately, no papers relating to *Marriage* remain in the collections of Abbey Press at St. Meinrad Abbey.

6. For a discussion of Catholic practitioners in the field of psychology, and their subsequent influence on Catholic culture in the 1960s and 1970s, see Gillespie, "Psychology and American Catholicism," 120–21. See also Nussbaum, "Profession and Faith."

7. The 571 articles were selected for analysis on the basis of their content. First, I chose articles that took gender as their focus. In addition, I selected articles on a range of topics that might lend themselves to commentary about changing gender roles, among them sexuality, rhythm and birth control, large families, lay action, parishes, prayer, vocation, suburban life, authority and obedience, parenting, and the general subject of married life.

8. Walker, *Women's Magazines*, 8–9.

9. See Kelly and Kelly, "Our Lady of Perpetual Help," for a discussion of laywomen reshaping their identity by dropping out of devotional practices.

10. McDannell, "Catholic Domesticity," 49; see Henold, *Catholic and Feminist*.

11. *Casti Connubii* (1930). For a helpful discussion of *Casti Connubii* and gender, see Kalbian, *Sexing the Church*.

12. Kalbian, *Sexing the Church*.

13. Kalbian, *Sexing the Church*.

14. Kalbian, *Sexing the Church*, 52, 97–98.

15. Rev. Richard Hopkins, "Role of Husband and Wife," *Act*, April 1959, CFM 110, UNDA, 9–10.

16. Lettie Morse, "Woman's Role in Next Year's Program," *Act*, July 1962, CFM 110, UNDA, 6–7; Dwyer-McNulty, "Moving Beyond the Home," 88.

17. Johnson, "The Home Is a Little Church," 114; Imbiorski, "Filling the Husband's Need," 34.

18. G. C. Nabors, MD, "Making Rhythm Work, pt. 1," *Marriage*, June 1964, 10; J. Cain, "Valentine for a Wife," *Marriage*, February 1963, 7; Mrs. Robert Jarmusch, "Town and Country Marriage," *Marriage*, January 1962, 11.

19. Aurelius Boberek, OSB, "God's Image in Woman," *Marriage*, March 1962, 42–43; Augustine Rock, OP, "His Care for Her," *Marriage*, May 1962, 22.

20. Sr. Mary Eva, OSB, "Femininity Can Be Taught," *Marriage*, September 1964, 24–28.

21. Mary Maino, "Getting to Know You," *Marriage*, September 1961, 15.

22. Richard and Margery Frisbie, "News and Notes," *Marriage*, April 1961, 5.

23. C. Q. Mattingly, book review of *The Flight from Woman*, *Marriage*, December 1965, 16; Charles and Audrey Riker, "The Role of Man and Woman in Marriage," *Marriage*, July 1963, 6; Karl Rahner, SJ, "Religion and the Man," *Marriage*, January 1964, 6.

24. Mary Maino, "Gifts of Mind," *Marriage*, June 1961, 59; Maino, "Getting to Know You."

25. Katherine Byrne, "Happy Little Wives and Mothers," *America*, January 1956, 474; Robin Worthington, "Prayers for the Reluctant Housewife," *Marriage*, August 1966, 51; Anne Topatimlis, "The Motherhood Wilderness," *Marriage*, May 1962, 45.

26. Marge Morton, "Motherhood . . . Bah!," *Marriage*, July 1968, 65; Lucille S. Harper, "What Being Feminine Is Not," *Marriage*, August 1964, 27.

27. Rosemary Lauer, "College Isn't Wasted on a Girl," *Marriage*, March 1965, 20.

28. Sidney Cornelia Callahan, "Marriage and Family in a 'New' Society," *Marriage*, August 1965, 36.

29. Kathleen Kinahan, "Reader Reaction," *Marriage*, April 1970, 72; Maureen Bond and Linda Erickson, "Reader Reaction," *Marriage*, July 1972, 70; Lucille W. Martin, "Reader Reaction," *Marriage*, March 1972, 69.

30. Johnson, "Taking Marriage 'One Day at a Time,'" 19–20. For a discussion of gender and headship in the context of Catholic devotions, see Chinnici, "The Catholic Community at Prayer," 65.

31. Griffith, *God's Daughters*; Neuffer, *Helen Andelin*, 32. Historian Robert O. Self also demonstrates how African American women in the 1960s were encouraged—through rhetoric originating in the Johnson administration, mainstream African American women's groups, and the black power movement—to recommit to male headship for the betterment of the black family. See Self, *All in the Family*, chap. 1.

32. Richard and Margery Frisbie, "Family Front," *Marriage*, January 1961, 5.

33. Richard and Margery Frisbie, "Family Front," *Marriage*, July 1964, 2.

34. Louise Shanahan, "A Catholic Marriage Clinic," *Marriage*, December 1962, 43; Alice Waters, "My Husband, the Boss," *Marriage*, February 1965, 54; Mrs. Bill Osbourne, letter to the editor, *Marriage*, July 1965, 69.

35. Henri J. Breault, MD, "Why Is a Father," *Marriage*, September 1961, 41; Harry J. Cargas, "Examination of Conscience for Family Men," *Marriage*, September 1964, 17.

36. Raban Hathorn, OSB, editorial, *Marriage*, May 1962; Raban Hathorn, OSB, editorial, *Marriage*, May 1964.

37. C. Q. Mattingly, editorial, *Marriage*, November 1964.

38. Mary Alice Zarella, editorial, *Marriage*, August 1965; Ann Ward, "What Do Women Really Want?" *Marriage*, November 1964, 6–12; "Reader Reaction," *Marriage*, February 1965, 57.

39. Marian Tompson, "The Head of the Wife," *Marriage*, June 1969, 11; Richard Brow, "What Is a Man?," *Marriage*, June 1969, 13; Lester A. Kirkendall, "Is Sexual Freedom a Mirage?," *Marriage*, July 1969, 58.

40. Louise Shanahan, "The Changing Husband Image," *Marriage*, February 1971, 46.

41. Shanahan, "The Changing Husband Image," 47; Louise Shanahan, "The Neuter Generation," *Marriage*, October 1969, 11.

42. Louise Shanahan, "Money: His and Hers," *Marriage*, November 1966, 16–20; Louise Shanahan, "Marriage: Act of Negotiating," *Marriage*, January 1971, 34.

43. Louise Shanahan, "Are You Planning to Run Away?," *Marriage*, June 1971, 54–57; Louise Shanahan, "Is Male Dominance a Thing of the Past?," *Marriage*, August 1970, 27.

44. Mrs. Carroll A. Thomas, letter to the editor, *Marriage*, August 1969, 71; Suzanne L. Bacznak, letter to the editor, *Marriage*, October 1969, 71.

45. Iris M. Rabasca, "What's a Mother to Do?," *Marriage*, July 1967, 63; Kathryn F. Clarenbach, "Women as Second Class Citizens," *Marriage*, December 1967, 34.

46. Gloria Skurzynski, "History's Woman Haters," *Marriage*, July 1971, 20–24.

47. Shanahan, "Is Male Dominance a Thing of the Past?," 24; Ashley Montague, "Why Dominates Who?," *Marriage*, June 1971, 7–8; Virginia Heffernan, letter to the editor, *Marriage*, November 1972, 70; Rev. John T. Catoir, "The Future of Christian Marriage," *Marriage*, January 1973, 55; Arthur Ciervo, "The Career Woman in a Man's World," *Marriage*, January 1973, 48; Louise Shanahan, "The Tyranny of Love," *Marriage*, January 1969, 12.

48. The open debate over working wives in *Marriage* in the 1960s and 1970s has precedent in the women's magazines of the postwar period. Historian Nancy Walker argues that most women's magazines managed to present alternatives to housewifery, usually in articles about prominent or famous working women. Walker, *Women's Magazines*, 8.

49. Coontz, *The Way We Never Were*, 161; Blackwelder, *Now Hiring*, 177.

50. Frisbie and Frisbie, "Family Front" (January 1961), 5; Marie Robinson, MD, "The Mature Woman," *Marriage*, February 1961, 10 (emphasis added); Mary G. Low, "I Enjoy

Being a Housewife!," *Marriage*, May 1965, 53–55; Nellie M. Stewart, "I Don't Want to Be Free," *Marriage*, December 1961, 24–27.

51. Coontz, *The Way We Never Were*, 162.

52. Mary Ann Black, "How to Untrap the Housewife," *Marriage*, May 1967, 62; Doris Evans, "Working Wife: To Get a Job, or Stay at Home," *Marriage*, December 1968, 62; Mrs. Patrick J. Boyle, letter to the editor, *Marriage*, June 1971, 4–5.

53. Marian Behan Hammer, "Danger: Working Wife!," *Marriage*, August 1971, 16.

54. Alice Ogle, "7,500,000 Working Mothers," *Marriage*, October 1961, 49; Marian Behan Hammer, "Should I Send My Child to a Day Nursery?," *Marriage*, December 1971, 63, 65.

55. "Think It Over," *Marriage*, February 1961, 25; Mary Place, letter to the editor, *Marriage*, August 1962, 62.

56. Hertz's work is consistent with women in the liturgical movement who hoped to encourage laywomen to bring liturgical innovations and a sacramental mindset into the home. See Harmon, *There Were Also Many Women There*, 244.

57. Richard and Margery Frisbie, "Family Front," *Marriage*, February 1964, 4; Solange Hertz, "Meditations While Mopping the Floor," *Marriage*, July 1965, 42. Hertz's writing did not appear in the magazine again after 1965, although she continued to publish elsewhere. By the early 1970s she had become an outspoken critic of the Second Vatican Council. Notably, she published a series of articles in the right-wing Catholic magazine *Triumph* in 1972 on the need for rigid gender roles. See Popowski, *Rise and Fall of "Triumph,"* 190.

58. Eleanor F. Culhane, "Part Time Jobs for Mothers," *Marriage*, June 1962, 44 (6) 45, 49.

59. Muriel Robertson, "A Good Word for Working Wives," *Marriage*, October 1964, 14; Antoinette Bosco, "Mothers without Aprons," *Marriage*, February 1968, 39–40.

60. Clarenbach, "Women as Second Class Citizens," 28, 31; Mattingly, editorial (November 1964); Bosco, "Mothers without Aprons," 40.

61. Donna McClesky, "The 'New Woman,'" *Marriage*, March 1968, 42–43; Betsy Bliss, "Book Review: What's Happening with He and She," *Marriage*, February 1971, 41.

62. Black, "How to Untrap the Housewife," 62–63; Lorraine Collins, "What's a Nice Place Like This Doing to a Girl Like Me?," *Marriage*, March 1973, 62–63; Louise Shanahan, "Woman 1970: A Counsellor's View," *Marriage*, January 1970, 32; Catoir, "The Future of Christian Marriage," 56.

63. Virginia Heffernan, "Expanding Woman's Role," *Marriage*, December 1971, 45.

64. Heffernan, "Expanding Woman's Role," 43; Joan Schaupp, "Benefits of the Working Mother," *Marriage*, October 1972, 57.

65. Richard W. O'Donnell, "Suicide and the Unhappy Housewife," *Marriage*, June 1970, 38–43.

66. Linda Hussmann, letter to the editor, *Marriage*, September 1970, 5 (emphasis in original).

67. Catholic sociologist Andrew Greeley reported in 1977 that "despite the conventional wisdom that Catholics believe a woman's place is in the home, the overwhelming majority of all the Catholic ethnic groups approve of working wives." I would argue that the debates that took place in Catholic magazines like *Marriage* probably helped foster this acceptance. Greeley, *The American Catholic*, 187.

68. Luise Cahill Dittrich, "To Share Is to Live," *Marriage*, August 1973, 2–7. Stephanie Coontz recounts a conversation with historian Ruth Rosen about fear of housewifery among upwardly mobile women in the feminist movement. Coontz believes some readers

found support for avoidance of the homemaker role in *The Feminine Mystique*. See Coontz, *A Strange Stirring*, 133.

69. Tentler, *Catholics and Contraception*. My analysis in the section builds specifically on Tentler's fifth chapter, "Rhythm, Education for Marriage, Lay Voices, 1941–1962." For discussions of the theological debates that rocked the American Catholic community over rhythm and artificial contraception, see Kalbian, *Sex, Violence, and Justice*; and Massa, *The American Catholic Revolution*.

70. Westoff and Bumpass, "The Revolution in Birth Control Practices," 41. By April 2011, the Guttmacher Institute published findings that 98 percent of sexually active American Catholic women had used birth control methods other than natural family planning. See Jones and Dreweke, "Countering Conventional Wisdom."

71. C. Q. Mattingly, editorial, *Marriage*, November 1966. For helpful discussions of the controversy surrounding the release of *Humanae Vitae*, see Massa, *The American Catholic Revolution*; and Kalbian, *Sex, Violence, and Justice*. For lay involvement in the papal birth control commission, see McClory, "Turning Point."

72. For one of the few studies of immediate post-Council, post–*Humanae Vitae* Catholic debates on sexuality, see Burns, "Sexuality after the Council," an examination of lay attempts to shift the conversation, particularly on LGBT issues, in the Archdiocese of San Francisco.

73. R. Marie Griffith points out that the field of Catholic studies has often left the intersections of sexuality and gender unexplored. She attributes this to a focus in Catholic women's history on women religious, and to a lack of gender analysis in most comprehensive histories that discuss laypeople in the larger context of American history. Griffith, "Crossing the Catholic Divide," 85.

74. Bailey, *Sex in the Heartland*, 202. The direction the magazine took in these years was not inevitable, and was one choice among many for a moderate Catholic magazine. For example, there was a significant movement against the teaching of sex education in Catholic schools in the late 1960s (an early sign of Catholic entry in the emerging culture wars), something that was never even reported in *Marriage*. See Chinnici, "An Historian's Creed."

75. Jim McCartin, "'Sex Is Holy and Mysterious': The Vision of Early Twentieth-Century Catholic Sex Education Reformers," prepublication manuscript; Tentler, *Catholics and Contraception*, 173, 199. I am indebted to Jim McCartin for his incisive comments on this section of the chapter.

76. Philip Scharper, "Person to Person: Christian Marriage Is an Eternal 'Yes,'" *Marriage*, March 1966, 19; Reginald F. Trevett, "Love and Sex," *Marriage*, December 1961, 14.

77. Angela Downs, "Marriage Mystery," *Marriage*, April 1968, 51; Diane McCurdy, letter to the editor, *Marriage*, November 1965, 68 (emphasis in original).

78. Maino, "Getting to Know You," 16, 18.

79. Downs, "Marriage Mystery," 52.

80. Elizabeth Mulligan, "Pre-marriage Counselling: Is It Working?," *Marriage*, September 1970, 66; Florence Weimrath, "Sex . . . Once Over Lightly," *Marriage*, June 1963, 7.

81. Jose de Vinck and John Catoir, "How to Enjoy Your Honeymoon," part 1, *Marriage*, May 1970, 40 (emphasis in original).

82. Gerhard, *Desiring Revolution*, 52–53. R. Marie Griffith notes that secular scholarship on the history of sexuality commonly only mentions Catholics when they stood in opposition to agents of change such as Alfred Kinsey. *Marriage* shows how Catholics did

in fact respond to Kinsey in positive, and far more subtle, ways. See Griffith, "Crossing the Catholic Divide," 95.

83. Beverly Bush Smith, "Starting the Day with Love," *Marriage*, October 1971, 21; Virginia Heffernan, letter to the editor, *Marriage*, October 1971, 3.

84. Henry Sattler, C.SS.R. "Why Female?," *Marriage*, May 1965, 8; Brian P. Hendley, letter to the editor, *Marriage*, July 1965, 68; James P. Considine, letter to the editor, *Marriage*, July 1970, 52.

85. Francis R. McGovern, "My Husband Is a Great Lover," *Marriage*, November 1963, 27.

86. Mario Panzen, "What I Like about Making Love," *Marriage*, February 1969, 14.

87. Pat Mainardi, "The Politics of Housework," 432.

88. Marie Robinson, MD, "The Mature Woman," *Marriage*, February 1961, 9. See Gerhard, *Desiring Revolution*, chap. 2: "By the 1940s, the vaginal orgasm became a standard through which women's sexual impulses were deemed healthy or pathological" (52).

89. Panzen, "What I Like," 67.

90. Susan R. O'Hara, "An Open Mind on Women's Lib," *Marriage*, June 1972, 54; Lynn Sallee, "When Your Husband Is Unemployed," *Marriage*, October 1971, 35; Hammer, "Danger: Working Wife," 12.

91. Lester A. Kirkendall, "Unfinished Business: The Double Standard, Part I," *Marriage*, June 1969, 69; Cliff Yudell, "The 'Successful' Marriage," *Marriage*, September 1971, 14.

92. Raban Hathorn, OSB, editorial, *Marriage*, February 1965, 2.

CHAPTER 4

1. Mother Mary Hennessey, RC, "Convention Address," 1966 Convention Minutes/ CDA/CUA, 162–64.

2. The Daughters do not fit easily into existing historiographic narratives of conservative women in the United States. They were sympathetic to some right-wing activism— particularly anticommunism—making them seem similar at times to the "housewife populists" described in *Mothers of Conservatism*, for example, but activism was never as central to their identities as Catholicism. Moreover, most studies see a steady increase in commitment to conservative ideology moving through the 1960s. The Daughters disrupt that narrative somewhat, since there appear to have been several years of reassessment in the 1960s, prompted specifically by Vatican II. See Nickerson, *Mothers of Conservatism*; and Kempker, *Big Sister*.

3. Marthaler and Clement, *Catholic Daughters of the Americas*, 46. See also Clement, *Daughters of Isabella*.

4. O'Connor, "Defenders of the Faith."

5. Marthaler and Clement, *Catholic Daughters of the Americas*, 94; Clement, *Daughters of Isabella*, 96.

6. The fifteenth-century Spanish queen was responsible for the expulsion of Jews and Muslims from Spain. Nevertheless, the D of I organized a campaign to champion Isabella for sainthood.

7. "The Supreme Directorate," *News and Views*, Spring 1958/CDA/CUA, 8; "A Close-up of the Delegation at the Cathedral," *Isabellan*, October/November 1962/DI/CUA, 9; "Junior Daughters of Isabella: The Most Outstanding," *Isabellan*, October/November 1961/DI/CUA, 29.

8. Francis M. Maher, "This Year of Our Lord, 1958," *News and Views*, Spring 1958/CDA/ CUA, 4; National Board Meeting Minutes, July 1966, folder National Board Meeting Minutes, 2/64–2/67/CDA/CUA; Convention Minutes, 1966/DI/CUA; National Regent's Report, National Board Meeting Minutes, 1969, folder National Board Minutes, 2/68–7/70/CDA/CUA, 8.

9. Bishop Vincent Waters, "My Dear Catholic Daughters," *News and Views*, Fall 1964/ CDA/CUA, 10; Vincent Waters, "Sermon at Mass," National Convention Minutes, 1962/CDA/CUA, 71; John J. Walde, "Convention Address," Convention Minutes, 1970/ CDA/CUA, 25; William G. Connare, "Junior Catholic Daughters of America—Our Responsibility," Convention Minutes, 1964/CDA/CUA, 150.

10. Report by Bishop Bernard Flanagan, National Board Minutes, 1972, folder National Board Minutes, 2/71–7/73/CDA/CUA.

11. Colleen McDannell argues that one of the dominant characteristics in Catholic domestic life in the period from 1940 to 1960 was the idea that women needed to defend the Catholic family against threats from secular society. The CDA and D of I clearly absorbed these ideas and carried them into the 1960s. See McDannell, "Catholic Domesticity," 49.

12. Maher, "This Year of Our Lord," 4; "More and More Good Reading Is a Fallout Shelter against Smut," *News and Views*, National Convention 1962, folder News and Views Fall 1962/CDA/CUA, 55.

13. Waters, "My Dear Catholic Daughters," 9.

14. For more on the Marylike Crusade, see Kane et al., *Gender Identities in American Catholicism*. See also Dwyer-McNulty, *Common Threads*, 138–41.

15. Martin Stepanich, OFM, "Catholic Fashion Shows?," *News and Views*, July 1965, folder News and Views July 1965/CDA/CUA, 15.

16. Lucy B. Callahan, "Storming Heaven for Vocations through All Night Prayer Vigils," *News and Views*, National Convention 1962, folder News and Views 1962 Fall/CDA/ CUA, 35.

17. Margaret Buckley, "Are You Growing or Standing Still?," *News and Views*, Spring 1958, folder News and Views Spring 1958/CDA/CUA, 8.

18. Vincent Waters, "St. Paul's Advice Is Recommended to Meet Challenge of the Sixties," *News and Views*, National Convention 1962, folder News and Views Fall 1962/ CDA/CUA, 6–7.

19. National Convention Minutes, 1962/CDA/CUA/30; National Convention Minutes, 1960/CDA/CUA, 45–47; "Saint Joseph, Universal Patron of the Vatican Ecumenical Council," *Isabellan*, October/November 1961/DI/CUA, 23.

20. Waters, "Sermon at Mass," 74.

21. Waters, "Sermon at Mass," 74.

22. Basil Frison, CMF, "God's Candles," *Isabellan*, February 1963/DI/CUA, 18.

23. Frison, "God's Candles," 18.

24. Anna K. Ballard, "The Laity—A Reservoir of Catholic Strength," *News and Views*, February 1963, folder News and Views 1962 Fall/CDA/CUA, 9; Margaret J. Buckley, "The Organization and the Program," *News and Views*, February 1963, folder News and Views 1962 Fall/CDA/CUA, 45 (emphasis added).

25. Philomena F. Kerwin, "A Lady of the Holy Sepulchre," *News and Views*, February 1964/CDA/CUA, 8.

26. Convention Minutes, 1966/DI/CUA.

27. "Junior Daughters of Isabella," 29; National Board Minutes, 1974, folder National Board Minutes, 1/74–7/76/CDA/CUA, 9.

28. Ballard, "The Laity," 9.

29. Bishop Augusten Frotz, "'Aggiornamento' Reaches the Women!," *News and Views*, February 1965, folder News and Views February 1965/CDA/CUA, 2; Pope Pius VI, "On the New Liturgy," *News and Views*, July 1965, folder News and Views July 1965/CDA/CUA, 23.

30. Mary Sparks, "Address," National Convention Minutes, 1966/CDA/CUA, 162 (emphasis in original).

31. Sister Mary Luke Tobin, "Women in the Church since Vatican II," *America*, November 1, 1986.

32. Philomena Kerwin, "Women at the Council," *News and Views*, July 1965, folder News and Views July 1965/CDA/CUA, 26.

33. Maria Fairfax, letter to the editor, *Isabellan*, October/November 1961/DI/CUA, 38; Patricia P. Adams, "Talk Given at 21st Annual Congress of Religious Education—CCD," Convention Minutes, 1966/DI/CUA, 2.

34. Connare, "Junior Catholic Daughters of America," 150.

35. Supreme Regent's Report, D of I Quarterly Newsletter, February 1967, folder Quarterly Newsletters, 1938–72/DI/CUA, 10; Hennessey, "Convention Address," 164 (emphasis in original).

36. Alexis McCarthy, O.Carm., "Address," National Convention Minutes, 1966/CDA/CUA, 81.

37. Anna K. Buckley, "Zeal for World Missions," *News and Views*, National Convention 1964, folder News and Views Fall 1964/CDA/CUA, 25; Mrs. Arthur L. Zepf, "Convention Banquet Speech," Convention Minutes, 1968/CDA/CUA, 96.

38. Joseph Beatty, "The Christian Woman," *The Isabellan*, August 1963, 12/DI/CUA 5; Vincent Waters, "Sermon," National Convention Minutes, 1966/CDA/CUA, 66.

39. Waters, "Sermon," 1966 (emphasis added); Second Vatican Council's "Message to the Women of the World," December 8, 1965, quoted in Bishop Stephen A. Leven, "Votive Mass for Peace," National Council of Catholic Women Conference Proceedings 1968, 1968/24/NCCW/CUA, 140.

40. "Message to the Women."

41. Beatty, "The Christian Woman," 5.

42. Rev. Hubert M. Newell, "Luncheon Address," 1962 Convention, 1962 Convention Proceedings/CDA/CUA, 83; Waters, Sermon, 1966, 68.

43. Waters, "Sermon," 1966, 68.

44. Lillian J. Kennedy, "This Is a Woman's World," *Isabellan*, June/July 1962/DI/CUA, 13.

45. Kennedy, "This Is a Woman's World."

46. Kennedy, "This Is a Woman's World."

47. Hennessey, "Convention Address," 163–64.

48. Zepf, "Convention Banquet Speech," 95–96.

49. Zepf, "Convention Banquet Speech."

50. Adams, "Talk Given at 21st Annual Congress," 2.

51. Bishop William Connare, excerpt of sermon, *News and Views*, July 1966, folder News and Views July 1966/CDA/CUA, 26.

52. Convention Minutes, 1964/CDA/CUA, 69–70; Convention Minutes, 1966/DI/CUA (emphasis in original).

53. Unfortunately, the ritual for arriving late or leaving early was not described in the archival material. It might have come in handy in my classroom.

54. "Liturgy: No Light Thing," editorial, *America*, August 18, 1962; Convention Minutes, 1962/CDA/CUA, 22.

55. Mary C. Kanane, "The Liturgical Conference," *News and Views*, National Convention, 1964, folder News and Views Fall 1964/CDA/CUA, 24; Helen D. Benett, "Report on 1967 National Liturgical Week," Convention Minutes, 1968/DI/CUA.

56. National Board Minutes, March 1971, folder National Board Meeting Minutes, February 71–July 73/CDA/CUA.

57. National Board Minutes, March 1973, folder NB Min 2/71–7/73/CDA/CUA, 25–26.

58. "Our Potentials—Limitless," Convention Minutes, 1964/CDA/CUA, 57; Connare, "Junior Catholic Daughters of America," 151.

59. Catharine G. Lee, "Marian Medal Revision Meeting," July 1971, Convention Minutes, 1972/DI/CUA, 54b–54i.

60. Marthaler and Clement, *Catholic Daughters of the Americas*, 101–2 (emphasis in original); *News and Views*, National Convention 1966, folder News and Views July 66/CDA/CUA, 26; Connare, "Sermon 1966 Convention," *News and Views*, July 1966, folder News and Views July 66/CDA/CUA, 22.

61. Ballard, "Report of the National Regent" National Board Minutes, February 1967, 3/CDA/CUA."

62. Ballard, "Report of the National Regent."

63. Anna Ballard, "National Regent Stresses Role of Women in the Apostolate of the Laity Movement," *CDA News* 1, no. 1 (May 1967), folder CDA News May 1976/CDA/CUA, 2–3; Marthaler and Clement, *Catholic Daughters of the Americas*, 98.

64. Ballard, "National Regent Stresses Role," 100.

65. Anna Baxter, National Regent's Report, National Board Minutes, February 1969, folder National Board Minutes, 2/68–7/70/CDA/CUA, 8–9.

66. Marthaler and Clement, *Catholic Daughters of the Americas*, 103; National Board Minutes, July 1973, folder National Board Minutes, 2/71–7/73/CDA/CUA; National Board Minutes, February 1974, folder National Board Minutes, 2/74–7/76/CDA/CUA.

67. Clement, *Daughters of Isabella*, 93; Marie Heyer, letter to the membership, Convention Proceedings, 1974/DI/CUA.

68. National Board Minutes, July 1974, folder National Board Minutes, 2/74–7/76/CDA/CUA.

69. For more on Catholics' fears of a declining culture, and their subsequent alliance with conservative Protestants in the culture wars of the late 1970s, see Flippen, "Carter, Catholics."

70. "The Sevenfold Program," *Around the World with the CDA*, 1969, folder 1969 Prior to Share/CDA/CUA, 8; National Board Minutes, July 1969, folder National Board Minutes, 2/68–7/70/CDA/CUA.

71. John Walde, "Address," Convention Minutes, 1968/CDA/CUA, 88–91; National Board Minutes, February 1970, folder National Board Minutes, 2/68–7/70/CDA/CUA.

72. McCarthy, "Address," 80; Adams, "Talk Given at 21st Annual Congress," 2.

73. Convention Minutes, 1979/DI/CUA; "The Sevenfold Program," 6.

74. Convention Minutes, 1970/DI/CUA; Convention Minutes, 1970/DI/CUA.

75. National Directorate Meeting Minutes, February 1967, folder National Board Minutes, 2/64–2/67/CDA/CUA; "Statement of Principles," Convention Minutes, box 11/CDA/CUA, 16.

76. Convention Minutes, 1974/DI/CUA. For more on IWY, see Olcott, *International Women's Year.*

77. Walde, "Convention Address" (1970), 24; Mary Cunningham, letter to National Regent Winifred Trabeaux, March 13, 1975, folder ERA/CDA/CUA. For a thorough discussion of the politics that attracted right-leaning Catholic women in the 1970s and later, see Taranto, *Kitchen Table Politics.*

EPILOGUE

1. San Martín, "Amid Focus on Women."

2. Statuto del Dicastero per i Laici, la Famiglia e la Vita, May 8, 2018, http://press.vatican.va/content/salastampa/it/bollettino/pubblico/2018/05/08/0329/00712.html#ing.

3. Glatz, "Pope Francis: Gender Theory Is the Problem."

4. Chapman, "Pope Francis: Gender Theory Is an Error of the Mind." For a scholarly reflection on the Vatican and its "war on gender," see Case, "Seeing the Sex and Justice Landscape."

5. Ferrone, "Francis's Words about Women."

Bibliography

ARCHIVAL COLLECTIONS

American Catholic History Research Center,
   Catholic University of America, Washington, D.C.
      Catholic Daughters of the Americas Papers
      Daughters of Isabella Records
      National Catholic Welfare Conference Records
      National Council of Catholic Women Records
Archdiocese of Chicago Archives and Records, Chicago, Illinois
      Albert Cardinal Meyer Collection
      Archdiocesan Council of Catholic Women Collection
University of Notre Dame Archives, Notre Dame, Indiana
      Christian Family Movement Records
      Lillian O'Connor Papers
Women and Leadership Archives,
   Loyola University Chicago, Chicago, Illinois
      Theresians of the United States Records

CATHOLIC PERIODICALS

Act	*The Isabellan*
America	*Liguorian*
Ave Maria	*Marriage*
Catholic School Journal	*Maryknoll*
Catholic Woman	*News and Views*
Emmanuel	*Sign*
Family Digest	*The Theresian*
Homiletic and Pastoral Review	*Today*
Information	*Word*

SECONDARY SOURCES

Bailey, Beth L. *Sex in the Heartland.* Cambridge, MA: Harvard University Press, 1999.
Blackwelder, Julia Kirk. *Now Hiring: The Feminization of Work in the United States,*
   1900–1995. College Station: Texas A&M University Press, 1997.
Blair, Melissa Estes. *Revolutionizing Expectations: Women's Organizations, Feminism, and*
   American Politics, 1965–1980. Athens: University of Georgia Press, 2014.
Bonner, Jeremy, Christopher Denny, and Mary Beth Fraser Connolly, eds. *Empowering the*
   People of God: Catholic Action before and after Vatican II. New York: Fordham University
   Press, 2014.

Bonner, Jeremy. "Who Will Guard the Guardians?" In *Empowering the People of God: Catholic Action before and after Vatican II*, edited by Jeremy Bonner, Christopher Denny, and Mary Beth Fraser Connolly, 222–48. New York: Fordham University Press, 2014.

Borromeo, Sister M. Charles, ed. *The New Nuns*. New York: New American Library, 1967.

Buchanan, Paul D. *Radical Feminists: A Guide to an American Subculture*. Westport, CT: Greenwood, 2011.

Burns, Jeffrey M. "Sexuality after the Council: Gay Catholics, Married Clergy, Rights, and Change in San Francisco, 1962–1987." In *Catholics in the Vatican II Era: Local Histories of a Global Event*, edited by Kathleen Sprows Cummings, Timothy Matovina, and Robert A. Orsi, 3–27. New York: Cambridge University Press, 2018.

Callahan, Daniel. *The Mind of the Catholic Layman*. New York: Charles Scribner's Sons, 1963.

Callahan, Sidney Cornelia. *The Illusion of Eve*. New York: Sheed and Ward, 1965.

Case, Mary Anne. "Seeing the Sex and Justice Landscape through the Vatican's Eyes." In *The War on Sex*, edited by David M. Halperin and Trevor Hoppe, 211–25. Durham, NC: Duke University Press, 2017.

Chapman, Michael W. "Pope Francis: 'Gender Theory Is an Error of the Mind That Leads to So Much Confusion.'" CNSNews, June 4, 2015. http://cnsnews.com/blog /michael-w-chapman/pope-francis-gender-theory-error-human-mind-leads-so -much-confusion.

Chinnici, Joseph P. "An Historian's Creed and the Emergence of Postconciliar Culture Wars." *Catholic Historical Review* 94, no. 2 (2008): 219–44. http://www.jstor.org /stable/25027276.

———. "The Catholic Community at Prayer, 1926–1976." In *Habits of Devotion: Catholic Religious Practice in Twentieth-Century America*, edited by James M. O'Toole, 9–87. Ithaca, NY: Cornell University Press, 2004.

Clement, Carol Dorr. *Daughters of Isabella: Our Legacy, Our Future, 1897–2007*. Rockville, MD: Mercury, 2008.

C. M. T. "Notes on Church-State Affairs." *Journal of Church and State* (1976): 151–96.

Cobble, Dorothy Sue. "More than Sex Equality: Feminism after Suffrage." In *Feminism Unfinished: A Short Surprising History of American Women's Movements*. New York: Liveright, 2014.

Conover, Pamela Johnston. "The Mobilization of the New Right: A Test of Various Explanations." *Western Political Quarterly* 36, no. 4 (1983): 632–49.

Coontz, Stephanie. *A Strange Stirring: "The Feminine Mystique" and American Women at the Dawn of the 1960s*. New York: Basic Books, 2011.

———. *The Way We Never Were: American Families and the Nostalgia Trap*. New York: Basic Books, 1992.

Copeland, M. Shawn ed. *Uncommon Faithfulness: The Black Catholic Experience*. Maryknoll, NY: Orbis Books, 2009.

Cott, Nancy F. *The Grounding of Modern Feminism*. New Haven, CT: Yale University Press, 1987.

Cressler, Matthew. "Black Power, Vatican II, and the Emergence of Black Catholic Liturgies." *U.S. Catholic Historian* 32, no. 4 (Fall 2014): 99–119.

Critchlow, Donald T. *Phyllis Schlafly and Grassroots Conservatism: A Woman's Crusade*. Princeton, NJ: Princeton University Press, 2005.

Cummings, Kathleen Sprows, Timothy Matovina, and Robert A. Orsi, eds. *Catholics in the Vatican II Era: Local Histories of a Global Event.* New York: Cambridge University Press, 2017.

Cunneen, Sally. *Sex: Female; Religion: Catholic.* New York: Holt, Rinehart, Winston, 1968.

Davis, Cyprian. *The History of Black Catholics in the United States.* New York: Crossroad, 1990.

del Rey, Sister Maria. *Bernie Becomes a Nun.* New York: Farrar, Straus and Cudahy, 1956.

Desmazières, Agnès. "Negotiating Religious and Women's Identities: Catholic Women at the UN World Conferences, 1975–1995." *Journal of Women's History* 24, no. 4 (2012): 74–98.

Dolan, Jay P. *The American Catholic Experience: A History from Colonial Times to the Present.* Garden City, NJ: Doubleday, 1985.

Dwyer-McNulty, Sally. *Common Threads: A Cultural History of Clothing in American Catholicism.* Chapel Hill: University of North Carolina Press, 2014.

Dwyer-McNulty, Sara. "Moving Beyond the Home: Women and Catholic Action in Post–World War II America." *U.S. Catholic Historian* 20, no. 1 (2002): 83–97. http://www.jstor.org/stable/27671152.

Ebaugh, Helen Rose, Jon Lorence, and Janet Saltzman Chafetz. "The Growth and Decline of the Population of Catholic Nuns Cross-nationally, 1960–1990: A Case of Secularization as Social Structural Change." *Journal for the Scientific Study of Religion* (1996): 171–83.

Echols, Alice. *Daring to Be Bad: Radical Feminism in America, 1967–1975.* Minneapolis: University of Minnesota, 1989.

Faggioli, Massimo. *A Council for the Global Church.* Minneapolis: Augsburg Fortress, 2015.

———. *Vatican II: The Battle for Meaning.* Mahwah: Paulist, 2012.

Ferrone, Rita. "Francis's Words about Women." *Commonweal,* April 5, 2017. https://www.commonwealmagazine.org/francis%E2%80%99s-words-about-women.

Flippen, J. Brooks. "Carter, Catholics, and the Politics of Family." *American Catholic Studies* 123, no. 3 (2012): 27–51. http://www.jstor.org/stable/44195421.

Friedan, Betty. *The Feminine Mystique.* New York: W. W. Norton, 1963.

Gerhard, Jane F. *Desiring Revolution: Second-Wave Feminism and the Rewriting of American Sexual Thought, 1920 to 1982.* New York: Columbia University Press, 2001.

Gillespie, C. Kevin. "Psychology and American Catholicism after Vatican II: Currents, Cross-currents and Confluences." *U.S. Catholic Historian* 25, no. 4 (2007): 117–31. http://www.jstor.org/stable/25156648.

Gilmore, Stephanie. *Groundswell: Grassroots Feminist Activism in Postwar America.* New York: Routledge, 2013.

Glatz, Carol. "Pope Francis: Gender Theory Is the Problem, Not the Solution." *National Catholic Reporter,* April 15, 2015. http://ncronline.org/blogs/francis-chronicles/pope-francis-gender-theory-problem-not-solution.

Greeley, Andrew M. *The American Catholic: A Social Portrait.* New York: Basic Books, 1977.

Griffith, R. Marie. "Crossing the Catholic Divide: Gender, Sexuality, and Historiography." In *Catholics in the American Century: Recasting Narratives of U.S. History,* edited by R. Scott Appleby and Kathleen Sprows Cummings, 81–108. Ithaca, NY: Cornell University Press, 2012.

———. *God's Daughters: Evangelical Women and the Power of Submission.* Berkeley: University of California Press, 1997.

Harmon, Katharine E. *There Were Also Many Women There: Lay Women in the Liturgical Movement in the United States, 1926–59*. Collegeville, MN: Liturgical, 2013.

Henold, Mary J. "Breaking the Boundaries of Renewal: The American Catholic Underground, 1966–1970." *U.S. Catholic Historian* 19, no. 3 (Summer 2001): 97–118.

———. *Catholic and Feminist: The Surprising History of the American Catholic Feminist Movement*. Chapel Hill: University of North Carolina Press, 2008.

———. "'Woman—Go Forth!': Catholic Women's Organizations and Their Clergy Advisors in the Era of the 'Emerging Laywoman.'" *U.S. Catholic Historian* 32, no 4 (Fall 2014): 151–73.

Hertz, Solange. *Women, Words, and Wisdom*. Westminster, MD: Newman, 1959.

Imbiorski, Rev. Walter J. "Filling the Husband's Need." In *The Basic Cana Manual*, edited by Rev. Walter J. Imbiorski. Chicago: Cana Conference of Chicago, 1963.

Johnson, Ann, and Elizabeth Johnston. "Unfamiliar Feminisms: Revisiting the National Council of Women Psychologists." *Psychology of Women Quarterly* 34, no. 3 (2010): 311–27. https://doi.org/10.1111/j.1471-6402.2010.01577.x.

Johnson, Karen J. *One in Christ: Chicago Catholics and the Quest for Interracial Justice*. New York: Oxford University Press, 2018.

Johnson, Kathryn. "The Home Is a Little Church: Gender, Culture, and Authority in American Catholicism, 1940–1962." PhD diss., University of Pennsylvania, 1997.

Johnson, Kathryn A. "Taking Marriage 'One Day at a Time': The Cana Conference Movement and the Creation of a Catholic Mentality." *Cushwa Center Working Paper Series* 22 (2001).

Jones, Rachel K., and Joerg Dreweke. "Countering Conventional Wisdom: New Evidence on Religion and Contraceptive Use." Guttmacher Institute, April 2011.

Kalbian, Aline H. *Sex, Violence, and Justice: Contraception and the Catholic Church*. Washington, D.C.: Georgetown University Press, 2014.

———. *Sexing the Church: Gender, Power, and Ethics in Contemporary Catholicism*. Bloomington: Indiana University Press, 2005.

Kane, Paula M., et al., eds. *Gender Identities in American Catholicism*. Maryknoll, NY: Orbis, 2001.

———. "Marian Devotion since 1940: Continuity or Casualty?" In *Habits of Devotion: Catholic Religious Practice in Twentieth-Century America*, edited by James M. O'Toole, 89–130. Ithaca, NY: Cornell University Press, 2004.

———. "'She Offered Herself Up': The Victim Soul and Victim Spirituality in Catholicism." *Church History* 71, no. 1 (2002): 80–119.

Kelly, Timothy. "Suburbanization and the Decline of Catholic Public Ritual in Pittsburgh." *Journal of Social History* 28, no. 2 (Winter 1994): 311–30.

———. *The Transformation of American Catholicism: The Pittsburgh Laity and the Second Vatican Council, 1950–1972*. Notre Dame, IN: University of Notre Dame Press, 2009.

Kelly, Timothy, and Joseph Kelly. "Our Lady of Perpetual Help, Gender Roles, and the Decline of Devotional Catholicism." *Journal of Social History* 32, no. 1 (1998): 5–26. http://www.jstor.org/stable/3789591.

Kempker, Erin M. *Big Sister: Feminism, Conservatism, and Conspiracy in the Heartland*. Urbana: University of Illinois Press, 2018.

Koehlinger, Amy L. *The New Nuns: Racial Justice and Religious Reform in the 1960s*. Cambridge, MA: Harvard University Press, 2007.

Laughlin, Kathleen A., and Jacqueline L. Castledine. *Breaking the Wave: Women, Their Organizations, and Feminism, 1945–1985.* New York: Routledge, 2011.

Mainardi, Patricia. "The Politics of Housework." In *Sisterhood Is Powerful: An Anthology of Writings from the Women's Liberation Movement,* edited by Robin Morgan. New York: Randon House, 1970.

Marthaler, Berard L., and Carol Dorr Clement. *Catholic Daughters of the Americas: A Century in Review.* Rockville, MD: Mercury, 2003.

Massa, Mark S. *The American Catholic Revolution: How the Sixties Changed the Church Forever.* New York: Oxford University Press, 2010.

———. *Catholics and American Culture: Fulton Sheen, Dorothy Day, and the Notre Dame Football Team.* New York: Crossroad, 1999.

Mathews-Gardner, A. Lanethea. "From Ladies Aid to NGO: Transformations in Methodist Women's Organizing in Postwar America." In *Breaking the Wave: Women, Their Organizations, and Feminism, 1945–1985,* edited by Kathleen A. Laughlin and Jacqueline L. Castledine, 111–24. New York: Routledge, 2012.

McCartin, James P. *Prayers of the Faithful: The Shifting Spiritual Life of American Catholics.* Cambridge, MA: Harvard University Press, 2010.

———. "The Sacred Heart of Jesus, Thérèse of Lisieux, and the Transformation of US Catholic Piety, 1865–1940." *U.S. Catholic Historian* 25, no. 2 (Spring 2007): 53–67.

McClory, Robert. *Turning Point: The Inside Story of the Papal Birth Control Commission and How* Humanae Vitae *Changed the Life of Patty Crowley and the Future of the Church.* New York: Crossroad Publishing, 1995.

McDannell, Colleen. "Catholic Domesticity, 1860–1960." *American Catholic Women: A Historical Exploration* (1995): 48–80.

———. *The Spirit of Vatican II: A History of Catholic Reform in America.* New York: Basic Books, 2011.

McGreevy, John T. *Parish Boundaries: The Catholic Encounter with Race in the Twentieth Century Urban North.* Chicago: University of Chicago Press, 1996.

Morrow, Maria C. "The Change in the Conception of Sin among Catholics in the United States, 1955–1975." *American Catholic Studies* 122, no. 1 (2011): 55–76.

Neuffer, Julie Debra. *Helen Andelin and the Fascinating Womanhood Movement.* Salt Lake City: University of Utah Press, 2014.

Nickerson, Michelle M. *Mothers of Conservatism: Women and the Postwar Right.* Princeton, NJ: Princeton University Press, 2012.

Nussbaum, Abraham. "Profession and Faith: The National Guild of Catholic Psychiatrists, 1950–1968." *Catholic Historical Review* 93, no. 4 (2007): 845–65. http://www.jstor.org/stable/25027163.

O'Connor, David. "Defenders of the Faith: American Catholic Lay Organizations and Anticommunism, 1917–1975." PhD diss., State University of New York at Stony Brook, 2000.

O'Gara, James. *The Layman and the Church.* New York: Herder and Herder, 1962.

O'Halloran, Ruth. "Organized Catholic Laywomen: The National Council of Catholic Women, 1920–1995." PhD diss., Catholic University of America, 1996.

Olcott, Jocelyn. *International Women's Year: The Greatest Consciousness-Raising Event in History.* New York: Oxford University Press, 2017.

O'Malley, James W. ed. *Vatican II: Did Anything Happen?* New York: Continuum, 2007.

Orsi, Robert A. *The Madonna of 115th Street: Faith and Community in Italian Harlem, 1880–1950.* 3rd ed. New Haven, CT: Yale University Press, 2010.

O'Toole, James M. "In the Court of Conscience: American Catholics and Confession, 1900–1975." In *Habits of Devotion: Catholic Religious Practice in Twentieth-Century America,* edited by James M. O'Toole, 131–85. Ithaca, NY: Cornell University Press, 2004.

O'Toole, James M., ed. *Habits of Devotion: Catholic Religious Practice in Twentieth-Century America.* Ithaca, NY: Cornell University Press, 2005.

Popowski, Mark D. *The Rise and Fall of "Triumph": The History of a Radical Roman Catholic Magazine, 1966–1976.* Lanham, MD: Lexington, 2011.

Robinson, Marie N. *The Power of Sexual Surrender.* New York: Signet, 1958.

Roche, Douglas J., and Remi De Roo. *Man to Man: A Frank Talk between Layman and Bishop.* Milwaukee: Bruce, 1969.

Rogow, Faith. *Gone to Another Meeting: The National Council of Jewish Women, 1893–1993.* Tuscaloosa: University of Alabama Press, 1993.

Rossi, Joseph S. "The Status of Women": Two American Catholic Women at the UN, 1947–1972." *Catholic Historical Review* 93, no. 2 (2007): 300–324.

San Martín, Inés. "Amid Focus on Women, Is the Vatican's Issue Less Gender than Laity?" *Crux,* May 10, 2018. https://cruxnow.com/vatican/2018/05/10/amid-focus-on -women-is-the-vaticans-issue-less-gender-than-laity/.

Schillebeeckx, Edward. *The Layman in the Church and Other Essays.* New York: Alba House, 1963.

Schreiber, Ronnee. *Righting Feminism: Conservative Women and American Politics.* New York: Oxford University Press, 2008.

Schulman, Bruce J. *The Seventies: The Great Shift in American Culture, Society, and Politics.* New York: Simon and Schuster, 2001.

Self, Robert O. *All in the Family: The Realignment of American Democracy since the 1960s.* New York: Hill and Wang, 2012.

Siegel, Reva B. "Text in Contest: Gender and the Constitution from a Social Movement Perspective." *University of Pennsylvania Law Review* 150, no. 1 (2001): 297–351.

Southern, David W. *John LaFarge and the Limits of Catholic Interracialism, 1911–1963.* Baton Rouge: Louisiana State University, 1996.

Sugrue, Thomas J. "The Catholic Encounter with the 1960s." In *Catholics in the American Century: Recasting Narratives of U.S. History,* edited by R. Scott Appleby and Kathleen Sprows Cummings, 61–80. Ithaca, NY: Cornell University Press, 2012.

Swidler, Arlene. *Sistercelebrations: Nine Worship Experiences.* Minneapolis: Fortress, 1974.

Taranto, Stacie. *Kitchen Table Politics: Conservative Women and Family Values in New York.* Philadelphia: University of Pennsylvania Press, 2017.

Tentler, Leslie Woodcock. *Catholics and Contraception: An American History.* Ithaca, NY: Cornell University Press, 2004.

Thorman, Donald J. *The Emerging Layman.* New York: Image, 1962.

von le Fort, Gertrud Freiin. *The Eternal Woman: The Woman in Time [and] Timeless Woman.* Milwaukee: Bruce, 1962.

Voss, Elwood C., and Patricia Mullen. *The Theresian Story: Women in Support of Women,* 35th anniversary ed. Colorado Springs, CO: Theresian, 1996.

Walker, Nancy A. *Women's Magazines, 1940–1960: Gender Roles and the Popular Press.* Boston: Bedford/St. Martin's, 1998.

Wallace, Ruth A. "Bringing Women In: Marginality in the Churches." *Sociological Analysis* 36, no. 4 (1975): 291–303.

———. "Joseph H. Fichter's Contributions to Feminism." *Sociology of Religion* 57, no. 4 (1996): 359–66.

Weaver, Janet. "Barrio Women: Community and Coalition in the Heartland." In *Breaking the Wave: Women, Their Organizations, and Feminism, 1945–1985,* edited by Kathleen A. Laughlin and Jacqueline L. Castledine, 173–88. New York: Routledge, 2011.

Weaver, Mary Jo. *New Catholic Women: A Contemporary Challenge to Traditional Religious Authority.* San Francisco: Harper & Row, 1988.

Westoff, Charles F., and Larry Bumpass. "The Revolution in Birth Control Practices of U.S. Roman Catholics." *Science* 179, no. 4068 (1973): 41–44. http://www.jstor.org/stable/1734937.

Wilkerson, Jessica. *To Live Here, You Have to Fight: How Women Led Appalachian Movements for Social Justice.* Urbana: University of Illinois Press, 2019.

Williams, Daniel K. *Defenders of the Unborn: The Pro-Life Movement before Roe v. Wade.* New York: Oxford University Press, 2016.

Index

abortion, 61, 71, 73, 75, 81–83, 91, 103, 111, 164, 187–88, 202n5

Act, 113

adulthood, of laywomen, 31, 67, 69–70, 72, 78–79. *See also* maturity

African Americans, 6, 11, 78, 195n5, 208n31. *See also* race

aggiornamento, 95–96

altar societies, 72–72, 78

America, 117, 178

Andelin, Helen, 133

androgyny, 14

anticommunism, 9, 71, 152, 158, 170, 211n2

antifeminism, 60–61, 71–72, 80–82, 99–103, 109, 111, 122, 127–28, 144, 173, 187–88

apostolate, 66; of laity, 49, 57, 111, 113, 159, 172, 182; of nuns, 47; of women's organizations, 31, 40, 48, 51–52, 58, 94, 163, 168. *See also* ministry

Archdiocesan Council of Catholic Women, Chicago, 1–3

authority, 150, 185; of clerics, 3, 6–8, 16, 34, 79, 111, 139, 153; of laity, 9, 111; of laywomen, 2, 13, 16, 25, 87, 107, 109, 193–94; in marriage, 122–25, 127–29, 131; of nuns, 34–35, 44, 48, 149; patriarchal, 9, 110, 113

autonomy: lay, 5, 9, 12, 113; of women, 72, 82, 85, 89–90, 92, 174, 176, 184

baby boom, 19, 26

Ballard, Anna, 148, 157, 162–63, 166, 181–82

baptism, 46–47, 49

Barrett, Mrs. Betty, 54, 67

Basic Cana Manual, The (Imbiorski), 114

Baxter, Anna, 182–83, 185

Bellosillo, María del Pilar, 96–98

Bernie Becomes a Nun (del Rey), 22–23

birth control. *See* contraception

bishops, 16, 26, 74, 90; criticism of, 70–72, 77, 95, 165, 167, 175, 189; and gender, 2, 12–13, 15, 72, 164, 167, 189; laywomen as agents of, 4, 7, 13, 46, 71–73, 93, 170, 178; support for, 74, 155–56, 161; and Vatican II, 1, 13, 77, 122, 149, 161, 177

Blessed Sacrament, prayer before, 24, 39–40

Body of Christ, 45, 49, 113, 161

Bordelon, Cynthia, 37, 40

Bosco, Antoinette, 105–7, 133, 147

Buckley, Anna K., 169

Buckley, Margaret, 158, 181

Callahan, Daniel, 120

Callahan, Sidney, 55, 83, 120

Campfire Girls, 180

Canada, 33, 51, 152

Cana Movement, 7, 9, 108, 111, 114, 119, 121, 140, 142

canon law, 97, 100, 174, 200n53

careers. *See* work, outside the home

Carmelites, 32

Casti Connubii, 111, 113–14

catechesis, 27, 53, 87, 194

Catholic Action, 2, 7, 46–47, 93, 157, 160, 166

Catholic Daughters of America, 2, 151–52; courts of, 152–53, 156, 158–59, 169, 177, 179, 184. *See also* Daughters

Catholic elementary schools, 12, 26–27, 32, 35, 42, 46, 210n74

Catholic Interracial Council, 7

Catholic Woman, 83, 103

chaplains, of the Daughters, 148, 153–56, 160–61, 169–72, 176–77, 179, 181, 183, 185, 188

charismatic renewal, 65, 184

charity, 35, 49, 115, 140, 152, 163, 168–70, 181, 184

childcare, 131, 136

children: and fathers, 122–23, 131; and feminism, 84, 112, 120; and mothers, 12, 19, 21–28, 38–39, 100, 133, 156, 158–59, 165, 172; and pregnancy, 6, 61, 112, 119, 138, 171

Christian Family Movement (CFM), 7, 9, 108, 111, 113–14, 140

Church Women United, 78

class, 5–6, 32, 58, 78, 81, 100, 107, 133, 152, 169

clericalism, 193

cloister, 32, 35

clothing, 18, 20, 53, 54, 75, 78, 152, 157, 161, 181. *See also* modesty

college, 6, 17, 33, 37, 89, 115, 117, 119, 120, 133

Colorado, 32–33, 39, 62, 66

Columbian Exposition, 151

communism. *See* anticommunism

complementarity, 9, 14–15, 192–93; Daughters and, 152, 172–73; *Marriage* and, 13–14, 56–57, 107, 111–18, 121, 124, 129, 136, 139, 141, 143–47; NCCW and, 14, 75, 84–85, 91–92, 103; Theresians and, 31, 38, 56–57, 59–60, 69. *See also* essentialism

confession, 6–7, 24, 111

Congregation for the Doctrine of the Faith, 191

Congress of Religious Education, 176

Connare, Fr. William, 168, 181–81

Connecticut, 38, 151

consciousness-raising, 1, 14, 63–64, 67, 137, 184

contraception, 7–8, 61, 74, 109, 111, 138–39, 141, 183–85, 210n70

convents, 17, 20, 26, 34, 37, 42

conversion, 76, 159, 186. *See also* evangelization

Cribari, Kathy, 29, 44, 53, 57, 62–63

crisis, sense of, 31, 50, 61, 75, 182–83, 185–86. *See also* evil; vocation crisis

crusading, 87, 156, 159, 163, 185, 187

Cunneen, Sally, 83

Daly, Mary, 89

Daughters (Catholic Daughters of America and the Daughters of Isabella), 2, 4, 152–53; and abortion, 164, 187–88; administration of, 177, 180; and chaplains, 148, 153–56, 160–61, 169–72, 176–77, 179, 181, 183, 185, 188; and charity, 152, 168–70, 174–75, 181, 184; and clergy, 149, 166–67, 170–73; and complementarity, 152, 172–73; and the conservative movement, 211n2; defensive posture of, 15, 61, 150, 156–59, 163–64, 169, 176, 179, 185–87, 189, 212n11; and duty, 165–66, 168–69, 188; and ecumenism, 160, 164, 181–82; and education, 168, 170, 181; and empowerment, 10, 170, 189; and equality, 171–73, 176; and the Equal Rights Amendment, 188; and essentialism, 57, 152, 161–62, 171–76; and evangelization, 160–61, 169, 186 and the family, 159, 165, 172, 212n11; and feminism, 10, 149, 152, 164–65, 170–76, 180, 184–85, 187–88; and the home, 153, 157, 162, 164–65, 169, 172, 184; and International Women's Year, 187–88; Junior Daughters, 154–55, 165–66, 179–80, 184; and leadership, women's, 149–50, 152–53, 155, 157–58, 165, 179–80, 183; and liturgy, 166, 170, 178–79; and love, 169–70; and marriage, 153, 157; and maturity, 175–76; membership of, 150, 152, 160, 177, 182, 184; and ministry, 172; and the modern world, 149–50, 153, 156, 162, 164, 169; and motherhood, 153, 162, 171–72; and obedience, 149–52, 155, 158–60, 177; and patriotism, 152, 181, 183; and prayer, 152, 158–59; and ritual, 151, 177, 179, 182, 187; and suffering, 25, 164; and tradition, 161, 163–65, 168, 174, 181–82; and Vatican II, 76, 148–50, 156, 159–64, 166–67, 169–71, 173–74, 176–83, 185–86, 188–89; and vocations to religious life, 25, 157–58; womanhood, ideas about, 10, 149, 152, 164, 168, 171–73, 175, 189; and women religious, 148–49, 152, 174. *See also* Catholic Daughters of America; Daughters of Isabella

Daughters of Isabella, 25, 150–52, 161, 168, 175–78, 184, 186–87, 211n6; circles of, 152–53, 171, 177. *See also* Daughters

deacons, women, 83, 191

Decree on the Apostolate of the Laity, 3, 46, 49, 148, 166

development, international, 93–94, 102, 106

devotional societies, 5

devotions: declining participation in, 7–8, 21–22, 111, 156, 186; home, 19, 21, 165; traditional, 6–8, 22, 39–40, 111, 121, 152, 159, 164. *See also* Mary: devotion to

Dicastery for Laity, Family, and Life, 191–92

discrimination against women: in the church, 64, 83, 87, 92, 194; in society, 81, 192

domesticity, 9, 31, 37, 62, 110, 130, 132, 212n11

duty, 3, 40, 78, 130, 159–60, 165–66, 168–69, 188–89

Eagle Forum, 102

ecumenism, 46, 78–79, 89, 160, 180–83

education, 13, 194; Daughters and, 160, 168, 170, 172, 178, 180–81, 188; *Marriage* and, 107, 113, 119, 133; NCCW and, 77, 88, 99; Theresians and, 32, 41–42, 48, 66–67, 115; WUCWO and, 93, 96

Ellis, John Tracy, 78, 166

Emmanuel, 20

empowerment, 111, 159, 166; Daughters and, 10, 170, 189; *Marriage* and, 110, 125; NCCW and, 72, 80, 88; Theresians and, 39–40, 46, 52, 56–57, 61–62

equality, 192–93, 205n45, 205n49; Daughters and, 171–73, 176; *Marriage* and, 118, 124, 128; NCCW and, 70, 86, 90–91, 101–2, 104; Theresians and, 31, 44, 51, 54–55, 59, 61–62, 64

Equal Rights Amendment (ERA), 4, 71, 73, 82, 99, 101–3, 188, 204n28

essentialism, 11, 13–15, 192–94, 205n49; Daughters and, 57, 152, 161–62, 171–76;

Marriage and, 109, 118–21; NCCW and, 4, 56, 75, 84–87, 96, 102–4, 163; Theresians and, 31, 38, 56–64, 69. *See also* complementarity

"eternal woman," 54, 58–61, 111, 153, 172

Eucharist. *See* Mass

evangelicalism, 121

evangelization, 160–61, 169, 186

evil, 75, 106, 157–59, 189. *See also* crisis, sense of

extramarital sex, 140

family, 9–10, 16, 20, 25, 111–12, 208n31; Daughters and, 159, 165, 172, 212n11; *Marriage* and, 15, 109–10, 121–23, 125, 128, 131, 136; NCCW and, 75, 78, 90, 102; WUCWO and, 93, 97. *See also* children; fatherhood; headship; marriage; motherhood

family planning. *See* contraception; rhythm (periodic continence)

Fascinating Womanhood (Andelin), 122

fashion. *See* clothing

fasting, 40

fatherhood, 38, 113, 115, 121–26

feminine genius, 191–93

Feminine Mystique, The (Friedan), 54, 81, 118, 201n53, 209–10n68

femininity, 8, 37, 59, 69, 86–87, 115–16, 119, 121–22, 126, 144, 174

feminism, 8–11, 56–58, 144; Catholic, 4–5, 9–10, 34, 54–56, 63–64, 70–71, 80–84, 96–97, 119–20, 167, 195n3, 200n42, 200n53, 202n76; cultural, 31, 67; and the Daughters, 149, 152, 164–65, 170–71, 173–76, 179–80, 188; goals of, 4, 10–11; liturgy and, 83, 98, 103, 204n31; and *Marriage*, 105, 109, 112, 118, 121, 124, 127–28, 130, 133, 137, 145, 147; moderate, 2–3, 9–11, 104, 203n28; and the NCCW, 30, 70–72, 80–92, 96, 99–104, 165, 174, 203n23, 204n24, 205n45; new, 206n62; radical, 185, 187, 206n62; and the Theresians, 15, 30, 44, 54–67; and Vatican II, 5, 30, 64, 80–81, 87–90, 98, 109, 204n24, 205n44; and WUCWO, 30, 97–99, 187. *See also* antifeminism; women's liberation; women's rights

Fichter, Fr. Joseph, 71

Flanagan, Fr. Bernard, 178, 183

formality, 174, 178, 187

Francis (pope), 191–3

Friedan, Betty, 54, 81, 105, 118, 130, 137, 200n53

Frisbie, Margery and Richard, 116, 122, 130, 132

fund-raising, 14, 73, 152–53, 156, 183

Galatians 3:28, 54, 84, 103, 172

Gaudium et Spes, 96

gender identity, 2–5, 8–10, 15, 69, 72, 92, 107, 109–11, 118, 126, 189. *See also* essentialism; womanhood

generosity, 25, 32, 58, 60

Girl Scouts, 180

global South, 5, 93

governance: church, 12, 56, 192; of women's groups: 47, 50, 151

grace, God's, 20, 28, 48, 66, 137, 158

graciousness, women's, 58, 70

Hallinan, Archbishop Paul, 181

headship, 15, 35, 38, 112–14, 121–29, 139, 145, 194, 208n31

Heffernan, Virginia, 136, 142

Heinzelman, Gertrud, 54

helpmate, 60, 115

Hennessey, Mary, RC, 148–49, 169, 174, 189

Hertz, Solange, 131–32, 209nn56–57

hierarchy: in the church, 1, 7, 15, 18, 34, 109, 149; and gender, 3, 11, 112–13; in women's organizations, 152, 155, 182. *See also* bishops

high school affiliates, Theresian, 33, 40, 42, 50. *See also* Junior Daughters

holy hour, of Theresians, 40, 42, 65

home: as devotional center, 9, 21, 100, 109, 165, 169, 203n13, 209n56; and marriage, 107, 109, 112, 123, 128–32; and men's authority, 38, 122–23; as woman's sphere, 12, 19–21, 32, 34–35, 46, 59, 61, 75, 78, 85, 102, 113, 115–16, 130, 132, 132, 153, 157, 162, 164, 172, 184

homemakers. *See* housewives

home mass, 65

Homiletic and Pastoral Review, 20

homosexuality, 140, 197n8

hostesses, 38, 58, 178

housewives, 58–60, 62, 79, 108, 117, 119, 122, 129–32, 135, 137, 200n53, 208n48, 209n68

housework, 129–32, 136, 144

Humanae Salutis, 160

Humanae Vitae, 139, 183, 185

Illusion of Eve, The (Callahan), 83, 120

Immaculate Conception, 12, 171

immaturity, 12

immodesty, 157

immorality, 61, 157

immutability: of the church, 77; of gender, 3, 13

International Declaration on Human Rights, 93

International Women's Year (IWY), 63, 99, 102, 187

Irish-American Catholicism, 34

Isabellan, the, 25, 161

Isabellans. *See* Daughters; Daughters of Isabella

Jericho meetings, 42–43

John Paul II (pope), 206n62

John XXIII (pope), 45, 89, 159–60, 162, 167

Johnson, Lyndon, 208n31

Journal of Ecumenical Studies, 83,

joy: and prayer, 40; and religious life, 17, 22, 27, 35, 43; as virtue, 115

Jubb, Dr. E. Dawne, 59–62

Junior Daughters, 148, 152, 154–55, 165–66, 179–80, 185. *See also* high school affiliates, Theresian

Kanane, Mary, 178

Kelly, Margaret Mary, 77, 79, 87–88

Kennedy, John F., 73

Kennedy, Lillian, 173–74

kingdom of God, 46, 75

Kinsey, Alfred, 142, 210–11n82

Knights of Columbus, 151, 153

laity, 1–2, 5–7, 25, 34, 40, 46, 93, 109, 111, 139, 179, 191–92; and Vatican II, 3, 12–13, 16, 22, 45–46, 49, 52, 55, 75, 87, 88, 164, 166, 168, 170

Latin America, 5, 191

Lauer, Rosemary, 119

laymen, 5, 11, 15, 21, 32, 56, 88, 91, 111, 114, 143, 153, 155, 194, 195n3

Leadership Conference of Women Religious, 63, 81

lectors, 178

legalism, 174–75

liberation theology, 65

liturgical experimentation, 59, 65

liturgical movement, 9, 76, 178, 209n56

liturgy: 9, 22, 203n13; Daughters and, 149, 166, 170, 178–81; feminist, 83, 98; *Marriage* and, 109; NCCW and, 76, 78–79, 82–85, 87–88, 101, 103; reform of, 46, 76, 78, 111, 166, 170; Theresians and, 59–60, 65

love, 18–22, 28, 197n8; Daughters and, 169–70; *Marriage* and, 115, 130–31, 137–38, 140–41; NCCW and, 78, 85; Theresians and, 47, 49, 57, 59, 66–67, 69

Lovette, Mrs. Charles H., 40–41, 44

Lumen Gentium, 3, 49, 96, 195n1

lunches, 38, 42

magazines: Catholic, 9, 17, 19, 21, 174, 209n57; women's, 62, 208n48. See also *America*; *Catholic Woman*; *Marriage*; *Theresian, The*; *Word*

Maher, Frances, 157

Mainardi, Pat, 144

Maino, Mary, 116–17, 141

male headship. *See* headship

Marian Medal, 180

marriage, 6–7, 18, 93, 107, 109, 117–18, 121–28, 135–37, 153, 157, 200n53

Marriage, 1, 4, 15, 107, 188; circulation, 108, 206n5; and clergy, 108, 115; and complementarity, 13–14, 56–57, 107, 111–18, 121, 124, 129, 136, 139, 141, 143–47; discussion of laywomen, vocation of, 109, 115, 124, 132; editorial policy of, 107–9, 118, 120–21, 124–25, 129–30, 134, 139, 145–47; and education, 119, 133; and empowerment, 110, 125; and equality, 118, 124, 128; and essentialism, 109, 118–21; and the family, 15, 109–10, 121–23, 125, 128, 131, 136; and family planning, 108, 111, 138–39, 141, 147; and fear, 137, 139–40, 209n68; and feminism, 105, 109–10, 118, 124–25, 127, 130, 133, 137, 144–45, 147, 167; and headship, 121–29, 131; and housewives, 62, 117, 119, 129–31, 134–37; and liturgy, 109; and love, 115, 130–31, 137–38, 140–41; and manhood, ideas about, 114–17, 119, 121–23, 128, 143–44, 146; and marriage, 107, 117–18, 121–28, 134–36; and marriage, egalitarian, 109, 128, 137, 145; and maturity, 130, 144; and motherhood, 106, 115, 119, 121, 131, 133; and prayer, 109, 117, 129, 132; and sex, 106, 108, 125, 138–45, 147, 210n74, 210–11n82; and suffering, 115, 132; and Vatican II, 107, 109, 120, 122, 146; and womanhood, ideas about, 106–7, 110, 115–17, 119, 141, 144; and women religious, 115, 146; and work outside the home, 106, 109, 129–37, 144, 147, 208n48, 209n67

Martin, Mrs. Lucille, 1, 14, 120

Mary: decline in devotion to, 103, 180, 186; devotion to, 6, 8, 45, 84, 152, 164, 182, 186, 188, 194; as model, 22, 25, 58, 103, 157–59, 164, 171, 173; theology of, 59, 159, 172

Maryknoll, 22–23

Mary Yolanda, BVM, 17–20, 27, 41

Mass, 6, 40, 84–85, 101, 178–79, 186. *See also* liturgy

Masters and Johnson, 142

materialism, 9, 17–18, 21, 28, 34, 44, 133, 158

maturity: Daughters and, 175–76; *Marriage* and, 130, 144; NCCW and, 72, 78–79, 89; Theresians and, 31, 64, 67, 69. *See also* adulthood, of laywomen

McGillicuddy, Frances, 83

Mealey, Margaret, 70–74, 77, 79–80, 82, 88–89, 91–92, 94–95, 97–99, 101, 104

meals, 21, 131, 165

menstrual cycle, 61, 138. *See also* rhythm (periodic continence)

Meyer, Cardinal Albert, 1–2

militarism, 163–64, 169, 174, 185

Millett, Kate, 63